Island Genres, Genre Islands

RETHINKING THE ISLAND

The Rethinking the Island series seeks to unsettle assumptions by comprehensively investigating the range of topological and topographical characteristics that lie at the heart of the idea of "islandness."

Series Editors:
Elaine Stratford, Professor of Cultural and Political Geography at the University of Tasmania, Interim Director of The Peter Underwood Centre, Deputy Director of Institute for the Study of Social Change.

Godfrey Baldacchino, Professor of Sociology at the University of Malta, UNESCO Co-Chair in Island Studies and Sustainability.

Elizabeth McMahon, Associate Professor in the School of the Arts and Media, University of New South Wales, Australia.

Titles in the Series:
Theorising Literary Islands: The Island Trope in Contemporary Robinsonade Narratives, Ian Kinane
Island Genres, Genre Islands: Conceptualisation and Representation in Popular Fiction, Ralph Crane and Lisa Fletcher
Postcolonial Nations, Islands, and Tourism: Reading Real and Imagined Spaces, Helen Kapstein (forthcoming)
Islands of Poetry: Exploring Imagination and Materiality, Rajeev S. Patke (forthcoming)
Caribbean Island Movements: Culebra's Trans-insularities, Carlo A. Cubero (forthcoming)

Island Genres, Genre Islands

Conceptualisation and Representation in Popular Fiction

Ralph Crane and Lisa Fletcher

London • New York

Published by Rowman & Littlefield International Ltd
Unit A, Whitacre Mews, 26-34 Stannary Street, London SE11 4AB
www.rowmaninternational.com

Rowman & Littlefield International Ltd.is an affiliate of Rowman & Littlefield
4501 Forbes Boulevard, Suite 200, Lanham, Maryland 20706, USA
With additional offices in Boulder, New York, Toronto (Canada), and Plymouth (UK)
www.rowman.com

Copyright © 2017 Ralph Crane and Lisa Fletcher

All rights reserved. No part of this book may be reproduced in any form or by any electronic or mechanical means, including information storage and retrieval systems, without written permission from the publisher, except by a reviewer who may quote passages in a review.

British Library Cataloguing in Publication Data
A catalogue record for this book is available from the British Library

ISBN: HB 978-1-7834-8205-4
ISBN: PB 978-1-78348-206-1

Library of Congress Cataloging-in-Publication Data

Names: Crane, Ralph J., 1957- author. | Fletcher, Lisa, 1972- author.
Title: Island genres, genre islands : conceptualization and representation in popular fiction / Ralph Crane and Lisa Fletcher.
Description: London ; New York : Rowman & Littlefield International, 2017. | Series: Rethinking the island | Includes bibliographical references and index.
Identifiers: LCCN 2016049706 (print) | LCCN 2017009797 (ebook) | ISBN 9781783482054 (cloth : alk. paper) | ISBN 9781783482061 (paperback) ISBN 9781783482078 (Electronic)
Subjects: LCSH: Islands in literature. | Fiction genres.
Classification: LCC PN56.I7 C73 2017 (print) | LCC PN56.I7 (ebook) | DDC 809/.9332142—dc23
LC record available at https://lccn.loc.gov/2016049706

Contents

Acknowledgements	vii
Illustration Acknowledgements	ix
Introduction: Reading Genre Islands	xi

PART I: ISLAND CRIME, CRIME ISLANDS	**1**
1 The Body on the Island: The Insular Geography of Crime Fiction	3
2 Whodunit?: Agatha Christie's Islands	19
3 The Postcolonial Geography of Island Crime: G. W. Kent's Solomon Islands Series	31
PART II: ISLAND THRILLERS, THRILLER ISLANDS	**43**
4 Top Secret Islands: The Geography of Espionage and Adventure	45
5 Paradise Threatened: The Bond Islands	57
6 The Proximity of Islands: Dirk Pitt's Insular Adventures	71
PART III: ISLAND ROMANCE, ROMANCE ISLANDS	**85**
7 I ♥ Islands: The Emotional Geography of Popular Romance	87
8 Love on the Isle of Man: Margaret Evan Porter's The Islanders Series	103

9 The Island Happy Ever After: Nora Roberts's Three Sisters
   Island Trilogy   119

PART IV: ISLAND FANTASY, FANTASY ISLANDS   **135**

10 Islands of the World: The Archipelagic Geography
   of Fantasy Fiction   137

11 Putting Islands on the Fantasy Map: Ursula K. Le
   Guin's Earthsea   153

12 An Imaginary Water World: Robin Hobb's The Liveship
   Traders Trilogy   165

Epilogue   177

Bibliography   179

Index   197

Acknowledgements

In writing this book we have, inevitably, incurred debts. We would like to acknowledge the support of the University of Tasmania which granted each of us a period of Study Leave in 2015, during which the bulk of the research and writing was carried out. We would like to thank Elizabeth Leane (University of Tasmania), Kim Wilkins (University of Queensland), and Jodi McAlister (University of Tasmania) for providing helpful suggestions and comments on draft chapters. We also wish to thank the editors of this series, Elaine Stratford, Godfrey Baldacchino, and Elizabeth McMahon for giving us the opportunity to embark on this island adventure, and the editorial staff at Rowman & Littlefield International for guiding the book to publication. And, as always, we wish to thank our families for their patience and support during the course of this project.

Illustration Acknowledgements

The authors and publishers wish to express their thanks to the following for permission to reproduce illustrations:

- Head Design for kind permission to reproduce the cover of *Entry Island* by Peter May (London: Quercus, 2014).
- Outer Hebrides Tourism for kind permission to reproduce a section of their brochure, "Peter May's Outer Hebrides."
- HarperCollins UK and HarperCollins US for permission to reproduce the map of Smugglers' Island from *Evil Under the Sun* by Agatha Christie (1941; repr., London: HarperCollins, 2008).
- Penguin Random House UK for kind permission to reproduce the map of the Falkland Islands from *Little Black Lies* by Sharon Bolton (London: Corgi, 2015).
- Little, Brown Book Group for permission to reproduce the book covers of *Devil-Devil* (London: Robinson, 2011), *One Blood* (London: Robinson, 2012), and *Killman* (London: C&R Crime, 2013) by G. W. Kent.
- Book cover from *Kissing a Stranger* by Margaret Evans Porter. Copyright © 1998 by Margaret Evans Porter. Reprinted by permission of HarperCollins Publishers.
- Margaret Evans Porter for kind permission to reproduce the e-book cover of the 2013 edition of *Kissing a Stranger* by Margaret Evans Porter.
- Curtis Brown, Ltd for permission to reproduce Ursula K. Le Guin's map of Earthsea. Copyright © 2012 by The Inter Vivos Trust for the Le Guin

Children. First appeared in A WIZARD OF EARTHSEA published by Houghton Mifflin in 1968, and reprinted in 2012 by HMH. Reprinted by permission of Curtis Brown, Ltd.

The authors have made every effort to trace copyright holders and would welcome correspondence via the publisher from those they have been unable to trace.

Introduction

Reading Genre Islands

On the dust jacket of the first American edition of Agatha Christie's *And Then There Were None* (1939), an enormous skeletal hand reaches from the night sky, its index finger pointing towards a lone white building on a black island. This cover signals not only the deaths to come, but also the isolated house and the closed, island setting where the deaths take place. Similarly, the dust jacket of Peter May's *Entry Island* (2014) shows the outline of a small island against a low horizon, with ominous dark clouds massing above it, filling the upper two thirds of the image (figure I.1), and presaging the menace of the bounded setting.

The image of an island on the cover of any popular genre novel draws on prevailing and powerful associations between place and story, and signals the type of narrative and concomitant emotional experience that awaits the reader. The ritual representations of islands in the marketing and telling of genre stories have undeniable appeal to writers, publishers, and readers alike. When measured in industry and commercial terms, popular fiction is a juggernaut compared to literary fiction (the novels most attended to by critics). If one of the goals of the Rethinking the Island series in which this book appears is to interrogate how prevailing ideas about "islandness" are produced and circulated, then the islands depicted in genre fiction merit very close attention.

Popular fiction offers literary geographers a potent site for identifying and unpacking habits of thinking about distinctive natural environments. *Island Genres, Genre Islands* considers four key popular genres—crime fiction, thrillers, popular romance fiction, and fantasy fiction—from the perspective of island (literary) studies. It asks: what role does popular fiction play in the world of islands? Our aim is to describe and account for the meaning and significance of islands in "the books everyone reads,"[1] to borrow David

Figure I.1. Front cover. Peter May, *Entry Island* (London: Quercus, 2014).

Glover and Scott McCracken's somewhat flippant, but nonetheless serious, definition of "popular fiction."

Some of our happiest experiences reading popular fiction have been *on* islands as well as *with* islands—and this is not just because we have both lived on islands for substantial parts of our lives, most recently Tasmania. McCracken begins his book about popular fiction with the sentence, "Some of my happiest experiences reading popular fiction have been on trains."[2] There is, for McCracken, "something about the combination of being trapped yet going somewhere that is particularly conducive to the pleasures of pulp."[3] While "pulp," which carries undeniably pejorative connotations, is not our preferred label for the fiction we discuss in this book, reading a popular novel on a train, whether the reader is a commuter or a long-distance traveller, is a stock scene of leisure reading, as, of course, is reading on a plane. This is why we have the term "airport novel." As Bianca Leggett explains, "airport novels aspire to remove us from the world of the airport,"[4] and, by an obvious extrapolation from the world of the plane. In these terms, popular fiction sells, and is read at airports because it offers readers the dual experiences of diversion and immersion. The happiness McCracken finds in reading novels on a train comes from the particular combination of his location—"trapped yet going somewhere"—and his choice of text. He sees, that is, a similarity between the controlled mobility of train travel and the reliability of genre novels: "While the popular narrative also traps in its predictability, despite, or maybe because of, that predictability, there is more hope for an escape into fantasy."[5] The link McCracken draws between the spatial experience of reading on a train and the cognitive and emotional experience of reading a novel translates readily to our own reflections about reading popular fiction on islands. The delimited narrative spaces of popular genres and the idea of "island bounds"[6] are mutually reinforcing in more ways than we could have anticipated when we commenced our research for this book.

We are highly conscious that we are not alone in finding a happy association between books and islands. Like train travel and airports, islands provide immediately recognisable, even stereotypical, locations for pleasurable reading: a palm-fringed beach; a sun-drenched island resort; or a cottage buffeted by the wind and rain of an island storm. If, as McCracken observes, "the reader of popular fiction likes reading about readers,"[7] then—if island-set novels are anything to go by—they also like reading about what Sheila Hones calls "the spatial event"[8] of reading and the attendant experiences of writing, buying, and living with books. Accordingly, popular fiction set on islands is replete with references to books and reading, which strike us as simultaneously metafictional and metageographical in their effects. That is, the novels that are our primary focus reflect, in many and various ways, on "the coincidence of literary and geographical forms."[9] Time and again, genre novels highlight a relationship—sometimes sympathetic, sometimes antagonistic—between their formal and stylistic qualities and features and the geographical qualities and features of islands.

Nora Roberts offers one example of a self-reflexive scene of island genre reading in her 1997 romance, *Sanctuary*, in which almost all of the action takes place on Lost Desire Island, a fictional addition to the Sea Islands on the Southeastern coast of the United States. The heroine, Jo Ellen Hathaway, "walk[s] through the waves to shore" after a long swim and sees her sister:

> Lexy was posed on a blanket, stretched out to show off her generous curves. She rested lazily on an elbow, turning the pages of a thick paperback novel. On the cover was a bare-chested man with amazing and improbable pecs, black hair that swirled over his gleaming shoulders, and an arrogant smile on his full-lipped mouth.
>
> Lexy gave a low, murmuring sigh and flipped a page.[10]

She looks, Jo muses, "like an ad for some sexy resort."[11] This seemingly inconsequential moment in the novel makes a connection between the practices and pleasures of reading romance—the genre in which this novel participates—and island tourism, both of which it frames as "escape into fantasy," to use McCracken's phrase. Importantly, Jo interprets Lexy's pose and behaviour as a deliberate performance and comments on her sister's ability to "Arrange [herself] so that every male in a hundred yards strains his neck to get a look at [her]."[12] The artificiality of Lexy's use of the landscape (beach as much as island in this instance) as a backdrop for seduction is reinforced here by her choice of novel: Karen Robards's historical romance, *Island Flame* (1981).

By linking Lexy's use of the visual clichés of travel brochures to those of paperback romance covers, this scene serves to emphasise the sincerity and uniqueness of Jo's response to the island, which is both her childhood home and the site of her mother's mysterious disappearance twenty years earlier. The irony here is that this scene appears in a genre novel by "the single most popular romance author of our time."[13] Jo's high sensitivity to the visual conventions for depicting people and places—and islands, in particular—is central to her characterisation as the heroine of *Sanctuary*. A successful photographer working on an art book commissioned by a major publisher, Jo traces her love of photography and her skill with a camera, to the summer in which a famous photographer visited Lost Desire to work on a picture book about the Sea Islands. Soon after the scene on the beach, Jo decides that her next project will be her own photographic book about the island and its people. Lexy is one of her most cooperative subjects—"She would pose endlessly"—but Jo's favourite shot of her sister captures her in an unguarded moment with her lover, Giff, "foolishly happy" as he "spin[s] her in circles just on the edge of the garden."[14] For us, images such as that of Lexy reading on the beach or swinging in her lover's arms on the boundary between the "tended gardens"[15] of the island's hotel and the "dark shadows"[16] of its forest, open pathways for exploring the synergies between genre novels and generic spaces. Further, they suggest a shared awareness among the writers and readers of genre fiction that the island "space itself warrants *reading*."[17] Our analyses of novels throughout this book are spatially oriented or, to use Stefan Ekman's term, "topofocal,"[18] with a specialised orientation towards insular spaces and places.

"What is an island?" For Godfrey Baldacchino, this is a "philosophical yet sterile question,"[19] but one which will continue to be asked. The implication in his discussion is that this question will be asked less often as island studies grows and matures as a field of study. To the contrary, asking "What is an island?" must remain "a foundational task," because it "modulates into the critical question, 'What is the proper object of island studies research?'"[20] The first question is a thread throughout this book as the meaning of "island" for different people and in multiple contexts is a recurring question in many of the texts we discuss. Further, as we demonstrate throughout the following chapters, responses to this question are genre-inflected: for example, a romance island is at once similar to and different from an island in a crime or fantasy novel. The second question was both the impetus for this book and one that resonates through its pages: island studies scholarship should include consideration of the "textual life of islands," to modify a phrase from Christopher Schaberg.[21]

Due, in part, to the influence of Pete Hay's 2006 article "The Phenomenology of Islands,"[22] the debate about the textual life of islands has been hindered by a preoccupation with the distinction between "real" islands and "islands as metaphors."[23] However, what if metaphor is not the most useful key concept for making sense of the literary and cultural geographies of islands? In many ways, this book argues that *genre* rather than *metaphor* is a better starting point for rethinking the island in literature, as in other forms of cultural production.

In broad terms, like John Frow, we are interested in the ways "genres actively generate and shape knowledge about the world."[24] More specifically, we are interested in how popular fiction genres—crime, thrillers, romance, and fantasy—generate and shape knowledge about island environments and populations. Frow's insights about the significance and operations of genre inform our thinking, but our focus on popular fiction means that, for the most part, we work with a narrower, and somewhat different, conception of genre. Frow follows Jacques Derrida's contention that "Every text participates in one or several genres, there is no genreless text."[25] This is persuasive if genres are understood as the procedures and systems organising all levels of, in Frow's terms, "verbal and non-verbal discourse"[26]—novels, news broadcasts, greeting cards, text messages, funeral notices, horror films, wedding vows, seed catalogues, shipping schedules, and so on in infinite variety—but would be an overstatement in a study limited to the genres of popular fiction. Frow dismisses "as irrelevant" approaches to studying genre, which focus on the "strongly defined" genres of popular culture—"the Western or heist movie" or "such popular genres as the detective story or science fiction."[27] He sees in terms such as "genre films" or "genre fiction" a flawed critical assumption that "genre is a term that applies to some texts and not to others."[28] Frow chooses not to engage with the lexicon of literary discourse beyond the academy. The term genre resonates differently, some might say more loudly, in certain textual domains than in others. One only has to type the phrase "genre fiction" into Google or browse the fiction shelves of a bricks-and-mortar bookshop to recognise that popular culture has staked a claim on the concept of genre which no work of scholarship can successfully dispute. Most importantly for us, the term "genre" signifies in particular and significant ways in relation to popular fiction, which would elude analysis if we granted priority to Frow's view of genre as a "universal dimension of textuality."[29] All of this is not to say that his approach to genre is irrelevant to popular fiction studies, or, in this case, to island literary studies. To the contrary, his account of genres as "performative structures that shape the world in the very process of putting it into speech"[30] strikes us as directly translatable to literary and popular fiction studies that take a narrower conception of genre as their starting point. As Ken Gelder contends, "Popular Fiction is, essentially, genre fiction."[31] The term "popular" in this context does not signify commercial success.[32] Rather it refers to a commercial and cultural division of the larger field of literature, the outer boundaries of which are typically plotted in relation to high literature, while the internal divisions are made along the lines of genre.

Island Genres, Genre Islands provides a geographically inflected analysis of popular genres and texts; that is, in making the case for studying genre, it lays upon the term "world" a stress that is different from Frow's. Our overarching premise here is not a new one, and will be familiar to scholars in that field variously termed literary geography or geocriticism: "geography can help us understand literature and literature can help us understand geography."[33] Our specific contention is that thinking about islands can help us better understand popular genres and reading genre novels can help us rethink islands.

While, as McCracken posits, popular fiction "is a quintessential product of the modern world,"[34] island studies scholars are only now beginning to appreciate that genre islands merit close reading. The present-day system of genre fiction—evident in the organisation of any bookshop in the English-speaking world—began to emerge in the closing decades of the nineteenth century. It almost goes without saying that, as broader literary culture was split by the division between "high" and "low" forms, islands were favoured settings for writers and readers. Some of the most prominent island texts, which were also influential in the history of popular fiction, have already been the subject of significant critical attention, including Robert Louis Stevenson's *Treasure Island* (1883), H. G. Wells's *The Island of Doctor Moreau* (1896), and H. de Vere Stacpoole's *The Blue Lagoon* (1908). Rather than follow this familiar, but by no means exhausted route, we focus on twentieth- and twenty-first-century bestsellers across four genres.

The book is organised into four parts, each of which includes an opening survey chapter that addresses how islands signify and function in a particular genre, and two further chapters that offer detailed case studies of the conceptualisation and representation of islands in seminal or otherwise significant texts.

Part I, "Island Crime, Crime Islands," examines the genre that most exploits the narrative potential of the island as a closed space. In crime fiction, the isolated and bounded isle facilitates both the initial murder and its investigation. The tropology of crime islands is nowhere more apparent than in the three golden age mysteries that are the focus of chapter 2: Agatha Christie's *And Then There Were None*, *Evil Under the Sun* (1941), and *The Caribbean Mystery* (1964). Chapter 3 examines G. W. Kent's Sister Conchita and Sergeant Kella Mysteries, a postcolonial crime series that exhibits the capacity of genre fiction to both conform to the conventions enabled by the island-as-container and attend to the historical and cultural particularities of their geographical setting. Part II, "Island Thrillers, Thriller Islands," reveals the pivotal role of islands in the hub-and-spokes logic of this genre's approach to real-and-imagined geographies. Chapters 5 and 6 chart the mutually constitutive relationship between heroes, villains, and islands in novels from Ian Fleming's iconic James Bond series and Clive Cussler's Dirk Pitt Adventures. Whereas in crime fiction and thrillers islands are invariably places where bad things happen, almost without exception, islands have positive connotations in popular romance, which is the subject of part III, "Island Romance, Romance Islands." Chapters 8 and 9 examine Margaret Evans Porter's historical romance series, The Islanders, and Nora Roberts's contemporary paranormal Three Sister's Island trilogy, where islands function as home, sanctuary, refuge, and paradise—ideal sites, that is, for the happy-ever-after ending which is a requirement of this genre. Part IV, "Island Fantasy, Fantasy Islands," interrogates the role of islands in the world-building project of fantasy fiction and argues that the genre deploys a literary cartography in which no island is "entire of itself." Chapter 11 looks to Ursula K. Le Guin's quintessential fantasy archipelago, Earthsea, to argue for the importance of island-to-island relations in fantasy fiction, while chapter 12 reads Robin Hobb's Liveship Traders Trilogy to make the case for paying greater attention to water in island literary studies.

NOTES

1. David Glover and Scott McCracken, "Introduction," in *The Cambridge Companion to Popular Fiction*, ed. David Glover and Scott McCracken (Cambridge: Cambridge University Press, 2012), 1.

2. Scott McCracken, *Pulp: Reading Popular Fiction* (Manchester: Manchester University Press, 1999), 1.

3. McCracken, *Pulp*, 1.

4. Bianca Leggett, "Departures: The Novel, the Non-Place and the Airport," *Alluvium* 1, no. 4 (2012), accessed 6 May 2015, http://dx.doi.org/10.7766/alluvium.v1.4.03.

5. McCracken, *Pulp*, 1.

6. This phrase is borrowed from Gillian Beer, "Island Bounds," in *Islands in History and Representation*, ed. Rod Edmond and Vanessa Smith (London: Routledge: 2003), 32–42.

7. Scott McCracken, "Reading Time: Popular Fiction and the Everyday," in *The Cambridge Companion to Popular Fiction*, ed. David Glover and McCracken (Cambridge: Cambridge University Press, 2012), 103.

8. Sheila Hones, "Text as It Happens: Literary Geography," *Geography Compass* 2, no. 5 (2009): 1302.

9. Catherine Brace and Adeline Johns-Putra, "The Importance of Process," in *Process: Landscape and Text*, ed. Catherine Brace and Adeline Johns-Putra (Amsterdam: Rodopi, 2010), 41.

10. Nora Roberts, *Sanctuary* (1997; repr., London: Hachette Digital, 2008), Kindle, location 6372.

11. Roberts, *Sanctuary*, location 6377.

12. Roberts, *Sanctuary*, location 6380.

13. An Goris, "Body, Mind, Love: Nora Roberts and the Evolution of Popular Romance Studies," *Journal of Popular Romance Studies* 3, no. 1 (2012): n.p., accessed 7 October 2014, http://jprstudies.org/2012/10/mind-body-love-nora-roberts-and-the-evolution-of-popular-romance-studies-by-an-goris/.

14. Roberts, *Sanctuary*, location 6576.

15. Roberts, *Sanctuary*, location 400.

16. Roberts, *Sanctuary*, location 70, 1110.

17. Christopher Schaberg, *The Textual Life of Airports: Reading the Culture of Flight* (New York: Continuum, 2012), 1. Adobe PDF eBook.

18. Stefan Ekman, *Here Be Dragons: Exploring Fantasy Maps and Settings* (Middletown: Wesleyan University Press, 2013), Kindle, location 123.

19. Godfrey Baldacchino, "The Lure of the Island: A Spatial Analysis of Power Relations," *Journal of Marine and Island Cultures* 1 (2012): 60.

20. Lisa Fletcher, "'… some distance to go': A Critical Survey of Island Studies," *New Literatures Review* nos. 47–48 (2011): 20.

21. Schaberg, *The Textual Life of Airports*.

22. Pete Hay. "A Phenomenology of Islands," *Island Studies Journal* 1, no. 1 (2006): 19–42. For a critique of this essay see Fletcher, "'… some distance to go'," 25–26.

23. Stephen A. Royle, *Islands: Nature and Culture* (London: Reaktion Books, 2014), 121–23.

24. John Frow, *Genre* (2005; repr., London: Routledge, 2009), 2.

25. Jacques Derrida, "The Law of Genre," *Glyph* 7 (1980), 212.

26. Frow, *Genre*, 1.

27. Frow, *Genre*, 1.

28. Frow, *Genre*, 1.

29. Frow, *Genre*, 2.

30. John Frow, "'Reproducibles, Rubrics, and Everything You Need': Genre Theory Today," *PMLA* 122, no. 5 (2007): 1633.

31. Ken Gelder, *Popular Fiction: The Logics and Practices of a Literary Field* (London: Routledge, 2004), 1.

32. See Glover and McCracken, "Introduction," 3.

33. Sarah Luria. "Spatial Literacies: Geotexts," in *GeoHumanities: Art, History, Text at the Edge of Place* (London: Routledge, 2011), 67, ePub eBook.

34. McCracken, *Pulp*, 6.

Part I

ISLAND CRIME, CRIME ISLANDS

Chapter One

The Body on the Island
The Insular Geography of Crime Fiction

Islands are everywhere in the atlas of crime fiction.

Agatha Christie sets three of her golden age mysteries on islands in Britain and the Bahamas. Nevada Barr's park ranger detective Anna Pigeon solves crimes on several islands: Lake Superior's Isle Royale (twice); Cumberland Island, off the Georgia coast; the group of tiny islands that make up the Dry Tortugas National Park off Key West; and the fictional Boar Island on the edge of the Acadia National Park in Maine. Pacific islands provide the locations for mystery series by John Enright, G. W. Kent, and Marianne Wheelaghan. Hawai'i is the setting for Earl Derr Biggers's first Charlie Chan mystery, *The House Without a Key* (1925), and Chip Hughes's Surfing Detective Mystery, *Murder on Moloka'i* (2004), straddles several islands of the Hawaiian archipelago. Paul Thomas's series featuring the Maori Detective Sergeant Tito Ihaka is set in New Zealand, as are four of Ngaio Marsh's Inspector Alleyn detective novels, and David Owen's Pufferfish series featuring Detective Inspector Franz Heineken is set in Tasmania. Garry Disher uses both Tasmania and Vanuatu as settings in *Port Vila Blues* (1996), the fifth of his series of eight hardboiled crime capers featuring the resourceful thief Wyatt; Sam Levitt's third outing takes him to Corsica in Peter Mayle's *The Corsican Caper* (2014); and Chris Ewan's *The Good Thief's Guide to Venice* (2011), the fourth in his series of comic capers featuring part-time crime writer and part-time thief, Charlie Howard, is set in Italy's island city. Donna Leon's Commissario Guido Brunetti Mystery series, also set in Venice, which began in 1992 with *Death in La Fenice*, now runs to twenty-five novels, and Sicily is the setting for Andrea Camilleri's numerous Inspector Montalbano crime novels. Inspector Singh investigates a murder in the island city-state of Singapore in Shamini Flint's *The Singapore School of Villainy* (2010), the third volume of her Asian cozy crime series, and another in Bali in *A Bali Conspiracy Most Foul* (2009), while each novel in Sandy Frances Duncan and George Szanto's cozy Islands Investigations International Mystery series is set on one of the islands off the coast of British Columbia and Washington State. Peter May's stand-alone crime novel, *Entry Island* (2014), is set in the Magdalen Islands situated between Newfoundland and Nova Scotia in the Gulf of St Lawrence, while Tangier Island, off the coast of Virginia, is the setting for Patricia Cornwell's police caper, *Isle of Dogs* (2001), and Susan M. Boyer's cozy Liz Talbot Mystery Series is set on the fictional Stella Maris, an island off the South Carolina coast. Leonardo Padura's quartet of crime novels featuring Inspector Mario Conde, which opens with *Havana Blue* (2000), is set in Cuba.

M. M. Kaye chose island locations for three of her colonial-era mystery novels *Death in Cyprus* (rev. 1984; originally published as *Death Walked in Cyprus*, 1956), *Death in Zanzibar* (rev. 1983; originally published as *The House of Shade*, 1959), and *Death in the Andamans* (rev. 1985; originally published as *Nights on the Island*, 1960). Crime fiction set on islands in the Mediterranean includes Marcello Fois's Sardinian mystery, *The Advocate* (1998); Marco Vichi's Inspector Bordelli mystery, *Death in Sardinia* (2004); Mark Mills's *The Information Officer* (2009), set on Malta during the Second World War; Daniel Silva's crime thriller, *The English Girl* (2013), set largely in Corsica; and the sixth outing of M. C. Beaton's cozy Agatha Raisin series, *Agatha Raisin and the Terrible Tourist* (1997) is set on Cyprus. Anne Zouroudi's seven Mysteries of the Greek Detective series, each themed around one of the seven deadly sins, are set mainly in the Greek islands, beginning with *The Messenger of Athens* (2007), set on the fictional island of Thiminos.

Islands also feature prominently in a range of Scandinavian crime novels. In Swedish crime fiction, which dominates the list of Scandinavian crime available in English, the island of Valo in the Fjällbacka archipelago is the setting for *Buried Angels* (2011), the eighth book in Camilla Lackberg's series featuring Detective Hedström and his wife, crime writer Erica Falck; Mari Jungstedt's *Unseen* (2006), set on the island of Gotland, is the first in a series featuring Detective Superintendent Anders Knutas and journalist Johan Berg; and Johan Theorin's *Echoes from the Dead* (2007) is the first in a quartet set predominantly on the Baltic island of Örland. Arnaldur Indridason's numerous Detective Erlendur crime novels are set in Iceland, as are those of his compatriot, Yrsa Sigurdardottir, which feature the lawyer Thora Gudmundsdottir as their central character. Danish crime fiction author Jussi Adler-Olson's *The Hanging Girl* (2015), his sixth Department Q novel, sees Copenhagen Detective Carl Morck investigate a cold case on the remote island of Bornholm. *The Last Refuge* (2014) by Scottish writer Craig Robertson is set in the Faroe Islands (an autonomous nation within the Kingdom of Denmark, situated about half way between Iceland and Norway).

The small islands around the coast of the Great Britain—the islands off the larger island—provide the settings for numerous British crime fictions. The best known of these are undoubtedly Ann Cleeves's Shetland series (two quartets), featuring Detective Inspector Jimmy Perez, and Peter May's Lewis trilogy, set in the Outer Hebrides, featuring Detective Inspector Fin MacLeod. Continuing round the coast in an anti-clockwise direction, the Isle of Man is the setting for Chris Ewan's *Safe House* (2012). Gillian E. Hamer's self-published *Crimson Shore* (2104) is set on the island of Anglesey off the North Wales coast, while Mark Billingham's *The Bones Beneath* (2014), part of his D. I. Tom Thorne series, takes place predominantly on Bardsey Island, the fourth largest island off Wales. In P. D. James's *The Lighthouse* (2005), the thirteenth book in her classic Adam Dalgliesh Mystery series, Dalgliesh is called in to investigate a mysterious death on the imaginary Combe Island off the Cornish coast, and in *The Skull Beneath the Skin* (1982) Cordelia Gray investigates a murder on the fictional Courcy Island off the Dorset coast, while Elizabeth George chooses the English Channel island of Guernsey as the setting for *A Place of Hiding* (2003). Guernsey is also the location for Canadian author Jill Downie's Moretti and Fall Mystery series, which debuted with *Daggers and Men's Smiles* (2011). The Isle of Wight is a key location for several of Pauline Rowson's D. I. Andy Horton Marine Mystery series, including *Blood on the Sand* (2010), while Tom Bale created a fictitious island in Chichester Harbour as the titular setting for *Terror's Reach* (2010). The island setting in Margery Allingham's *Mystery Mile* (1930) is based on the real Mersea Island, which lies just off the Essex coast. Scolt Head Island, off the North Norfolk coast, provides the scene of the crime in Jim Kelly's *Death's Door* (2012), the fourth instalment in his D. I. Peter Shaw and D. S. George Valentine series. Further up the east coast, Sheila Quigley's trilogy of D. I. Mike Yorke novels—*Thorn in My Side* (2011), *Nowhere Man* (2012), and *The Final Countdown* (2013)—is based on and around Northumberland's Holy Island, and M. C. Beaton's *Death of a Snob* (1992) takes Hamish Macbeth to the fictitious island of Eileencraig off the coast of Sutherland in the Scottish Highlands.

While there are a number of excellent crime novels set in Ireland—including Matt McGuire's Belfast-based D. S. O'Neill novels, *Dark Dawn* (2012) and *When Sorrows Come* (2014), and the six Dublin-based Quirke Mysteries by Benjamin Black (John Banville's *nom de crime*)—these capture the tenor of the cities in which they are set rather than that of Ireland as an island. The same is true of the bulk of British crime fiction: a sense of place is always important but not a sense of mainland Britain as island place. So, too, in Australia, where island crime fiction is focused on islands such as Tasmania, "the island off the island" as Heineken calls it in *Pig's Head* (1994), the first of Owen's Pufferfish mysteries,[1] or Thursday Island, an island in the Torres

Strait Islands archipelago which provides the setting for Catherine Titasey's debut crime fiction, *My Island Homicide* (2013).

The allure of islands as settings for crime fiction is succinctly summed up by Barbara Pezzotti in her section on island locations in *The Importance of Place in Contemporary Italian Crime Fiction*:

> The island is an ideal setting for a detective story. The sense of mystery it generates is a vital element for crime fiction. Moreover, an island provides a crime writer with a small community where many of the inhabitants are interrelated, where secrets are deeply hidden, and from which a quick escape can be physically difficult or impossible.[2]

For Pezzotti, the island itself lends mystery to the mystery. Islands have long been associated with paradise on the one hand, and prison on the other—a dichotomy that is exploited to good effect by many crime writers, from Christie to Cleeves. In this chapter we want to explore the prevalence of stereotypical island topologies in the popular imagination, the meaning and significance of which cannot be taken for granted.

In countless crime novels readers—and in many cases the detective, too—first encounter the island from a distance, as a bounded and isolated space, and frequently an air of mystery veils that initial sighting. In the first chapter of Dennis Lehane's *Shutter Island* (2003), "islands appeared out of the fading dusk, huddled together, as if they'd been caught at something,"[3] alerting the reader to the potential of the island as a crime scene, and its peculiar culpability. There is a clear suggestion here that places produce stories. More than an issue of the personification of landscape for symbolic effect, this view of the island signals the agency of place. Not only can islands function as settings, they can also operate on the level of character, and influence plot. In May's *Entry Island*, the titular island is revealed to both the reader and to Detective Sime MacKenzie as a remote, bounded space, which is again invested with agency:

> stretched out on the far side of the bay, the sun only now rising above a gathering of dark morning cloud beyond it. The island drew Sime's focus and held it there, almost trancelike, as the sun sent its reflection careening towards him, creating what was almost a halo effect around the island itself. There was something magical about it. Almost mystical.[4]

Sime and the other members of the investigating team already know a body awaits them, but they do not know what to anticipate in terms of the island itself. During the course of the novel, as Entry Island reveals itself to him, so Sime moves towards solving the crime; an understanding of the one goes hand-in-hand with an understanding of the other. Knowledge of the island, its geography and its culture, is invariably a prerequisite to solving an island crime: the author must ensure that both the detective and the reader are able to make sense of the island—to read the island—during the course of the novel. Thus island crime fiction contains not just two stories, "the story of the crime and the story of the investigation"[5] identified by Tzvetan Todorov in his classic essay "The Typology of Detective Fiction," but also the story of the island.

Similarly, in Billingham's *The Bones Beneath* the reader first encounters the remote Welsh island known to the English as Bardsey Island and to the Welsh as Ynes Enlli, the Island of Tides, as Tom Thorne and his team escort the psychopath Stuart Nicklin back to the island so that he can reveal the whereabouts of a corpse he buried twenty-five years ago: "The first view was of cliffs and the snowflake specks of wheeling seabirds against the black crags. The island was shaped like a giant, humpbacked tadpole; no more than a mile from end to end and about half as wide."[6] Thorne and his team know there is a body on the small island, but, unusually, they do not know where it lies. Knowledge of the island is invested in the killer, Nicklin, rather than in the detective, and a sense of foreboding is built up through the description of the island as a "giant, humpbacked tadpole," with the seabirds "wheeling" ominously "against the black crags."

While the detective may or may not know that a body awaits him or her, the reader of island crime fiction is always already alert to the *potential* of the island as a crime scene. Neither Hercule Poirot nor Miss Marple anticipate a body when they embark on their island sojourns in *Evil Under the Sun* (1941) and *A Caribbean Mystery* (1964), respectively, and in both instances Christie's detective is already on the island at the time of the murder. In *Raven Black* (2006), the first novel in Cleeves's Shetland series, Jimmy Perez is stationed on Mainland, the largest, most populous island of Shetland and the centre of the archipelago's sea and air connections. And even though the members of the Inverness investigation team have to be flown in from Aberdeen, their arrival into Lerwick is not described beyond the observation that their plane was running late. But the very fact of their arrival from elsewhere sets them apart as outsiders whose ability to decipher the geography, history, and culture of the island is necessarily limited. Similarly, at the outset of *The Blackhouse* (2011), the first volume of May's Lewis trilogy, we encounter Fin MacLeod returning to home territory, to the island of his birth, so his arrival is muted: "Fin had barely lifted his bag from the luggage carousel when a large hand grabbed the handle and took it from him."[7] When George Gunn, the policeman who has taken his bag, tells him that he will "probably see a few changes,"[8] Fin is presented to the reader as someone with knowledge of the island, an insider, but no longer an intimate one. In both novels, the sense of the island is established early through references to geography and meteorology. In *Raven Black* the remoteness of the islands, which must be reached by ferry or plane, is emphasised when the investigation team arrives too late for the body to be shipped back to Aberdeen on that evening's ferry. And in both novels the reader is introduced to the islands, the Shetland Islands and the Outer Hebrides, through references to the weather which defines life there: "In Shetland, when there was no wind it was shocking,"[9] while Fin is reminded that on Lewis there is "One thing that never changes [...]. The wind. Never gets tired of blowing."[10] In *Raven Black* and *The Blackhouse* the islands are first encountered from near rather than far, reflecting the proximity of the detective, and lending a heightened sense of insularity to the ever-present awareness of bounded space. Islands initiate particular types of story, particular modes of storytelling, and generate a sense of closeness, of intimate proxemics, that can be detected in various genres, but most obviously in crime fiction and popular romance.

In Owen's *Pig's Head*, while Tasmania is not first viewed as a bounded space, its sense of islanded isolation is nevertheless established in the opening sentence, "You cannot enter this state by road,"[11] and reinforced shortly thereafter through reference to Tasmania as a "sea-locked state."[12] Indeed, Owen never allows the reader to forget the island geography of his setting through multiple, comic, and ultimately overdone allusions to Tasmania as: the "Apple Isle"[13]; the "Gentle Isle"[14]; the "Divided Isle"[15]; the "Friendly Isle"[16]; the "Delectable Isle"[17]; the "Sceptered ... Isle"[18]; the "Penal Isle"[19]; the "Holiday Isle"[20]; the "Southern Isle"[21]; the "Quiet Isle"[22]; the "Green Isle"[23]; the "Left-Off-the-Map Isle"[24]; the "Unimportant Isle"[25]; the "Resilient Isle"[26]; the "Surprising Isle"[27]; and, along with New Zealand (the "Shaky Isles"[28]), a "Piffly Isle."[29]

In *Form and Ideology in Crime Fiction* Stephen Knight explains that a sense of bounded and isolated space is an integral part of the structure of the clue-puzzle mystery:

> Christie perfected a structure, best called the clue-puzzle, which invited and empowered the careful reader to solve the problem along with the detective. The individualism and the sense of *isolation* inherent to the audience who shared the basic bourgeois values were themselves activated by the overall form of the novel. It is true that many readers could not solve the puzzle, and hardly tried to do so; indeed some novels are not quite fairly open to such solving. But these facts do not remove the crucial ideological force of the clue-puzzle, which marshalled the simple skills of a respectable, leisured, reading public and applied them in their own personalised defence system, with an inquiring agent to represent the reader who could only aspire to such observing and ordering powers. (emphasis added)[30]

This structure, especially the sense of isolation, remains current in contemporary island crime fiction. As Pezzotti accurately observes, "the island with its natural boundaries seems to guarantee an enlarged version of the mystery of the enclosed chamber."[31] The device of the locked room that proved so enduring in the golden age is augmented in contemporary crime fiction by the device of the locked island—a development heralded by Christie herself as early as 1939 in *And Then There Were None*. The novels in Cleeves's Shetland series, for example, can all be usefully seen as the descendants of the clue-puzzle mysteries of the golden age,[32] albeit with the contained space of Christie's islands expanded to encompass the Shetland chain of islands. Regardless of the form—clue puzzle or noir, cozy crime or crime caper—island history or folklore frequently plays a part in the narrative, too. The supernatural story of Peerie Lizzie is woven into the fabric of Cleeves's *Thin Air* (2014); the Manx Halloween, Hop-tu-naa, lends structure to Ewan's *Dark Tides* (2014); and Samoan history and folklore informs the four novels in John Enright's cross-cultural mystery series featuring the idiosyncratic Detective Apelu Soifua: *Pago Pago Tango* (2012), *Fire Knife Dancing* (2013), *The Dead Don't Dance* (2014), and *Blood Jungle Ballet* (2014). In all these island crime fictions, as in earlier clue-puzzle mysteries, there is the sense that the murderer is in one's midst, and the fear is thus heightened for characters and readers alike. The island, frequently regarded prior to the crime as a stable, hospitable environment, is transformed during the period of the investigation into an unstable, inhospitable one—a sinister environment under threat from a murderer, who, of course, is more often than not a local (a sense of evil within rather than an invasion from outside, as is invariably the case in Christie's novels). The role of the detective, who may be either a local like Jimmy Perez, or an outsider like Hercule Poirot, is to restore order and return the island to its previous safe state.

Part of the appeal of islands as settings for detective fiction is that they provide a manageable crime scene, the perimeter of which is defined by the geography of the island. This practical concern, what we might think of as the efficiency of storytelling, is important to writers of genre fiction who may be contracted to produce several titles in a year. Like the variant settings of clue-puzzle mysteries from the golden age—country-house mysteries, locked-room mysteries, and the many variations thereof, including snow-bound mysteries, murders on trains or ships—the restricted setting of the island limits the number of suspects to those on the island at the time of the murder, while the watery boundary restricts (but does not always prevent) the movement of suspects and others from and to the island.

Thus on one level, it can be argued that crime fiction is not interested in challenging the dominant tropes of islandness, that the bounded nature of islands produces a predictable type of mystery, and that the geography of islands enables the resolution of the mystery. However, while this is true of many island crime fictions, it is not always the case. In a number of island-based crime novels—from Allingham's *Mystery Mile* to Stieg Larsson's *The Girl with the Dragon Tattoo* (2005)—there are criminals who exploit the assumption that island boundaries are absolute, while both the detective and the reader must recognise that this is not the case. In Christie's *Evil Under the Sun*, for example, Poirot must consider the possibility that the murderer may have arrived on and departed from Smugglers' Island either via the causeway that links it to the mainland at low tide or by boat.

It is perhaps not surprising, then, that many island crime fictions include maps, which, as John Scaggs notes, "fix a particular event in spatial terms"[33] and reinforce the importance of setting and a sense of place in crime fiction. Maps were common in novels of the golden age: Allingham provides the reader with a map of the island of Mystery Mile in her novel of the same name, and Christie includes a map of Smugglers' Island in *Evil Under the Sun*, to highlight two well-known examples. While perhaps not as commonplace as they once were, maps nevertheless remain a relatively frequent element of paratext in contemporary crime novels. Barr, for instance, includes a detailed map of Cumberland Island in her fifth Anna Pigeon mystery, *Endangered Species* (1997).

Barr's map, drawn by Jackie Aher, includes scale and orientation as well as other decorations. Like her map of the islands of Dry Tortugas National Park in *Flashback* (2003),[34] and Meighan Cavanaugh's map of the Isle Royale National Park in *Winter Study* (2008), it furnishes readers with geographical and topographical specificity that assists them to follow the spatial and temporal movements of characters in the novel. Further, they are able to do this confident that what Sally Bushell calls a literary map—"a graphic representation of spatial relations among places or objects (real or imagined) that is presented alongside the literary work at the time of first publication and is authorial or authorially approved"[35]—and Barr's narrative maps—the descriptions of the island's topography in the text of the novel—are accurate reflections of each other. To similar ends, in *The Chessmen* (2013), the third volume of his Lewis trilogy, May includes a paratextual map of the Outer Hebrides, which identifies key locations, real and invented, from the three novels; Duncan and Szanto include two maps in each of the four volumes of their Island Investigations International Mystery series,[36] the first (common to each novel) of the coast and islands of the Pacific Northwest, and the second, a larger scale one, of the specific island that is the setting for that novel; and Zouroudi includes a relief map by John Gilkes of the fictional Island of Thiminos in *The Messenger of Athens*—which, in both style and the choice of font, is reminiscent of the maps in fantasy fiction.[37] While in May's trilogy the narrative map follows the real geography of the Outer Hebrides, Gilkes has drawn a map to illustrate Zouroudi's description of the fictional Thiminos—in a way that is reminiscent of the process of illustration in nineteenth-century adventure fiction. Regardless of whether the description of the island follows the geography of a real island, or the map follows the description of a fictional island, in each case the inclusion of a map recognises the importance of setting and the relationship between the geography of the mystery and the physical topography of the island.

The landscape of Thiminos is described in considerable detail by Zouroudi over the course of her novel. An early, detailed description of the island highlights topographical characteristics and emphasises its boundedness:

> From the sea, the island of Thiminos showed exactly what it was: rock, one huge rock, so undercut by the salt water of the southern Aegean it seemed to float free, rising and falling in the swell. Mostly, the cliff faces of its coasts were sheer; where the slopes were gentler, they were all thin dirt and stone. There was little else: a few black pines rooted into the mountainsides at improbable angles; thorny, run-down shrubs between the boulders. And yet, here and there, it held a colourful surprise—on an empty beach, a tiny, white chapel in a garden of fresh, fuchsia-blossomed evergreens.
>
> It was an island with no beauty of its own, but around its shores, where the sea ran the gamut of all blues—turquoise and lapis lazuli, sapphire, ultramarine and cobalt—the water and sunlight changed it. Grey rocks on the beach shone silver; there was gold in the dull soil on the mountain slopes. Fool's gold, Tricks of light.
>
> There was one way in and one way out: by sea.[38]

Seen thus from the water the island is a world of its own, surrounded and threatened by an encroaching sea. The "huge rock" which forms the island is "undercut," the cliffs "sheer," and even the gentler slopes are coated in "thin dirt and stone." Covered in "boulders," "black pines," and "thorny, run-down shrubs" the island presents an inhospitable face to the world. The colour and appeal of the island is in the introduced environment, the chapel and the fuchsias which signal a transformation of space to place. But, like the tricks played by sun and sea, these are only illusory; the insularity of the island is ultimately magnified by the sea, the only way in or out.

In *The Information Officer,* Mills provides detailed descriptions of parts of the island of Malta. In this passage the eponymous Max Chadwick, who embarks on a private investigation to track down a murderer, finds himself in "one of the few corners of the island which he had never explored"[39]:

> The track elbowed its way up a hillside of stunted trees and lumpy fields. It then dipped away sharply towards the cliffs, before veering to the right and hugging the coastline. To his left the ground descended in narrow, cultivated terraces until the slope became too steep to hold them. On his right rose a rocky escarpment. True to form, the Maltese had responded by pouncing on this meager

scrap that Nature had tossed them, this precarious step of land at the edge of the world.[40]

Like Zouroudi in her description of the imagined Thiminos, Mills emphasises the ruggedness of Malta, and also the attempts made by the islanders to tame the landscape with precariously perched "cultivated terraces." And although Malta is in the middle of the Mediterranean, in this passage its insularity is succinctly captured in the key phrase, "at the edge of the world," used to describe the island's coastline.

A different form of "mapping" is offered by Billingham, who includes (as well as a map on the inside front cover, and a translation of the island's Welsh place names on the inside back cover) a three-page "Author Note" at the end of *The Bones Beneath*, which provides basic geographical information about Bardsey Island and the addresses of seven websites where curious readers can find out more about its history, mythology, and scientific importance. And while Leon includes maps in some but not all of her Brunetti novels, Toni Sepeda's *Brunetti's Venice: Walks Through the Novels* "accompanies"[41] Brunetti across Venice, through various *sestieri*, and around the islands of the Venetian lagoon, providing readers with richly detailed commentary and maps. These examples highlight the impact of islands on genres and genres on islands and illustrate some of the ways islands operate as spaces of cultural production, emphasising the intersections between touristic and genre discourses. These effects can be subtle and difficult to explain. Popular fiction genres are sources of distraction and entertainment for billions of readers. They are also systems of meaning, which have an immeasurable impact on our spatial awareness and imagination, leading to tourists in Venice seeing the island city saturated by the imagery of the Donna Leon novels, or visitors to the Outer Hebrides experiencing the islands by following the "Peter May Trail," based on locations from the Lewis trilogy, and set out in a glossy brochure produced by Outer Hebrides Tourism (figure 1.1).[42] This type of epitextual material, which exploits the voyeuristic desire of readers to see the locations of crime in paradise, demonstrates the way popular genre fiction spills into broader cultural spaces.

Scaggs convincingly argues that Miss Marple, who "always sees everything,"[43] "becomes in Christie's fiction the embodiment of Bentham's Panopticon."[44] The idea that Miss Marple is able to observe everything, to keep under constant surveillance every suspect, has application in terms of island crime fiction. The "textual Panopticon of detective fiction"[45] has particular resonance when the setting of the crime is a bounded, isolated island that is rendered a prison under constant surveillance by the detective—a panoptic view which, of course, the reader shares. The possibilities of the panoptic architecture of islands are manifest in a scene late in Christie's *Evil*

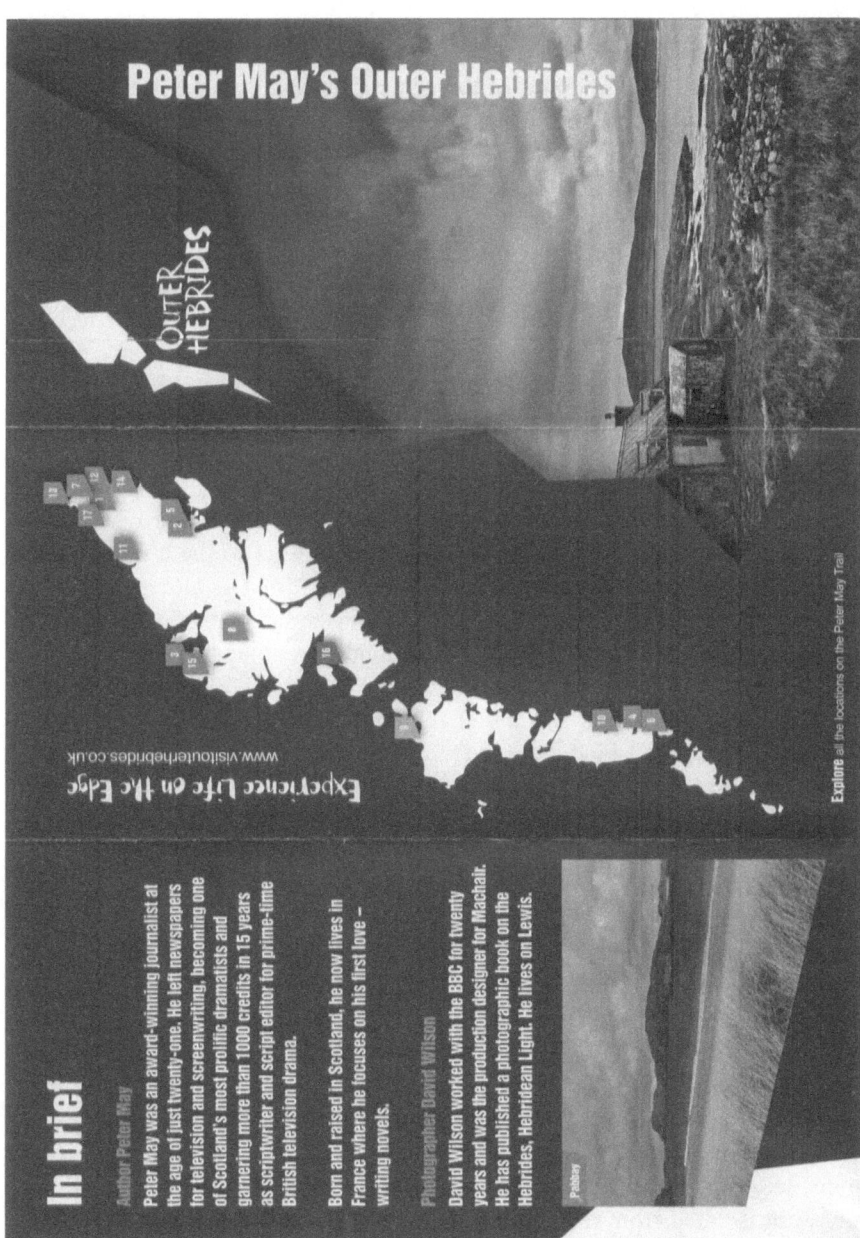

Figure 1.1. The Peter May Trail (leaflet produced by Outer Hebrides Tourism).

Under the Sun in which Hercule Poirot is described sitting on the summit of Smugglers' Island reviewing the evidence he has gathered through his surveillance of the suspects. Because in much island crime the murderer (along with other potential suspects) is already on the island, the detective inevitably performs the role of the operator of the central tower.

What Peter Messent calls "Vision and supervision in detective fiction" are, he argues, "crucially connected to location—and to *city space* in particular."[46] Despite his insistence on the importance of urban settings in the genre, he does acknowledge that crime can be committed anywhere and that detectives do operate in rural settings, though he does not mention islands. Setting is a key element in crime fiction, and island crime zones influence character and plot just as much as city crime zones do. Ian Rankin's Inspector Rebus is crucially connected to Edinburgh but only in the same way Jimmy Perez is crucially connected to the Shetland Islands. And, of course, while the relationship of the detective and the island (the story of the investigation) is well documented, the parallel relationship between the criminal and the island (the story of the crime) also needs to be examined.

Setting in island crime fiction is more than simply either "the where and when" or "the locale."[47] In simple terms the key events of the crime novels discussed in this section occur in island locales. The term "locale" can be seen as a synonym for "place" as the latter is distinguished from the more abstract "space" by Yi-Fu Tuan: "What begins as undifferentiated space becomes place as we get to know it better and endow it with value."[48] Or, as Eric Prieto succinctly puts it, place is a "*human* relation."[49] The relationship between the detective and the island—the detective's understanding of the island as place, his or her understanding of its geographical, historical, and cultural specificity—is a defining element in, if not the foundation stone of island crime fiction. He or she either already has, or must acquire, knowledge of the island. Thus in contemporary island mysteries considerable local knowledge is frequently invested in the detectives, who in most cases are serving police officers (thus bringing back the detailed police activity that Christie previously eschewed): Jimmy Perez, Fin MacLeod, Inspector Montalbano, Commissario Brunetti, or Sergeant Kella in G. W. Kent's Solomon Islands series. However, this is not always the case. Zouroudi's enigmatic Hermes Diaktoros, like Hercule Poirot before him, must study the proxemics of the islands and their inhabitants before he can solve his cases.

In his much quoted "Meditation" from the *Devotions*, John Donne uses the imagery of the island and the continent to advance the idea that individuals are not isolated from one another but are interconnected: "No man is an island, entire of itself; every man is a piece of the continent, a part of the main."[50] It is worth reflecting on Donne's homily on isolation versus interconnectedness when considering the nature of islands in crime fiction. For example, can islands be used by crime writers as microcosms of larger societies, as discrete spaces in which the issues of larger societies can be forensically examined? Pezzotti argues that this is so in Camilleri's Montalbano series. She notes that as the series progresses Camilleri stops referring to Sicily as an island because he wants it to stand for Italy and that the village of Vigàta operates as the closed "island" space in his novels.[51] In Pezzotti's reading of Camilleri's Montalbano series his "island" is both a real place (Sicily) and a metaphorical one (Vigàta). It would be difficult, though, to argue that Cleeves's Shetland or May's Outer Hebrides stand for Scotland (or Britain) in the way Pezzotti suggests Camilleri's Sicily stands for Italy. The distinction is similar to the difference between nissology—the study of islands on their own terms—and geography, which can include the study of islands, but is not exclusively the study of islands. Islands may once have been part of the main, but it is their present boundedness—their individuality—that attracts writers of crime fiction and not their ability to stand for a larger whole. Each island crime setting is distinct, not least because to arrive there involves crossing an expanse of water.

NOTES

1. David Owen, *Pig's Head* (1994; repr. Sydney: Arrow, 2003), 167.
2. Barbara Pezzotti, *The Importance of Place in Contemporary Italian Crime Fiction: A Bloody Journey* (2012; repr. Madison, NJ: Fairleigh Dickinson University Press, 2014), 125.
3. Dennis Lehane, *Shutter Island* (2003; repr. London: Bantam Books, 2004), 21–22.
4. Peter May, *Entry Island* (London: Quercus, 2014), 14.
5. Tzvetan Todorov, "The Typology of Detective Fiction," in *The Poetics of Prose*, trans. Richard Howard (Oxford: Blackwell, 1977), 44.
6. Mark Billingham, *The Bones Beneath* (London: Sphere, 2014), 148.
7. Peter May, *The Blackhouse* (London: Quercus, 2011), 37.
8. May, *The Blackhouse*, 37.
9. Ann Cleeves, *Raven Black* (2006; repr. London: Pan, 2010), 1.
10. May, *The Blackhouse*, 37.
11. Owen, *Pig's Head*, 1.
12. Owen, *Pig's Head*, 2.
13. Owen, *Pig's Head*, 4, 243.
14. Owen, *Pig's Head*, 9.
15. Owen, *Pig's Head*, 13.
16. Owen, *Pig's Head*, 57.
17. Owen, *Pig's Head*, 65.
18. Owen, *Pig's Head*, 72.
19. Owen, *Pig's Head*, 72.
20. Owen, *Pig's Head*, 90.

21. Owen, *Pig's Head*, 103.
22. Owen, *Pig's Head*, 133.
23. Owen, *Pig's Head*, 149.
24. Owen, *Pig's Head*, 155.
25. Owen, *Pig's Head*, 164.
26. Owen, *Pig's Head*, 167.
27. Owen, *Pig's Head*, 236.
28. Owen, *Pig's Head*, 254.
29. Owen, *Pig's Head*, 254.
30. Stephen Knight, *Form and Ideology in Crime Fiction* (London: Macmillan, 1980), 107.
31. Pezzotti, *The Importance of Place in Contemporary Italian Crime Fiction*, 125.
32. Donna Leon acknowledges the debt future mystery writers owe to Christie in *Death in La Fenice* (1992), the first of her Commissario Brunetti novels set in the island city of Venice. Both Dr Barbara Zorzi, who initially attends the corpse, and Brunetti admit to recognising the smell of cyanide "only from reading Agatha Christie" (1992; repr. London: Arrow, 2009), 157.
33. John Scaggs, *Crime Fiction* (London and New York: Routledge, 2005), 51.
34. Aher has drawn the maps for several of Barr's novels including *Endangered Species* and *Flashback*, as well as *Blind Descent* (1998), set in the Carlsbad Caverns National Park, and *Deep South* (2000), set on the Natchez Trace Parkway in Mississippi.
35. Sally Bushell, "The Slipperiness of Literary Maps: Critical Geography and Literary Cartography," *Cartographica* 47, no. 3 (2012): 149.
36. *Never Sleep with a Suspect on Gabriola Island* (2009); *Always Kiss the Corpse on Whidbey Island* (2010); *Never Hug a Mugger on Quadra Island* (2011); and *Always Love a Villain on San Juan Island* (2013).
37. A specialist in drawing maps for a range of publications, Gilkes prepared the maps for all seven books in Zouroudi's Mysteries of the Greek Detective series: *The Messenger of Athens* (2007); *The Taint of Midas* (2008); *The Doctor of Thessaly* (2009); *The Lady of Sorrows* (2010); *The Whispers of Nemesis* (2011); *The Bull of Mithros* (2012); *and The Feast of Artemis* (2013). See http://www.johngilkesmapart.co.uk.
38. Anne Zouroudi, *The Messenger of Athens* (2007; repr., London: Bloomsbury, 2011), 24.
39. Mark Mills, *The Information Officer* (London: Harper, 2009), 244.
40. Mills, *The Information Officer*, 244.
41. Toni Sepeda, *Brunetti's Venice: Walks Through the Novels* (2008; repr. London: Heinemann, 2009), 19.
42. See also the Visit Outer Hebrides website at: http://www.visitouterhebrides.co.uk/see-and-do/trails-and-journeys/peter-may-lewis-trilogy. There is also a "Peter May's Lewis Trilogy App" available free from the iTunes App Store, which features an interactive map of the islands showing locations featured in the books, photographs, an audio guide to Gaelic pronunciation, and background material to the books.

43. Agatha Christie, *The Murder at the Vicarage* (1930; repr. London: HarperCollins, 2002), 26.

44. Scaggs, *Crime Fiction*, 45.

45. Scaggs, *Crime Fiction*, 46.

46. Peter Messent, *The Crime Fiction Handbook* (Chichester: Wiley-Blackwell, 2013), 62.

47. J. A. Cuddon, *Dictionary of Literary Terms and Literary Theory*, 5th ed., rev. by M. A. R. Habib (Chichester: Wiley-Blackwell, 2013), 650.

48. Yi-Fu Tuan, *Space and Place: The Perspective of Experience* (Minneapolis: University of Minnesota Press, 1977), 6.

49. Eric Prieto, *Literature, Geography, and the Postmodern Poetics of Place* (London: Palgrave Macmillan, 2013), xx.

50. John Donne, *Devotions Upon Emergent Occasions and Death's Duel* (London: Vintage, 1999), 103.

51. Pezzotti, *The Importance of Place in Contemporary Italian Crime Fiction*, 127–29.

Chapter Two

Whodunit?
Agatha Christie's Islands

A small island provides the perfect geography for the clue-puzzle mysteries that dominated the golden age of crime fiction—generally understood to refer to the period between the First and Second World Wars. And the writer most commonly identified with the golden age is Agatha Christie. Her novel *The Mysterious Affair at Styles* (1920) is widely regarded as the first publication of the golden age, and as Stephen Knight persuasively argues, "Agatha Christie had the intellect and the technical skill to make of the clue-puzzle" the narrative mode of the period.[1] Julian Symons insists "she is alone among Golden Age writers in remaining as readable as ever."[2] Identifying a "modernist spirit"[3] in Christie's work, Alison Light suggests that

> if literary modernism, as many critics have argued, is more drawn to spatial than to temporal forms, the crime puzzle can be seen as a compromise between the two; like the jig-saw (itself an inter-war craze) this is a narrative whose breakup of linear development and continuities is only a temporary fragmentation, the pieces deliberately scattered for the express pleasure of putting them back together again.[4]

Thus, it is not only a *timeline* that must be reconstructed; in many of Christie's novels a *map* must also be pieced together before the murder can be solved and the murderer revealed.

In an essay on "The Golden Age" Knight clearly sets out the key elements of the clue-puzzle: murder is the central crime; the setting is enclosed; the social circle is similarly restricted; wider political issues of the moment are ignored; the victim will be a person of means; the method of detection is rational; the writing style, in keeping with the rational nature of the detection, will be plain; there will be several suspects; and the criminal is identified at the end of the story.[5] Of particular interest to us is the convention of restricted setting, a key feature of the classic detective game, *Cluedo*, launched in 1949, and the murder mystery game series, *How to Host a Murder*, the first of which was released in 1983. Frequently, of course, the location for a clue-puzzle mystery—or for the later cozy mysteries (or cozies), a benign sub-genre of contemporary crime fiction which imitates the golden age—is a country house, but they can also take place in other contained locations or intimate communities: in a small village, on board a train, ship, or plane, in a hotel or guest house, or on an *island*. All are depicted as closed or bounded spaces, ideal places for a group of strangers—instantly recognisable types, who are rarely developed beyond the requirements of cardboard or flat characters—to become a temporary community of potential murderers, their gaze turned inwards on one another, until they are released following the denouement in which the murderer in their midst is revealed. Nevertheless, there is a degree of tension in Christie's novels between the nature of settings as closed or open. While her settings are ostensibly closed, they remain open insofar as the mystery is triggered by the arrival or presence of outsiders: guests in a country house, passengers on a train, or holidaymakers on an island. Further, while islands afford similar narrative possibilities to the other closed settings listed above, as containers for action their geography is less prescribed. And, of course, an island can contain any or all of the venues for crime listed above.

Three of Christie's whodunits are set on islands: *And Then There Were None* (1939)[6]; *Evil Under the Sun* (1941), featuring Hercule Poirot; and *A Caribbean Mystery* (1964), featuring Miss Marple.

And Then There Were None is Christie's bestselling novel (with over 100 million copies sold worldwide) and is considered by many critics to be her masterpiece. Ten people are lured to an island under a variety of pretexts by a mysterious employer-cum-host that none of them has met. On their first night on the island a gramophone recording accuses each of the guests of getting away with murder and informs them that they have been brought to the island to pay for their past crimes. Marooned by a violent storm, the ten are murdered one by one in a gruesome parody of the nursery rhyme, "Ten Little Soldiers." In the absence of a Poirot or Marple to deliver the denouement, a postscript to the novel in the form of a message from the killer reveals his identity and method.

In *Evil Under the Sun,* Poirot is enjoying a quiet holiday at the instructively if conventionally named Jolly Roger Hotel on Smugglers' Island when the beautiful and flirtatious Arlena Marshall is found murdered on one of the small island's secluded beaches. Poirot and the police interview the guests, all of whom have secrets and motives that make them suspects.

A Caribbean Mystery takes place in the Golden Palm Hotel on the island of St Honoré, where Miss Marple is convalescing following a bout of pneumonia. Half-listening to another of Major Palgrave's long-winded stories, Miss Marple's attention is caught when he begins to tell her a story about a man who got away with murder. As he is about to show her a photograph of the murderer he glances over her shoulder, sees someone, and hastily returns the photo to his wallet while loudly launching into a different story. The next day he is found dead, apparently of natural causes. Miss Marple, however, is convinced he was murdered, and that the murderer is the person the Major saw behind her.

The descriptions of the fictional island of St Honoré are most likely based on St Lucia, an island in the West Indies that Christie had visited on holiday. Similarly, both Soldier Island, where the victims unwittingly gather in *And Then There Were None*, and Smugglers' Island, the setting for *Evil Under the Sun*, draw on Christie's first-hand knowledge of Burgh Island off the south coast of Devon. However, her islands are *not* St Lucia or Burgh Island. Referential meaning is not important in Christie's fiction. As Kim Wilkins explains,

> Each genre is structured by its own regimes of verisimilitude, which are consistent with what is commonly held to be true for that genre at that time. Verisimilitude, therefore, operates at the levels of *plausibility* and *probability*.[7]

For Wilkins, "regimes of verisimilitude give genres their distinctive qualities. They signal the genre to the reader, then they fulfill the expectations of the reader."[8] In Christie's island murder mysteries geographical verisimilitude only matters to the extent that it permits the mechanics of the clue-puzzle mystery, whereas in Chris Ewan's crime thrillers *Safe House* (2012) and *Dark Tides* (2014), both set on the Isle of Man, geographical verisimilitude is expected by the reader. Each island Christie builds is a separate crime location. Its topography, insofar as it is described, is painstakingly imagined and constructed, unlike, for example, the real island settings of the Shetland Islands in Ann Cleeves's Jimmy Perez series, or the Pacific island of Tarawa (an atoll in the Gilbert Islands and the capital of the Republic of Kiribati) in Marianne Wheelaghan's *Food of Ghosts* (2012), where the topography always already exists. Christie's islands are places where a small group of individuals are exposed as possible victims and placed under scrutiny as possible suspects; they are circumscribed spaces in which the number of potential suspects is carefully contained and where the topography can be manipulated to aid the plot in the way that the topography of "real" islands cannot.

First and foremost, then, Christie's islands are bounded spaces; second, the topography of her islands is part of the fabric of the clue-puzzle, and integral to the plot in just the same way the layouts of Styles Court in *The Mysterious Affair at Styles* and Fernly Park in *The Murder of Roger Ackroyd*

(1926), for example, are integral to those plots. If Styles offers a "bucolic dream of England,"[9] which is shattered by the murder of Emily Inglethorp, so Christie's islands, where people go for their holidays or to convalesce, to relax and escape from the stresses of everyday life, are ripe to be disturbed by murder. The victims in *And Then There Were None* are lured to the island by the murderer (and final victim)—a framework later adopted in island horror fiction such as Richard Laymon's *Island* (1991), as well as in film and television horror, including the CBS mini-series, *Harper's Island* (2009).

Christie's *A Caribbean Mystery* trades on reader familiarity with touristic discourses of islands. Life on St Honoré "was sunshine, sea, and social pleasure,"[10] where visitors could enjoy (or otherwise in Miss Marple's case) the relaxed routine: "Lovely and warm, yes—and *so* good for her rheumatism—and beautiful scenery, though perhaps—a trifle monotonous? So *many* palm trees. Everything the same every day—nothing ever *happening*."[11] This sense of idyllic island life is further enhanced through references to cultural topography, to the steel bands which "were one of the main attractions of the islands,"[12] and to a troupe of dancers who entertain the resort's guests in the evening. The strictly observed ritual of gathering on the beach each day, to sunbathe or swim in "the deep blue of a Caribbean Sea,"[13] provides an important contact zone for the guests. In this novel, while there are references to specific natural and cultural locations on the island—Castle Cliff, Pelican Point, and Jamestown, all of which offer pleasant alternatives to "a quiet morning on the beach"[14]—the physical geography of the island is not developed. This absence of physical description highlights the efficiency of the island setting for the crime fiction genre in particular, as well as for other genres. The tropes of islandness are so well known to readers of all forms of genre fiction that Christie only has to gesture towards the island to establish her setting in *A Caribbean Mystery*, whereas rich description is needed to establish other settings such as the country house or hotel, none of which *automatically* carry with them the sense of isolation or containment that (literary) usage has invested in the island.

In *A Caribbean Mystery* the setting is less St Honoré, and more the island's Golden Palm Hotel; in this novel it is the grounds of the hotel that contain both killer and suspects rather than the sea than encircles the island as a whole. Indeed, beyond the reader's own knowledge of the West Indies, there is little sense of the island, which is barely referenced beyond the gates of the hotel. The qualities of islandness, the senses of solitude, isolation, and insularity that a small island generates in popular fiction are untethered from the notion of a tract of land surrounded by water. Gillian Beer argues that

> islands, as the language of bio-geography reminds us, need not be only parcels of land; they can in that discourse be ponds or lakes, clearings in the wood, or

clusters of trees on the plain. That is, in this bio-geographical usage islands are enclosures within which intimate ecological relations prevail and from which their population cannot escape and survive (not fish in the wood, or tree-insects on the plain).[15]

In this sense, then, *A Caribbean Mystery* is an "island" crime novel in two senses: both for its setting on St Honoré and the treatment of the hotel as a metaphorical island. Indeed, if we were to apply Beer's notion of islands as enclosures, *all* Christie's contained locations—country houses and hotels, trains and ships—might be read as islands.

Islands in Christie's crime oeuvre are places where individuals are exposed to danger and/or placed under scrutiny. The bounded island location (literal or metaphorical) also means that there are always a limited number of suspects. This is famously the case in *And Then There Were None*. In this novel ten seemingly disparate characters are drawn to Soldier Island, "a little island off the Devon coast," by the promise of a free holiday in "the luxurious modern house" that had been built there some years previously.[16] Despite not knowing their host, they accept their invitations because, as one of the party so succinctly puts it, "There was something magical about an island—the mere word suggested fantasy. You lost touch with the world—an island was a world of its own."[17] This generic response, which neatly captures the popular mythology of islands, also highlights, in the particular instance, the fact that only one of the party appears to be familiar with the island: "[Mr Blore] remembered Soldier Island as a boy ... Smelly sort of rock covered with gulls—stood about a mile from the coast. It had got its name from its resemblance to a man's head."[18] This initial description of the island clearly emphasises its physicality: its location and its ruggedness. The physical reality is emphasised from an early point in the narrative, when the travellers get their first glimpse of the island "jutting up out of the sea."[19] For one of the group, Vera Claythorpe, the island seems "a long way out"[20]; and she shivers, feeling that "There was something sinister about it."[21] Her sense of foreboding is heightened when the boatman who ferries the group across from the mainland cheerfully informs them that it is impossible to land on the island in a south-easterly, and that sometimes "'tis cut off for a week or more."[22] In similar fashion, the boatman taking Inspector Thorne and his party over to Bardsey Island in Mark Billingham's Welsh crime thriller *The Bones Beneath* (2014) announces that one group was "stuck out there for three weeks earlier in the year"[23] due to the bad weather. Once she has the party of strangers on the island, Christie continues to emphasise the watery perimeter of the island; looking south from the house, "there was no land to be seen anywhere—just a vast expanse of blue water."[24] The geography of the island is crucial in this novel. Once the group has been marooned by the storm, they realise that there is no way for them to communicate with the mainland. Looking back from the summit of the island they find that "The actual village of Sticklehaven could not be seen, only the hill above it, a jutting out cliff of red rock concealed the actual little bay."[25] It is apparent at this point to the members of the group that they have been lured to the island to be murdered one by one and that "Soldier Island is to be isolated until Mr. Owen has finished his job."[26]

The island geography thus enables a degree of isolation that is not achievable, for example, in a country house. It is almost always possible to escape from a house, a hotel, or a village, but with no boat and the storm raging, there is no way off the island. This device of using a violent storm to isolate the island is not uncommon in island crime fiction or in hybrid genres such as romantic suspense. It is also used very effectively, for example, in M. M. Kaye's *Death in the Andamans* (1960), where the storm not only isolates the guests at Government House but also threatens to destroy any clues to the initial murder.[27] In Ann Cleeves's *Blue Lightening* (2010), Fair Isle is isolated by a raging autumn storm, and in Peter May's *Entry Island* (2014), the storms that lash the titular island, an English-speaking enclave among Quebec's Îles de la Madelaine (Magdelen Islands), strand Detective Sime Mackenzie. Indeed, the weather, and violent storms in particular, is a common crossgeneric trope, also employed frequently, for example, in romance fiction where the island storm forces the principal characters to stay together, and in fantasy fiction where island storms frequently signify the presence of magic.

In *And Then There Were None* the topography as well as the geography of the island is crucial to the plot. As three of the party search "the more or less bare rock,"[28] Christie provides a detailed description of the island's topography in order to show that there is no hiding place for their host, U. N. Owen, whom they now suspect is the murderer. Moreover, as the village is not visible from the island, the possibilities of heliographing for help are also severely restricted by geography.

In this novel more than in any other of her island crime fictions (stories as well as novels), Christie not only exploits the geography and topography of her island, she also plays with island tropes, stranding her victims, having them explore their "desert island"[29] looking for boats or some means of communicating with the mainland, having them scavenge for food (albeit in the well-stocked larder), and having the murderer deliver his confession in a sealed bottle tossed into the sea. "The practice of throwing a bottle into the sea with an important document inside," he writes, "was one that never failed to thrill me when reading adventure stories as a child."[30] Christie's intertextual reference directs the reader back to Jules Verne, who employed a message in a bottle in both *In Search of the Castaways* (1873) and *The Mysterious Island* (1874), and Edgar Allan Poe's short story "MS. Found in a Bottle" (1833), and through those tales to the wider tradition of island adventure stories, from

Daniel Defoe's *Robinson Crusoe* (1719) through Robert Michael Ballantyne's *The Coral Island* (1857) to Robert Louis Stevenson's *Treasure Island* (1883). Light, however, prefers to read the novel "As a metaphor for the corruptions of insularity, [which] can be read on many levels, not least as an image of the mental universe of the British middle classes in the late 1930s, shut in and clannish, and increasingly marooned." It can, she continues, "be read as a veiled warning that those who live on an island must beware of becoming cut off."[31] Or, as Peter Messent succinctly puts it, "Golden Age crime fiction was socially as well as spatially enclosed."[32] In "one of Christie's coldest, most precise studies of human venality,"[33] British middle-class life is reflected in the unredeeming topography of Soldier Island. The island is also at once exotic and familiar, part of England but not quite—which raises the question of whether Christie's use of insular settings is linked to the anxiety and vulnerability of the British *Isles* in the inter-war years in *And Then There Were None* and into the Second World War in *Evil Under the Sun*.

As in *A Caribbean Mystery*, the contained space of the clue-puzzle is a hotel in *Evil Under the Sun*, though in this work the guests are not confined by the hotel grounds but roam freely around the island, as they do in *And Then There Were None*. The island—as a physical setting—takes on much greater significance in *Evil Under the Sun*. Importantly, Christie includes a literary map of Smugglers' Island (figure 2.1) immediately before the narrative commences.

This visual paratext, which unlike the floor plan in *The Mysterious Affair at Styles* or the plan of the Calais coach in *Murder on the Orient Express* (1934) is never referred to in the narrative, provides the reader with a clear impression of the imaginary geography of the island before the narrative itself commences. This map in many ways highlights the connections between geography and literature that are of interest to us in this book and in particular the importance of islands in terms of place and setting in popular genre fiction as a whole. Indeed, Christie's island as depicted in the map bears more than a passing resemblance to Nora Roberts's islands and to many of the islands imagined along the American east coast by romance writers. There are three core questions, identified by Sally Bushell, that need to be asked when interpreting literary maps: "What does the map add to the text? What does the reading of the map do to the reading of the text, and vice versa? What might the map reveal about the text, or the text about the map?"[34]

The presence of the map at the beginning of *Evil Under the Sun* signals the importance of spatiality in Christie's crime fiction (as in all locked-room mysteries). In this case the island space depicted in the map provides a bounded environment which allows "for a limited number of possible intersections of person, event, and location."[35] Christian Jacob's discussion of "fictive maps" is useful in this context: he observes that islands "occupy a privileged

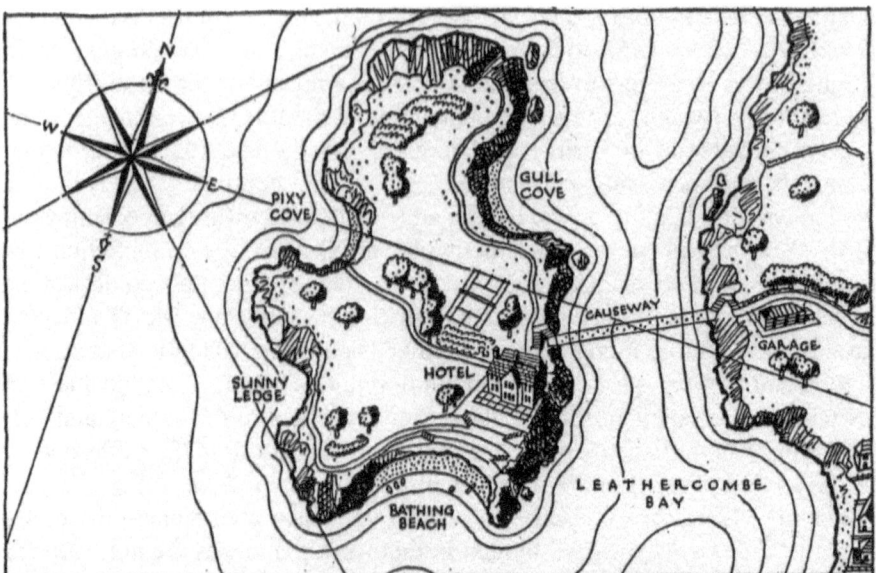

Figure 2.1. Map of Smugglers' Island in Agatha Christie, *Evil Under the Sun* (1941; repr., London: HarperCollins, 2008).

place" in the cartography of fiction.[36] For Jacob, "A form surrounded by the sea, perfectly detached and visible on the surface of the enframed map, the island, because of its limited size, is less likely to be cluttered with excessive and confusing information."[37] As Poirot attempts to piece together who was doing what, where, and when, the map (presumably the hotel map referred to in the novel[38]) offers the reader a seemingly reliable means of confirming and *understanding* the movements of the various suspects in spatial terms, and indeed, if the map were to scale (though the comparative sizes of the hotel and tennis court suggest otherwise), temporally, too. The map, then, aids what in his discussion of *The Murder of Roger Ackroyd* Knight has referred to as Poirot's "rigid attention to an objectified sense of time and place," "his superior attention to the clock and the map."[39] At the same time, the limited narrative of the map emphasises the apparent impossibility of the crime, or of any of the island suspects being the murderer; indeed the tidal causeway graphically keeps open the possibility of the murderer being an outsider, just as the bridge, the closure of which temporarily isolates Hedeby Island from the mainland, keeps open the possibility of outsider involvement in the disappearance of Harriet Vanger in Stieg Larsson's *The Girl with the Dragon Tattoo* (2005). In the end, like Poirot, the reader must be prepared to look beyond the empirical evidence of a map for other clues. As Bushell notes,

Poirot "repeatedly asserts the limits of mere empirical evidence in favour of psychological interpretation of the individual."[40] The map is not only a visual version of the narrative map Christie draws in the text: it is simultaneously both a clue and a red herring.

Smugglers' Island is immediately established as a tidal island, cut off twice a day at each high tide, despite the concrete causeway that joined it to the mainland. The various island zones are established early, too: the "beaches, coves, and queer little paths,"[41] and the series of terraces that lead from the hotel to the sea. The hotel guests spend their time sunbathing, swimming, or in boats—all activities immediately associated with islands and their proximity to the ocean. The narrative map of the island is drawn in some detail:

> When you came out of the hotel on the south side the terraces and the bathing beach were immediately below you. There was also a path that led off round the cliff on the south-west side of the island. A little way along it, a few steps led down to a series of recesses cut into the cliff and labeled on the hotel map of the island as Sunny Ledge. Here cut out of the cliff were niches with seats in them.[42]

It is noticeable, too, that the topography is frequently introduced in conjunction with characters: "Rosamund Darnley and Kenneth Marshall sat on the short springy turf of the cliff overlooking Gull Cove. This was on the east side of the island."[43] Similarly, during the course of the investigation the knowledge different characters have of the island's topography is revealed to the reader; thus the reader is alerted to the fact that Patrick Redfern, who is later revealed as the murderer, and his victim, Arlena, met secretly, and "used to go off for a stroll together to different parts of the island."[44]

The "sense of space"[45] associated with islands in the Shetlands of Cleeves's *Thin Air* (2014) is never present on Christie's islands, and here, as in *And Then There Were None*, the weather is used to establish and maintain the atmosphere of the locked-room mystery: "Rain was falling and mist encircled the island."[46] Using the weather, particularly dramatic weather events such as tempests, snowstorms, or heavy fog, is a common means of turning the tide of the story and/or the investigation in crime fiction. And given the unpredictability of the weather, even of violent weather, the author is able to manipulate it to his or her design. The atmosphere of the locked-room mystery is further enhanced by the size of the island, which is small enough to be circumnavigated in a rowing boat before lunch even when setting off at half past eleven. This carefully constructed sense of containment or bounded space means that from the outset the police are able to conclude that "our murderer must be pretty well within a limited radius"[47]—that is, a guest at the island hotel rather than an outsider. As Poirot makes clear, "A man bent on murder could not risk coming in broad daylight across the causeway and past the hotel. Someone might have seen him."[48] Further, the distance from the mainland, the strong currents between the harbour and the island, and hotel staff keeping a lookout for uninvited visitors makes the likelihood of the murderer arriving by boat extremely small.

In the end it is knowledge of the island—of possible routes to the murder spot, and specifically the distance from the hotel to the ladder down to Pixy Cove and on to the beach—that give Poirot the power to solve the mystery. It is significant, then, that "Hercule Poirot sat on the turf on the summit of the island,"[49] monarch of all he surveyed,[50] as he pieced together the final clues in the murder puzzle. The symbolism of his position in relation to both the mystery and the island is unmistakable. In Christie's crime fiction an island *can* be controlled. From his vantage point atop the island, Poirot is able to produce the map and the timeline of events leading up to Arlena Marshall's murder, restoring the island to the comprehensible, orderly, and safe place it had previously been.

NOTES

1. Stephen Knight, *Crime Fiction Since 1800: Detection, Death, Diversity*, 2nd ed. (London: Palgrave Macmillan, 2010), 89.

2. Julian Symons, *Bloody Murder: From the Detective Story to the Crime Novel: A History* (London: Faber, 1972), 129.

3. Alison Light, *Forever England: Femininity, Literature and Conservatism Between the Wars* (London and New York: Routledge, 1991), 61.

4. Light, *Forever England*, 91–92.

5. Stephen Knight, "The Golden Age," in *The Cambridge Companion to Crime Fiction*, ed. Martin Priestman (Cambridge: Cambridge University Press, 2003), 77–79.

6. First published in Britain as *Ten Little Niggers*, the title was later changed to *Ten Little Indians* before the American title, *And Then There Were None*, was adopted for all English-language editions in the 1980s. Similarly, the island was previously called Nigger Island and Indian Island.

7. Kim Wilkins, "The Process of Genre: Authors, Readers, Institutions," *Text* 9, no. 2 (2005), accessed 27 July 2015, http://www.textjournal.com.au/oct05/wilkins.htm.

8. Wilkins, "The Process of Genre."

9. David Grossvogel, "Agatha Christie: Containment of the Unknown," in *The Poetics of Murder*, ed. Glenn W. Most and William W. Stowe (New York: Harcourt Brace Jovanovich, 1983), 256.

10. Agatha Christie, *A Caribbean Mystery* (1964; repr., London: HarperCollins, 2006), 43.

11. Christie, *A Caribbean Mystery*, 12.

12. Christie, *A Caribbean Mystery*, 22.

13. Christie, *A Caribbean Mystery*, 8.

14. Christie, *A Caribbean Mystery*, 141.

15. Gillian Beer, "Island Bounds," in *Islands in History and Representations*, ed. Rod Edmond and Vanessa Smith (London: Routledge, 2003), 33.

16. Agatha Christie, *And Then There Were None* (1939; repr., London: HarperCollins, 2013), 5.

17. Christie, *And Then There Were None*, 33.

18. Christie, *And Then There Were None*, 17–18.

19. Christie, *And Then There Were None*, 23.

20. Christie, *And Then There Were None*, 23.

21. Christie, *And Then There Were None*, 23.

22. Christie, *And Then There Were None*, 27.

23. Mark Billingham, *The Bones Beneath* (London: Sphere, 2014), 145.

24. Christie, *And Then There Were None*, 32.

25. Christie, *And Then There Were None*, 92.

26. Christie, *And Then There Were None*, 101.

27. Originally published in Great Britain under the title *Night on the Island*.

28. Christie, *And Then There Were None*, 102.

29. Christie, *And Then There Were None*, 229.

30. Christie, *And Then There Were None*, 239.

31. Light, *Forever England*, 98.

32. Peter Messent, *The Crime Fiction Handbook* (Chichester: Wiley-Blackwell, 2013), 128.

33. Robert Merrill, "Christie's Narrative Games," in *Theory and Practice of Classic Detective Fiction*, ed. Jerome H. Delamater and Ruth Prigozy (Westport: Greenwood, 1997), 99.

34. Sally Bushell, "The Slipperiness of Literary Maps: Critical Geography and Literary Cartography," *Cartographica* 47, no. 3 (2012): 153.

35. Bushell, "The Slipperiness of Literary Maps," 154.

36. Christian Jacob, *The Sovereign Map: Theoretical Approaches in Cartography Throughout History*, ed. Edward H. Dahl, trans. Tom Conley (Chicago: Chicago University Press, 2006), 286.

37. Jacob, *The Sovereign Map*, 286.

38. See page 40, for example.

39. Stephen Knight, *Form and Ideology in Crime Fiction* (London: Macmillan, 1980), 119.

40. Bushell, "The Slipperiness of Literary Maps," 158.

41. Agatha Christie, *Evil Under the Sun* (1941; repr., London: HarperCollins, 2008), 36.

42. Christie, *Evil Under the Sun*, 40.

43. Christie, *Evil Under the Sun*, 44.

44. Christie, *Evil Under the Sun*, 116.

45. Ann Cleeves, *Thin Air* (2014; repr. London: Pan, 2015), 238.

46. Christie, *Evil Under the Sun*, 52.

47. Christie, *Evil Under the Sun*, 79.

48. Christie, *Evil Under the Sun*, 197.

49. Christie, *Evil Under the Sun*, 208.

50. William Cowper's "Verses, Supposed to be written by Alexander Selkirk, during his solitary abode in the island of Juan Fernandez" (1782), begins:

>I am monarch of all I survey,
>My right there is none to dispute;
>From the centre all round to the sea
>I am lord of the fowl and the brute.

Chapter Three

The Postcolonial Geography of Island Crime

G. W. Kent's Solomon Islands Series

The covers of the original UK paperback editions of G. W. Kent's three Sister Conchita and Sergeant Kella mysteries, set in the Solomon Islands, each depict a highly stylised image of an island (figures 3.1, 3.2, 3.3). These two-dimensional illustrations present naïve topographical maps of an island, surrounded by water and with contours depicting both the shoreline and the littoral zone. For Christian Jacob, "the island is a space suited par excellence to vertical, cartographical viewing."[1] On the covers of Kent's crime novels, the aerial perspective creates a sense of omniscience while simultaneously inviting closer scrutiny.

Each map includes the outline of at least one body as well as bright red blood splatters, which clearly signal the genre. Additionally, each illustration has several other features linked to the particular murder mystery enclosed within the book's bright cover: a skeleton, a pistol, and a boat on the cover of *Devil-Devil* (2011); a skull, a church, three crosses, and three nuns on the cover of *One Blood* (2012); and a boat, a Japanese flag, several animals, a couple of figures (a nun and suited man), and a solitary figure (in red shorts and short-sleeved shirt) on the cover of *Killman* (2013). These props gesture to the board and playing pieces in a game of *Cluedo*—suspects, weapons, and locations that help the players determine the murderer and here point to the style of mystery: more clue-puzzle than noir. Further, both the placement of clues on the map and the tagline which appears on the front covers of *One Blood* and *Killman*—"Move over Botswana, the Solomon Islands is the place to be"[2]—assume the reader's acquaintance with the detective fiction genre in general and Alexander McCall Smith's No. 1 Ladies' Detective Agency series in particular. Specifically, the gestures to McCall

Figure 3.1. G. W. Kent, *Devil-Devil* (London: Robinson, 2011).

Figure 3.2. G. W. Kent, *One Blood* (London: Robinson, 2012).

Figure 3.3. G. W. Kent, *Killman* (London: C&R Crime, 2013).

Smith's work signal that the novels in Kent's series are also postcolonial or anthropological detective fictions in which indigenous culture plays a significant role, and that, as in McCall Smith's novels, readers of Kent's mysteries will be immersed in *place*. The palm trees, seagulls, and dolphins that feature on each of the three covers emphatically signal the Pacific island setting.

Kent's detective, Sergeant Ben Kella, is a Solomon Islander, one of the salt-water people from the Lau Lagoon on the north-east coast of the island of Malaita. He is also the *aofia*, the traditional peacemaker of the Lau people, and distinctly not a member of the colonial elite that still ruled the Solomons in the early 1960s, the historical milieu of the novels. His sidekick, Sister Conchita, a Boston-Irish nun (who chose her religious name expecting to be posted to South America), is an excellent foil to the native policeman. In part this is because as a nun she, like Kella, is beyond the expatriate pale (though not as far outside). More importantly though, it is because she is not simply a "spectator," as Franco Moretti suggests Watson is in the Sherlock Holmes stories.[3] Rather, she plays an active and at times thoroughly independent role that clashes with, as well as complements, Kella's investigations. While Kent's crime novels follow a conventional pattern—the body found, the protagonists in place, the clues followed, and the mystery solved—the combination of his native policeman and white sidekick allows him to shift the framework to accommodate a postcolonial perspective. Thus, for example, Kent pits against each other indigenous and colonial methodologies as well as pagan and Catholic superstitions. While solving the crime remains the primary focus of Kent's novels, his choice of a postcolonial detective adds a second strand to the narrative. For the reader there is an added layer of interest insofar as the investigation in each case invites questions about the nature of colonialism and the position of the expatriate community in a group of islands moving inexorably towards independence.

Importantly, as Ed Christian notes, "Most indigenous postcolonial detectives have been created not by indigenous authors but by ex-colonisers, generally white men who have lived in the countries they write about or who have studied them sympathetically."[4] This is true of Kent's Sergeant Kella. For eight years Kent lived and travelled widely in the Solomon Islands, where he ran the educational broadcasting service, so he is familiar with his setting, albeit as an outsider and a cog in the colonial machine. As he explained in an interview following the publication of *One Blood*, during the period he lived in the Solomons he "was lucky enough to spend much of [his] time in the remoter parts of [the] islands, travelling on foot and by canoe through jungles and across rivers[,] reefs and mountains," meeting thousands of islanders in their homes, encountering expatriates, including "white-robed Marist Catholic sisters of all nations," and "indigenous policemen" who "would travel on foot for 100s of miles in pursuit of culprits, often defying the all-powerful district headmen and *ramos*, or hired killers." These experiences proved to be the stimulus that led to the pairing of his fictional detective and sidekick:

> As the years passed and I grew to know the islands a little better, I began to wonder what might happen if one of these tough pagan police officers should be forced to link up with a young American nun, two people from completely different cultures forced to combine to track a malevolent killer. Decades later this proved to be the inspiration for my Sergeant Kella and Sister Conchita series.[5]

Clearly his novels—colonial-era mysteries with a postcolonial awareness—are aimed at a Western readership, rather than an indigenous (Melanesian/Polynesian) one, and for the non-Solomon Islands reader Kent appears to present both an accurate and sympathetic portrait of the geography and culture of his island locations. So while Stephen Knight is right to highlight the potential for so-called postcolonial detective fictions to perform a "culturally recolonizing role,"[6] it is also true, as Knight recognises, that crime fiction "can be used proactively both to explore and deplore oppressions and crimes with a focus on race and ethnicity" and that they can "develop plot and resolve crimes with reference to the experience and evaluative systems of their communities"[7]; or as Christian more prosaically puts it, "indigenous detectives often count on their cultural knowledge to help them solve crimes."[8] Whether Kent's crime fictions further the postcolonial agenda in Knight's terms may be a moot point, but his detective certainly uses his cultural instinct and his knowledge of Solomon Islands' myth and ritual to solve the crimes he encounters.

With just two exceptions, one of which is a death that took place eighteen years earlier during the Second World War, all the murder victims in Kent's series are Solomon Islanders, as are the murderers. As the deaths are often "custom killings," Kella must use his indigenous cultural knowledge to solve the crimes—a level of understanding of the geography and customs of the Solomon Islands to which his white superiors have little or no access. On the one occasion a white man's death is investigated by Kella and Sister Conchita (in *One Blood*) the killer turns out to be an expatriate, thus ensuring that racial tension does not become the focus of these island mysteries. Moreover, Kent is always alert to "geographic and ethnic niceties,"[9] and does not homogenise the Solomon Islands or the Solomon Islanders in his novels, as his colonial officials are wont to do. Instead he is alert to the cultural differences between the islands and islanders as well as the more nuanced divisions between tribal groups within particular islands. On the other hand, English, Australian, and American expatriates are collectively referred to as "whitey" by the islanders, with no regard to the cultural differences between them.

If we accept Peter Messent's suggestion that "one of the most productive ways of thinking about [crime fiction] is its relationship to the dominant social system: to the hierarchies, norms, and assumptions of the particular area, country, and historical period it represents,"[10] then it may be useful to consider further Kent's novels through a postcolonial lens. Kent's islands are what Mary Louise Pratt terms "contact zones," "social spaces where disparate cultures meet, clash, and grapple with each other, often in highly asymmetrical relations of domination and subordination."[11] And while it is clear that cultural methods of detection are always treated as subordinate to Western ones by Kella's superiors, it is also clear that the contact zones in the novels are also spaces of interaction where cultural exchange takes place, not least between Kella and Sister Conchita, who together use traditional as well as Western forms of knowledge to solve the crimes they encounter. If Kella's role, like that of any detective in crime fiction, is to solve the crime and restore order and the rule of law, in these novels there is always in the background a vexed question: which rule of law should be restored, the colonial one or the cultural one? The answer is not, of course, straightforward. All Kella's actions are complicated by his loyalty to both tribal custom and his position as a member of the Solomon Islands Police Force, a situation that is highlighted regularly throughout the three novels. Early in *Devil-Devil*, for example, after a village headman questions Kella's authority, he responds by telling the headman first that "I speak as the government's policeman,"[12] and then adding, in a raised voice so that the gathered crowd of villagers can hear, "I speak as your *aofia*, directed by the spirits to keep the peace."[13] Here, as elsewhere, Kella is aware that his cultural status carries more weight with the native population than his legal one.

A number of authors have used Pacific island settings for their crime fiction since 2011, including Kent, John Enright, whose Jungle Beat Mystery series set in American Samoa runs to four novels, Catherine Titasey, whose *My Island Homicide* (2013) is set on Thursday Island, and Marianne Wheelaghan, whose two Scottish Lady Detective novels, *Food of Ghosts* (2012) and *The Shoeshine Killer* (2015), are set on Tarawa and Fiji, respectively. In all these novels place, the real geography (physical and cultural) of the islands—the Solomon Islands, American Samoa, Thursday Island, Tarawa in Kiribati, and Fiji—is a critical element in the story. The importance of place is emphasised by the inclusion of maps in several of these crime fictions. In *Food of Ghosts* Wheelaghan provides the reader with a literary map of the Tarawa Atoll, the specific setting of the novel, and a much smaller-scale map which locates Tarawa in both Kiribati and in the wider region of Oceania. Similarly, *Devil-Devil* includes a literary map of the Solomon Islands, with an inset smaller-scale map of the western South Pacific Ocean which faces the opening page of the novel.

While, like the map in Agatha Christie's *Evil Under the Sun*, this visual paratext is not referred to in the narrative, it clearly identifies the various islands Kella and Sister Conchita visit in this novel (and in the later novels in his series) and provides an important sense of scale (the map scale is clearly provided in the top left). The wide expanse of ocean evident in both the main and inset maps highlights the island geography that plays such a strong role in each mystery. The inclusion of a map at the beginning of the first book in Kent's series foregrounds the bounded nature of each of the islands in the archipelagic state and highlights their physical proximity to each other. It also introduces the location to readers who may not be familiar with this part of the Pacific. Readers of crime fiction set in exotic locations expect to be transported to a place that most of them will never be able to visit. So the *place*, the *island*, is especially important in crime fiction set in the South Pacific, in the Solomon Islands, Samoa, Kiribati, or Fiji. The island setting is even more important in Kent's mysteries, as it is in Enright's, where the novel's topographies, the Solomon Islands, or American Samoa, reveal to the reader something about the character of the indigenous detectives, Ben Kella or Enright's Apelu Soifua, and the societies in which they operate.

Whereas the map in *Evil Under the Sun* serves to limit the number of suspects Poirot must consider, the map that prefaces Kent's series, rather than providing a clue of any sort, serves to emphasise the difficulty of the task facing Kella, who must engage with the geography of an extensive archipelago rather than a single small island. In other words, Kent's literary map emphasises a sense of island/ocean space—like that exploited in Ann Cleeves's Shetland quartets, for example—rather than the sense of containment Christie favours in her island mysteries. The purpose of the literary map provided at the outset of *Devil-Devil* is achieved in *One Blood* by a narrative map, a description of the Solomon Islands archipelago early in the book: "The Solomons consisted of a string of hundreds of beautiful and remote tropical islands, five hundred miles east of Papua New Guinea and a thousand miles north-east of Australia."[14] Nevertheless, the setting is not entirely open, despite the extensive geography. As in a game of *Cluedo*, the movements of the suspects are not confined to a single room (island), but they are limited by the extent of the house (archipelago). "The islands were difficult to reach"[15] and thus difficult to escape. In the final analysis it is knowledge of the islands—of both their topography and customs—that enables Kella to solve the crime(s). In general terms, the crimes in these novels play out in similar ways to those in Christie's novels discussed in the previous chapter. However, given that the islands in Kent's series are almost all true places that can be found on any map of the region, geographical verisimilitude is crucial,[16] and neither the topography nor the customs of real islands—nor the means and time of travelling between them—can be altered to suit the plot. Thus, when the plot requires place to be significantly altered, Kent must invent an island. The signs of desecration of the interior rainforest and the damage to the reef which Kella finds on "the ruined logging island of Alvaro"[17] (named with more than a little irony after the Spanish navigator, Alvaro de Mendana, the first European to visit the Solomon Islands) would have been incongruous if located on a real island in the archipelago.

In *Devil-Devil* Kella is sent to his home island of Malaita to search for a missing American anthropologist. He soon finds himself examining a "custom death,"[18] being cursed by a local magic man, catching Sister Conchita re-interring the bones of an Australian beachcomber who had probably been murdered eighteen years earlier, and getting caught up in a smuggling operation that leads to several murders, all of which he solves with the help of the strong-willed nun. In the second novel, *One Blood*, Kella is sent to investigate the sabotage of international logging interests in the Western District, far from his home island of Malaita. Meanwhile, in the same district an American tourist is murdered in the church of the run-down Marakosi Mission (on Gizo) that Sister Conchita has been sent to supervise until a replacement priest can be found to head the mission station. Some of the political and environmental concerns facing the country as it transitions towards independence are confidently introduced as Kella and Sister Conchita join forces to solve a web of crimes which are also linked back to the sinking of the torpedo boat PT-109, under the command of then Lieutenant John F. Kennedy, by the Japanese in August 1943. In *Killman* the death of the leader of a religious sect is followed by two more murders that suggest a professional killer is on the loose and that he may be a Japanese soldier still hidden in the jungle fifteen years after the end of the war. In their search for the "killman," the lines of enquiry pursued by Kella and Sister Conchita take them from Malaita to the remote Polynesian outlier island of Tikopia in the far southeast of the Solomons.

Devil-Devil opens with a scene of arrival as Sister Conchita fights to paddle her dugout canoe to shore after she is abandoned by her Malaitan guide a hundred yards from the coastal village where a large crowd of cheering locals gather to monitor her efforts. This opening scene introduces the reader not only to Sister Conchita (Kella is introduced in the next chapter) but also to the island–sea–custom triad that she must learn everything about if she intends "serving God in the Solomons"[19] or, as yet unbeknown to her, helping Kella unravel the mysteries in which they find themselves embroiled. By being introduced in the act of *arriving*, Sister Conchita is presented as an outsider. However, her refusal to panic when she is abandoned by the native paddler and left "to fight the sea alone"[20] earns the applause and respect of the watching villagers and is an early indication that while she may be an outsider, she will prove to have unusual insight into and empathy with the islands and islanders. As the expatriate John Deacon, who is amongst the crowd on the beach, explains, "They wanted to see what you were made of. You didn't do so bad. Most shielas just stay in the boat screaming bloody murder."[21] In contrast, native characters, who are always already there, are frequently introduced through their association with specific islands and customs: Solomon Bulko is from Choiseul in the Western Solomons; Mendana Gau is from the Santa Cruz island group; Sergeant Ha'a is from New Georgia; and so on. But even then, the islands themselves are divided both topographically and culturally. The old priest, Father Pierre, head of the mission station at Ruvabi on Malaita, explains to Sister Conchita that "On this one island alone we have thirteen different clans"[22] and that Kella is

> a Sulufou man. The Malaitans are the hardest men in the Solomons, and the ones from Sulufou are the pick of the bunch. They don't only build their own houses, they construct whole islands, stone by stone, out in the lagoon, when they're not fighting the bush people inland, or taking their canoes hundreds of miles out to sea.[23]

Kella, then, is a Malaitan before he is a Solomon Islander. Each island is clearly defined by its distinct topography and multiple cultural identities, and each Solomon Islander is in turn defined by his or her island. This is particularly true of the Sulufou men who literally build their own islands: the artificial islands in the Lau Lagoon. The distinction and divisions between the islands are seen, too, in the Labour Lines in the capital Honiara on Guadalcanal, where itinerant workers are housed in "long breeze-block buildings [...] each one reserved for the workers of a different island,"[24] and in the town's bars where the workers drank "in island coteries."[25]

In *One Blood* Sister Conchita's increased identification with the islands is reflected in an early scene in which she confidently "guided her narrow-draught canoe across the Roviana Lagoon, one hand on the tiller of the diesel-driven Yamaha outboard motor."[26] She remains, however, an outsider: as Father Pierre warns her, "If she wanted to make a success of her mission in the islands, she would have to learn much more about the local religions, and perhaps even experience their true meanings and wellsprings."[27] In other words, she must understand her native congregation if she is to be of any use to them, or, indeed, to Kella.

The identity of the native characters in the novel is again forcefully determined by their island locales. Faced with the prospect of being sent to the Western District on an assignment, Kella tells his superiors—Robinson, the Secretary for Internal Affairs, and the irascible Chief Superintendent Grice—"I know nothing of the customs and traditions of other parts of the Solomons," adding "I would be of no use to you outside my own island."[28] For Kella, "Sending a Lau man to investigate a crime in the Western Solomons would be akin to asking an Inuit to intervene in an inter-tribal squabble in Dahomey."[29] In the case of Australian-educated Mary Gui, her island identity is literally inscribed on her body in the tattooing ceremony Kella stumbles upon in a Kolombangara village:

> Twenty or so women were gathered around a slight figure seated hunched on a tree stump outside one of the leaf houses. [...] blood was pouring down her back in rivulets as she was hunched forward, writhing in agony on her seat. One woman standing behind her, frowning in concentration, was tracing a maze of patterns on the girl's soft skin with a pointed bone of a bat, while another woman was rubbing coloured herbs into the bleeding wounds.[30]

When Kella asks her why she has done this to herself she answers: "I'm proud of my traditions and I wanted to go through the ceremony. *Now everyone will know that I come from Kolombangara*" (emphasis added).[31] Similarly, Kent's readers will appreciate that character and (island) place are inextricably linked.

And just as individual characters are strongly identified with specific islands, so each island is specifically described. The large volcanic island of Kolombangara is "a dank, inhospitable place."[32] The small island of Kasolo in the Roviana Lagoon, where Kennedy and his crew swam ashore after their torpedo boat had been rammed and sunk, and where Sister Conchita finds the semiconscious white youth, Andy Russell, is "about a hundred yards wide by seventy yards long, with a ring of white sandy beach and a profusion of the spiky green foliage of the tall casuarina trees covering its centre."[33] And "the notorious Kundu Hite, more commonly known as Skull Island"[34] is "flat, less than fifty yards long and not as wide. Trees grew right down to the water's edge, leaving no room for a beach."[35] The carefully defined topography—the size and physical characteristics of each island—establishes the setting (in terms of locale) and contributes to the characterisation and plot of each novel.

In *Killman* the nature of islands is emphasised through the importance of boats as a means of transport. When Sister Conchita approaches the tiny artificial island of Foubebe where the burial of Papa Noah, the murdered (we later discover) leader of the breakaway cult, the Church of the Blessed Ark, is to take place, she is met with the sight of "several hundred canoes in the lagoon ahead of her," which "varied from simple dugouts with a single occupant to large, plank-built craft containing whole families"[36] that have transported the mourners to the island. Elsewhere there are references to the government boat, the *Commissioner*, which "Every three months made a heavily subsidised seven-day trip to the tiny remote island of Tikopia,"[37] and

Kella is frequently seen approaching islands in his dugout canoe or aboard other, larger vessels.

Beyond Kella's "home island"[38] of Malaita, the Polynesian island of Tikopia features strongly in *Killman*. As *The Spirit of the Islands* approaches Tikopia, with Kella, Sister Conchita, and several other characters who are key to the plot among its passengers, the principal features of the island are fulsomely described:

> At first Tikopia had been a mere child's unformed pencil smudge on the flat far edge of the sea. As the ship drew nearer, the vague land form filled out to reveal sandy beaches, a thickly forested interior and a central volcanic mountain. The outline of a lake shimmered at the foot of the volcano. Flocks of grey ducks floated lethargically over its surface, while pied cormorants flapped watchfully overhead, looking for shoals of mullet in the brackish water. A guidebook had informed Sister Conchita that the whole island was only three miles long and about half that wide.[39]

Here the details of the topography and fauna transform the generic "island" into a specific one as the boat draws closer. The "notoriously rebellious and feckless"[40] Tikopians are carefully linked to Polynesian culture, perhaps most notably via the *vaka tapu*, the great canoe which carries the body of Shem on its final journey out to sea. Kella's indirect allusion to *Te Toki-a-Tāpiri*, a traditional Māori war canoe from the early 1800s, and an important signifier of Polynesian identity—"I thought there was only one left, in a museum in Auckland"[41]—serves to distinguish Tikopia from the Melanesian islands of the Solomons.

The trip to Tikopia also serves to highlight what might here usefully be called geography of the sea: the risk of missing an island as small as Tikopia without the aid of a compass and "sail[ing] into nothingness,"[42] and the ability of the islanders to steer by the stars: "for three days and nights, Shem had sat stoically, without sleep, in the bows of *The Spirit of the Islands*, steering by the tides and stars,"[43] to guide the ship to his home.

In all three novels, knowledge of the topographical and cultural geography of the islands, and of routes between the islands of the archipelago, gives Kella the power to solve the various crimes he and Sister Conchita investigate. He understands instinctively, for example, the full implications of Ed Blamires discovering Andy Russell hiding on Kasolo with a canoe, "which meant that he could go anywhere in the Roviana Lagoon."[44] Archipelagic thinking and custom knowledge are the keys to Kella restoring order to the islands. The scale of Kella's task is evident if we compare the literary map Kent includes at the beginning of *Devil-Devil* with the one Christie includes in *Evil Under the Sun*. Poirot's power to solve the murder of Arlena Marshall stems from the knowledge he acquires of the tiny Smugglers' Island. The *extent* of the task facing Kella in each of the Sister Conchita and Sergeant Kella mysteries (the deceptive order in which their names appear on the cover of *Devil-Devil* and the title pages of *One Blood* and *Killman*) is evident in the literary map of the Solomons. His knowledge must extend across an archipelago; his power is derived both from this knowledge, and from his position as *aofia*, which gives him the custom knowledge he needs to complement his topographical knowledge of the islands.

Tzvetan Todorov convincingly argues that detective fiction "contains not one but two stories: the story of the crime and the story of the investigation."[45] On one level, the literary map in Christie's novel helps the reader understand the story of the crime; on another it is a clue the reader can use in his or her attempt to solve the crime puzzle. The literary map in Kent's novel, however, only serves the first of these two purposes. Both the *scale* of the location and the concomitant lack of cultural knowledge prevent the reader from any serious attempt to solve the clue-puzzle in Kent's exotic locations.

NOTES

1. Christian Jacob, *The Sovereign Map: Theoretical Approaches in Cartography Throughout History*, ed. Edward H. Dahl, trans. Tom Conley (Chicago: Chicago University Press, 2006), 286.

2. G. W. Kent, *One Blood* (London: Robinson, 2012); G. W. Kent, *Killman* (London: C&R Crime, 2013).

3. Franco Moretti, "Clues," in *Signs Taken for Wonders: On the Sociology of Literary Forms* (1983; repr., London: Verso, 2005), 147.

4. Ed Christian, "Ethnic Postcolonial Crime and Detection (Anglophone)," in *A Companion to Crime Fiction*, ed. Charles J. Rzepka and Lee Horsley (Chichester: Wiley-Blackwell, 2010), 283.

5. Peter Moore, "GW Kent: The Secrets Behind His Solomon Island Murder Mysteries," *Wanderlust*, July 19, 2012, accessed 1 June 2015, http://www.wanderlust.co.uk/magazine/articles/interviews/g-w-kent-the-secrets-behind-his-solomon-island-murder-mysteries?page=all.

6. Stephen Knight, *Crime Fiction Since 1800: Detection, Death, Diversity*, 2nd ed. (London: Palgrave Macmillan, 2010), 200.

7. Knight, *Crime Fiction Since 1800*, 203.

8. Christian, "Ethnic Postcolonial Crime and Detection (Anglophone)," 291.

9. Kent, *Killman*, 187.

10. Peter Messent, *The Crime Fiction Handbook* (Chichester: Wiley-Blackwell, 2013), 11.

11. Mary Louise Pratt, *Imperial Eyes: Travel Writing and Transculturation* (London: Routledge, 1992), 4.

12. G. W. Kent, *Devil-Devil* (London: Robinson, 2011), 12.

13. Kent, *Devil-Devil*, 13.

14. Kent, *One Blood*, 3–4.
15. Kent, *One Blood*, 4.
16. Kent makes a rare error when in *One Blood* he refers on several occasions to "the island of Munda" (31); Munda is not an island, but the largest town on the island of New Georgia.
17. Kent, *One Blood*, 42.
18. Kent, *Devil-Devil*, 28.
19. Kent, *Devil-Devil*, 1.
20. Kent, *Devil-Devil*, 2.
21. Kent, *Devil-Devil*, 2.
22. Kent, *Devil-Devil*, 46.
23. Kent, *Devil-Devil*, 45.
24. Kent, *Devil-Devil*, 144.
25. Kent, *Devil-Devil*, 140.
26. Kent, *One Blood*, 31.
27. Kent, *One Blood*, 67.
28. Kent, *One Blood*, 24.
29. Kent, *One Blood*, 26.
30. Kent, *One Blood*, 86.
31. Kent, *One Blood*, 88.
32. Kent, *One Blood*, 114.
33. Kent, *One Blood*, 40.
34. Kent, *One Blood*, 204.
35. Kent, *One Blood*, 204.
36. Kent, *Killman*, 74.
37. Kent, *Killman*, 92.
38. Kent, *One Blood*, 43.
39. Kent, *Killman*, 145.
40. Kent, *Killman*, 93.
41. Kent, *Killman*, 154. *Te Toki-a-Tāpiri* is on display at the Auckland War Memorial Museum. This massive war canoe is twenty-five metres long and could carry up to a hundred warriors.
42. Kent, *Killman*, 135.
43. Kent, *Killman*, 145.
44. Kent, *One Blood*, 255.
45. Tzvetan Todorov, "The Typology of Detective Fiction," in *The Poetics of Prose*, trans. Richard Howard (Oxford: Blackwell, 1977), 44.

Part II

ISLAND THRILLERS, THRILLER ISLANDS

Chapter Four

Top Secret Islands

The Geography of Espionage and Adventure

In "The Typology of Detective Fiction," Tzvetan Todorov distinguishes between the whodunit and the thriller. He argues that the whodunit presents two stories, "the story of the crime and the story of the investigation,"[1] while the thriller "suppresses the first and vitalises the second."[2] In the thriller:

> We are no longer told about a crime anterior to the moment of the narrative; the narrative coincides with the action. No thriller is presented in the form of memoirs: there is no point reached where the narrator comprehends all past events, we do not even know if he will reach the end of the story alive. Prospection takes the place of retrospection.[3]

In arguing that the thriller should be recognised as a genre, Todorov identifies several characteristics, including its "tendency toward the marvelous and the exotic, which brings it closer on the one hand to the travel narrative, and on the other to contemporary science fiction."[4] Given this tendency, it is perhaps not surprising that many thriller writers have been drawn to the island—topographical shorthand for the marvellous and the exotic across popular genres and beyond—as a setting for their fiction.

If, as Stephen Heath suggests, literature (as a whole body rather than a field of writing; literature rather than Literature) is structured by "the power of genre conceptions,"[5] and if readers of popular fiction choose to feed voraciously at the table of a particular genre, it follows that fans of thrillers may be drawn not only to particular authors (Ian Fleming; Clive Cussler) or series (James Bond; Dirk Pitt) but also to particular types of thrillers (spy thrillers; adventure thrillers) or to particular settings (the Antarctic; islands). As Elizabeth Leane reminds us, "*Where* the action happens is […] of utmost importance when it comes to writing and selling thrillers."⁶ In David Poyer's *Louisiana Blue* (1994), when the hero Tiller Galloway's thoughts wander back to his native Hatteras Island he reflects that "the natural condition of an island [is] isolation."⁷ This view, while not peculiar to thrillers, takes on a particular inflection in the genre, as isolation, both geographical and social, becomes the prime condition for the pleasures and perils of a certain kind of adventure. Kingsley Amis recognises the link between geography and genre in his introduction to his James Bond continuation novel, *Colonel Sun* (1968). "The matter of setting, of *where*," is "so important in all Bond's adventures,"⁸ Amis writes, alerting us to the way setting (and he chooses the Greek islands for his contribution to the series) dictates the *type* of adventure Bond will have.

Small islands provide the perfect geography for whodunits, or clue-puzzle mysteries; similarly, islands—large as well as small—have proved fertile ground for thrillers. In British spy fiction Britain's awareness of its insular geography and its vulnerability to foreign invasion and the concomitant need for the island to be protected from incursion is so ubiquitous that the invasion novel has become a recognised sub-genre of the spy thriller. In Erskine Childers's classic *The Riddle of the Sands* (1903), for example, two amateur spies thwart a German plot to invade England when they discover a fleet of barges hidden amidst the shifting sands of the Frisian Islands. The novel is not only set among islands, it is also about protecting a vulnerable island nation from foreign invasion; in Childers's novel islands are at once sites of adventure and territory to be defended. Islands beyond the shores of the British Isles can thus also function as sites of threat as well as threatened sites. More generally, islands in thrillers are bounded spaces that serve to intensify the action, bases from where the villains can pursue their illicit activities undetected, and landscapes against which the heroes must pit themselves. Islands from around the globe have enabled the narratives of entrapment, escape, and rescue that are characteristic of thrillers, and have provided the exotic settings in which heroes and villains play out their dreadful contests. In his introduction to Ian Fleming's *Live and Let Die*, Andrew Taylor argues that, "[i]n broad terms, spy thrillers work because they tap into the political fears and insecurities of their readers; the genre's heroes make our world safe for us."⁹ This is true, too, for other types of thrillers, from adventure thrillers to psychological thrillers, though the fears and insecurities they tap into may not be political. When the setting is an island, the battleground carefully contained by the sea and isolated from larger landmasses, geography is employed to aid the hero in the pursuit of his mission.

In thrillers, particularly spy thrillers and adventure thrillers, islands are not a permanent base for the protagonist: while the detective in a crime fiction may be stationed on the Shetland Islands, typically the hero of a thriller only passes through the insular locations he or she visits. While not a tourist, per se, the hero of a thriller is nevertheless a visitor whose engagement with the island is often described in touristic terms. For the reader this provides an opportunity to visit vicariously an exotic location—or what Louis Turner and John Ash, writing about the tourist industry, usefully label the "pleasure periphery."[10] In Desmond Bagley's *Bahama Crisis* (1980), the unlikely hero, the entrepreneur Tom Mangan, must avert a politically motivated, cold-war plot that threatens his own successful tourism business, the viability of Bahaman tourism more generally, and ultimately the future of the Bahaman economy and the island nation itself. While other thriller writers borrow from the litany of tourism, Bagley brings the link between islands and tourism to the fore. His hero is not a visitor to the pleasure periphery, but a white Bahamian, a resident like many of the detectives in island crime fiction.

The islands of the West Indies, with their links back to nineteenth-century pirate fiction, provide the settings for numerous thrillers. Fleming sends James Bond to the Caribbean island of Jamaica in three of his 007 fictions, and to the Bahamas in a fourth, and there are references to various islands in the Antilles archipelagos in several others, too. Desmond Bagley chooses West Indian settings for two of his thrillers: *Wyatt's Hurricane* (1966), an early eco-thriller, is set on the fictional island of San Fernandez, and *Bahama Crisis* in the Bahamas. Dennis Wheatley's classic Gregory Sallust thriller, *The Island Where Time Stands Still* (1954), opens on a mysterious South Pacific island, while two of his Duke de Richleau stories, *Strange Conflict* (1941) and *Dangerous Inheritance* (1965), are set in Haiti and Sri Lanka, respectively. Haiti is also a background presence in Fleming's *Live and Let Die* (1954), and the setting for Nick Stone's dark, grisly Max Mingus thriller, *Mr Clarinet* (2006), the first in a trilogy to feature the ex-cop, ex-PI, ex-con. In the final volume in the series, *Voodoo Eyes* (2011), set in Cuba, Stone captures the atmosphere of America's *bête noire* as assuredly as he had earlier brought Haiti to life. David Poyer chooses the waters around Hatteras Island, off the North Carolina coast, and the Bahamas for the first two volumes of his Tiller Galloway underwater thriller series—*Hatteras Blue* (1989) and *Bahamas Blue* (1991)—while Michael Crichton, writing as John Lange, sets his underwater adventure thriller, *Grave Descend* (1970) in Jamaican waters. And Crichton's more recent thriller *State of Fear* (2004) takes readers from Paris to a number of remote locales, including the Solomon Islands.

The islands of the Mediterranean provide the settings for numerous thrillers. Jack Higgins's *The Dark Side of the Island* (1963) and *Night Judgement at Sinos* (1970) are set in the Greek Islands, while the action of Chris Allen's *Hunter* (2012), the second book of his Intrepid Series, largely takes place on Malta and Gozo, the largest two islands in the Maltese archipelago. The

Canary Islands are the site of a terrorist operation that Charlie Dean must foil in Stephen Coonts and William H. Keith's *Deep Black: Death Wave* (2011).

The titular island of John Buchan's last thriller, and the fifth and final outing of his popular hero, Richard Hannay, *The Island of Sheep* (1936)—"a spiritual place which you won't find on any map"[11]—is most often identified with the Faroe Islands by critics, including Patrick Parrinder, and John Gornall. Gornall suggests that "although a *locus amoenus*, a place as much of the imagination as of geography, the Island of Sheep is also set firmly within the archipelago, from which, on another level, it may equally well have derived its name (Faroes 'Islands of Sheep')."[12] The Faroe Islands are also the setting for several of Jógvan Isaksen's crime thrillers, including the eco-thriller *Walpurgis Tide* (2005), the first of his novels to have been translated into English. Welsh author Ken Follett sets his spy thriller, *Eye of the Needle* (1978), on the fictitious Storm Island, "a cold cruel island in the North Sea,"[13] off the coast of Scotland, and the titular island of Mo Hayder's horror-infused thriller, *Pig Island* (2006), takes readers to another imagined Scottish island. Two of Sharon Bolton's thrillers are set on islands: *Sacrifice* (2008) on the remote Scottish island of Shetland, and *Little Black Lies* (2015) on the Falkland Islands. Chris Ewan's *Safe House* (2012) and *Dark Tides* (2014) are set on the Isle of Man, which is also where his novel *Long Time Lost* (2016) opens.

Desmond Bagley's *Running Blind* (1970) follows ex-MI6 spy Alan Stewart on a mission in Iceland. Alistair MacLean's locked-room thriller, *Bear Island* (1971), takes place on the *Morning Rose* as it pushes north through the Barents Sea, and on the eponymous island in the Svalbard archipelago in the Norwegian Arctic. Jeremy Duns's cold-war thriller *The Moscow Option* (2012) is largely set in the archipelago of Aland, between Sweden and Norway. Indeed, Scandinavian islands have become popular locations for thrillers since the publication of Peter Hoeg's *Miss Smilla's Feeling for Snow* (1992). Hoeg's thriller is infused with the language, culture, and even the smell of Greenland, despite the fact that only a small section of the novel is actually set on the island; Greenland is a similarly evocative presence in Bernard Besson's eco-thriller, *The Greenland Breach* (2013). Islands also feature prominently in numerous other Scandi-thrillers, including works by three Swedish authors: Camilla Lackberg sets her psychological thriller, *The Lost Boy* (2009), on Graskar, a small island near Fjällbacka on Sweden's west coast; Johan Theorin sets his quartet of crime thrillers—*Echoes from the Dead* (2009), *The Darkest Room* (2010), *The Quarry* (2013), and *The Voices Beyond* (2015)—on the desolate Baltic island of Öland; and Mari Jungstedt sets her Anders Knutas crime thrillers on the island of Gotland.

Islands from around the world provide locations for Clive Cussler's Dirk Pitt adventure thriller series, from the quiet Greek island of Thasos in his first outing in *The Mediterranean Caper* (1973), to the icy waters of Greenland in *Treasure* (1988), and from the fictional Japanese Ajima Island in *Dragon* (1990), to Seymour Island in the Antarctic and islands in the four corners of the Pacific in *Shock Wave* (1996).

As this journey round the world of thrillers demonstrates, island thrillers are predominantly set on existing islands or on fictional islands off real landmasses. In other words, they are able to employ the existing geographical and social spaces of the real world, instead of having to map entire worlds, as fantasy writers must do.

Ken Gelder suggests that the thriller may be "popular fiction at its purest, soliciting the reader's belief as it unfolds and using its sheer pace to carry that belief along intact."[14] As the brief survey above indicates, islands are ubiquitous in thrillers—from Erskine Childers to Camilla Lackberg, from the Faroe Islands to the Falkland Islands—because they satisfy three essential requirements of the genre: spatial verisimilitude, immediately familiar symbolism, and the duality of local sites and global networks. And where thrillers are invested in the boundedness of islands, the hero's role is in part to work out how to gain access to and egress from that contained location. The hero is thus a mobile figure, who challenges the villain's attempts to exploit the apparently sealed environment of the island, as we see, for example, in Fleming's *Dr No* (1958) and Cussler's *Dragon*.

From the perspective of the thriller genre, islands are discrete entities, physically isolated and detached from larger landmasses, surrounded and contained by the sea, their space finite, at once scrutable and inscrutable. As in detective fiction, the reader frequently first encounters the island from a distance, from the sea, or from the air. In Sharon Bolton's *Little Black Lies* the reader first glimpses the outline of the Falkland Islands from Catrin's boat: "In the distance, the mountains are dark against a paler night sky and the water around me has the appearance and texture of an old glass mirror."[15] The outline of the archipelago is dark and forbidding, spatially ripe for crime. The reader does not share Catrin's knowledge of the island, and neither the reader nor Catrin knows what has happened on the island in the short time she has been at sea.

In Douglas Preston and Lincoln Child's Gideon Crew novel, *The Lost Island* (2014), a techno-thriller that borders on lost-world island fantasy, Gideon and Amy also first encounter the island they have been searching for from the sea:

> The landforms slowly rose up as they approached. Gideon could make out three of them. A massive, initial island thrust steeply out of the sea, rising more than a thousand feet into the clouds. A smaller but even steeper and taller island lay beyond it. Right in front of them was the twisted place: a volcanic sea stack or eroded plug that stuck up like a witch's finger, a black bent spire of rock.[16]

In this initial (fantasy-infused) description of the island words like "massive," "thrust," "twisted," and "black," together with the metaphor of "a witch's finger," lend a sense of foreboding to their arrival; they neither know the island nor what awaits them there. Viewed in this way from the water, the reader is immediately alert to the potential danger on the island. Similarly, when first viewed from the ship, the island in MacLean's *Bear Island* "presented the most awesome, awe-inspiring and, in the true sense of the word, awful spectacle of nature." It "was black, black as widow's weeds," an "ebony mass towering 1500 vertical feet" out of the water. The repetition of black and its synonym ebony add to the sense that the island is "an evil and dreadful and sinister place."[17]

In Stone's *Mr Clarinet*, Max Mingus's first view of Haiti is from the air rather than from the water:

> Shaped like a lobster's pincer with most of the top claw chewed off, Haiti from the air looked completely out of place after the dense luscious green of Cuba, and all the other smaller islands they'd passed. Arid and acidic, the country's rust on rust coloured landscape seemed utterly bereft of grass and foliage. When the plane circled over the edges of the bordering Dominican Republic you could clearly see where the two nations divided—the land split as definitely as on any map; a dry bone wasteland with an abundant oasis next door.[18]

A deformed, arid wasteland, Haiti is presented as a stark contrast to the lush islands that surround it, a place that repels rather than pleases. Whether approached by sea or air, the first sight of these islands casts them as hostile, and defines the protagonists as vulnerable outsiders whose knowledge of the islands is limited, and who do not know what perils await them. On the other hand, readers always know that the hero will be pitted against a villain who has the advantage of being already familiar with the topographical and cultural geography of the island. Unlike the detectives in some crime fiction, the heroes of thrillers are rarely already on the island and are rarely equipped with detailed prior knowledge of the island terrain they will encounter (Tom Mangan in Bagley's *Bahama Crisis* is a rare exception). James Bond may be familiar with Jamaica, but the Isle of Surprise in *Live and Let Die* and Crab Key in *Dr No* are both unknown to him at the beginning of his missions.

For this reason, compared to crime fiction, maps are a less frequent element of paratext in island thrillers, though in the work of Cussler and others they may be included as the hero discovers the geography of the island or simply as an aid to the reader. MacLean includes a map of the titular island at the beginning of *Bear Island*, and Bolton provides the reader with a map of the Falkland Islands at the outset of *Little Black Lies* (figure 4.1).

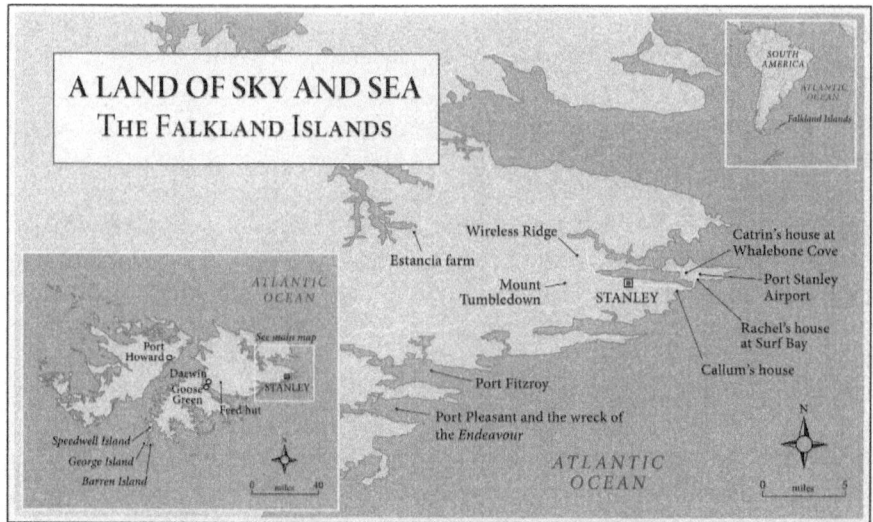

Figure 4.1. Map of The Falkland Islands. Sharon Bolton, *Little Black Lies* (2015; repr., London: Corgi, 2015).

Similarly, in *Miss Smilla's Feeling for Snow* Hoeg supplies an intratextual map of Greenland—embedded within the text rather than before it—as Smilla Jaspersen sets out for the island aboard the *Kronos*. However, few of these maps, regardless of where they appear in the text, offer the level of topographical detail that is commonly found in the literary maps that accompany island crime fictions. The maps of Bear Island and the Falkland Islands both include scale and orientation, as well as identifying key locations that feature in the novels, but the lack of topographic detail (contour lines and so on) makes it impossible for the reader to unpack the geography of the novel except as it unfolds in the narrative. Or to put it another way, the maps do not in any way detract from the suspense of the novel. In a crime novel the reader is engaged in the activity of trying to solve the crime that has already taken place; in the thriller the crime unfolds in the narrative present.

More commonly in thrillers the topography of the island is presented as a narrative map. In *Eye of the Needle*, for example, Follett provides a detailed description of Storm Island which extends over three pages and is bracketed by the repeated sentence "It is for places like this that the word 'bleak' had been invented"[19]:

> The island is a J-shaped lump of rock rising sullenly out of the North Sea. It lies on the map like the top half of a broken cane, parallel with the Equator but

a long, long way north; its curved handle towards Aberdeen, its broken, jagged stump pointing threateningly at distant Denmark. It is ten miles long.[20]

This passage is followed by vivid topographical descriptions and details of the flora and fauna which flesh out the desolate geography of the island whose "most constant visitor is the wind."[21] Frequently, however, the descriptive passages provided in thrillers are deliberately short of detail. In Allen's *Hunter*, Malta is a strategic island and a staging post for trafficking and modern-day piracy that provides an ideal base from which to launch the kidnap at the heart of the novel. There are references to "the rocks and crashing waves that were the hallmark of the Gozo coastline,"[22] and to "Fort Manoel, located strategically on Manoel Island to cover the sea entrance to the city,"[23] but the only map of the archipelago is in Alex Morgan's head: "The image of a map of Malta formed in his mind's eye and Morgan studied it intently. Then it came to him. The ferry had to be the Gozo Channel ferry, connecting the main island of Malta to the northern island of Gozo."[24] Bound and bundled into the boot of a car, Morgan has little sense of geography, while the reader, too, is deliberately left in the dark as to his location. The suspense inherent in the "combination of investigation, entrapment and hair's-breadth escape" that "was to become a standard ingredient in the James Bond novels,"[25] and in thrillers more generally, is heightened when the island is at best only partially known. In other words, the intensity of the action may best be served by the *absence* of topographical detail. Fleming's Bond novels are unusual in that, as David Seed notes, "they constantly slow down or suspend their urgency in order to explore the worlds of wine-tasting, West End clubs, or gambling."[26] Or, in the case of the Caribbean novels, they take time out to explore Jamaica, to provide a tourist's view of the island—"often lending them their interest and a certain degree of verisimilitude"[27]—before resuming the pace of the action on an uncharted peripheral or satellite island: the Isle of Surprise or Crab Key.

Such is the appeal of islands as exotic or remote locations that MacLean's adventure thriller *Santorini* (1986) takes its title from the Greek island, and includes a paratextual literary map of the Aegean Sea, with an inset map of Thera (Santorini), even though the action of the novel takes place near rather than on the island—primarily aboard the frigate *Ariadne*. Islands are not simply exotic locations in thrillers, however. They are devices whose natural boundaries both contain and structure the action. And they are often places where the rules of society no longer operate. They represent a confined territory in which, or over which, two rivals (nations, agencies, individuals) compete, like boxers in a ring, repeatedly coming out of and retreating into their respective corners as the novel progresses. Moreover, islands provide settings that lend themselves to what Todorov calls the *"rules of the genre"*[28]—the generic verisimilitude that identifies a novel as a thriller, as well as a broader verisimilitude, which

Todorov calls "*public opinion*,"²⁹ that allows readers to believe in the "reality" of the novel—through the inclusion of literary maps or references to the island's bordered space or to its cultural as well as geographical boundaries. Thus, for example, the "rules of the genre" and "public opinion" (generic and cultural verisimilitude) may work together to persuade the reader of Bolton's *Little Black Lies* that following the disappearance of the three-year-old child, Archie West, it is indeed possible to seal the island, as Major Wooton's immediate response to the news implies: "'close the ports,' [...] 'No one leaves the islands.'"³⁰

While it is inevitable that we have focused thus far on the bounded nature of islands in their conceptualisation and representation, islands are not represented exclusively as contained or sealed locales in thrillers (or any other popular genre). Often thrillers are equally invested in the mobilities that connect islands: to each other and to continental landmasses. As Phillip Vannini notes, mobilities or immobilities of transport can insulate and isolate an island, "filter[ing] out almost everything that is noxious about the outside world,"³¹ but they can also, as Tim Cresswell explains, facilitate rapid local and global movement.³² Thrillers are fascinated both by the limits to mobilities that typically define island geographies and by the place and purpose of islands in networks of mobility. Thus the next two chapters, on Ian Fleming's James Bond novels and Clive Cussler's Dirk Pitt series, focus on the movements to and from islands, as well as on their representation as bounded. Thrillers, as we shall see, are highly invested in narrative pace, which is achieved in part through mobile geography, by the speed with which the hero is able to move from place to place—specifically, the ease with which he is able move to, from, and between islands. Thus islands in thrillers operate as nodes in local and global networks, where the mobility of the hero—his ability to "flit on and off islands"³³—is augmented by the technologies of transport (which in turn help define island geographies): ferries, small boats, planes, helicopters, ultralight power gliders, and so on. In *Live and Let Die* James Bond swims to Mr Big's island, while in *Dragon* Dirk Pitt emerges onto a beach on Marcus Island in a futuristic Deep Sea Mining Vehicle (DSMV). Island thrillers, as the following chapters illustrate, are attentive to both topographical space and to what Cresswell terms "constellations of mobility,"³⁴ to the connectivity of islands as well as their insularity, and to what Edward Relph calls the "machinery and paraphernalia of travel"³⁵ as well as the geography of the destination.

NOTES

1. Tzvetan Todorov, "The Typology of Detective Fiction," in *The Poetics of Prose*, trans. Richard Howard (Oxford: Blackwell, 1977), 44.
2. Todorov, "The Typology of Detective Fiction," 47.

3. Todorov, "The Typology of Detective Fiction," 47.
4. Todorov, "The Typology of Detective Fiction," 48.
5. Stephen Heath, "The Politics of Genre," in *Debating World Literature*, ed. Christopher Prendergast (London: Verso, 2004), 173.
6. Elizabeth Leane, "Unstable Places and Generic Spaces: Thrillers in Antarctica," in *Genre Settings: Spatiality and Popular Fiction*, ed. Lisa Fletcher (London: Palgrave Macmillan, 2016), 26.
7. David Poyer, *Louisiana Blue* (1994; repr., n.p.: Northampton House Press, 2014), 222.
8. Kingsley Amis, introduction to *Colonel Sun*, by Kingsley Amis, writing as Robert Markham (1991; repr., London: Vintage, 2015), xii.
9. Andrew Taylor, introduction to *Live and Let Die*, by Ian Fleming (London: Vintage, 2012), xiii.
10. See Louis Turner and John Ash, *The Golden Hordes: International Tourism and the Pleasure Periphery* (London: Constable, 1975).
11. John Buchan, *The Island of Sheep* (1936; repr., Oxford: Oxford University Press, 1997), 225.
12. See Patrick Parrinder, "John Buchan and the Spy Thriller," in *The Bloomsbury Introduction to Popular Fiction*, ed. Christine Berberich (London: Bloomsbury, 2015), 200–212; John Gornall, "John Buchan's *The Island of Sheep* and *Faereyinga Saga*," *Saga-Book* 24, no. 5 (1997): 352.
13. Ken Follett, *Eye of the Needle* (1978; repr., New York: Harper, 2010), 66. The novel was originally published under the title *Storm Island*.
14. Ken Gelder, *Popular Fiction: The Logics and Practices of a Literary Field* (Abingdon: Routledge, 2004), 61.
15. Sharon Bolton, *Little Black Lies* (2015; repr., London: Corgi, 2015), 17–18.
16. Douglas Preston and Lincoln Childs, *The Lost Island* (New York: Grand Central Publishing, 2014), 221–22.
17. Alistair MacLean, *Bear Island* (1971; repr., New York: Sterling, 2012), 137.
18. Nick Stone, *Mr Clarinet* (2006; repr., London: Penguin, 2011), 86.
19. Follett, *Eye of the Needle*, 50 and 53.
20. Follett, *Eye of the Needle*, 50.
21. Follett, *Eye of the Needle*, 52.
22. Chris Allen, *Hunter: Intrepid 2* (Sydney: Momentum, 2012), 153.
23. Allen, *Hunter*, 93.
24. Allen, *Hunter*, 130.
25. David Seed, "Crime and the Spy Genre," in *A Companion to Crime Fiction*, ed. Charles J. Rzepka and Lee Horsley (Chichester: Wiley-Blackwell, 2010), 234.
26. David Seed, "Spy Fiction," in *The Cambridge Companion to Crime Fiction*, ed. Martin Priestman (Cambridge: Cambridge University Press, 2003), 125.
27. Michael Denning, *Cover Stories: Narrative and Ideology in the British Spy Thriller* (London: Routledge & Kegan Paul, 1987), 103.
28. Tzvetan Todorov, *Introduction to Poetics*, trans. Richard Howard (Minneapolis: University of Minnesota Press, 1981), 18.
29. Todorov, *Introduction to Poetics*, 19.

30. Bolton, *Little Black Lies*, 72.

31. Phillip Vannini, "Constellations of Ferry (Im)mobility: Islandness as the Performance and Politics of Insulation and Isolation," *Cultural Geographies* 18, no. 2 (2011), 257.

32. See Tim Cresswell, "Towards a Politics of Mobility," *Environment and Planning D: Society and Space* 28, no. 1 (2010), 24–25.

33. Clive Cussler, *Shock Wave* (1996; repr., New York: Pocket Star Books, 2008), 506.

34. Cresswell, "Towards a Politics of Mobility," 17.

35. Edward Relph, *Place and Placelessness* (London: Pion, 1976), 87.

Chapter Five

Paradise Threatened
The Bond Islands

Islands are privileged sites in what Meaghan Morris terms in passing "Bondspace," "the luxury hotels, resorts, and hi-tech communications command centres,"[1] which are iconic settings for spy thrillers. Morris's Bondspace is a refined space cut off from, and inaccessible to, mere mortals; it is a space occupied by powerful heroes and dastardly villains. At stake is the ability to control the resources and expand the limits of the purified space. Islands work particularly well as Bondspace because they are defined locations from which the mundane can easily be excluded. As the compound noun implies, the hero and the environments through which he is empowered to move are mutually defining (as are thrillers and the environments in which they are set); Morris's Bondspace, or what Michael Denning calls Ian Fleming's "world system"[2] is inhabited not only by James Bond, but by Jason Bourne and others, too.

Several of Fleming's fourteen books (twelve novels and two collections of short stories) featuring the British secret agent, James Bond, utilise islands as key locales: *Live and Let Die* (1954), *Dr No* (1958), and *The Man With the Golden Gun* (1965) have Jamaican settings; *Thunderball* (1961), Fleming's bestselling Bond novel,[3] is set in the Bahamas; and three of the five stories in *For Your Eyes Only* (1960) have island settings—"For Your Eyes Only" (Jamaica), "Quantum of Solace" (the Bahamas), and "The Hildebrand Rarity" (the Seychelles). There are also, as Vivian Halloran notes, "repeated references to Nassau, the Cayman Islands, Haiti, Cuba, and Jamaica in the Bond fiction"[4]; in *Goldfinger* (1959), for example, the eponymous villain is "[d]omiciled in Nassau,"[5] and there are references to the capital of the Bahamas throughout the novel. Drawing on Rebecca Weaver-Hightower's contention that "the island, with its natural geographic borders, becomes the perfect imaginary space for an individual person to inhabit and solely command,"⁶ this chapter will unpack the link between the masculine hero and islandness in the three key Bond island novels, *Live and Let Die*, *Dr No*, and *Thunderball*. It will also interrogate the extratextual resonances of the Bond island in broader popular culture, from the iconic image of a bikini-clad girl rising from the Caribbean Sea in *Dr No*, the initial Bond film (a loose adaptation of the novel of the same name, starring Sean Connery as Bond and Ursula Andress as Honey Ryder, the first of a long line of "Bond girls" on screen), to Goldeneye, the estate Fleming built in Jamaica, which now operates as the GoldenEye tourist resort (the spelling reflecting that of the title of the seventeenth film in the Bond series).

Bond's assignment in *Live and Let Die*, the second novel in Fleming's series (in Matthew Parker's view "possibly Fleming's best. [...] Certainly [...] the book that established the winning formula"⁷), is to investigate the activities of Mr Big, a Soviet agent and underworld kingpin, whom MI6 suspect is selling seventeenth-century gold coins, part of the hoard hidden in Jamaica by the pirate Sir Henry "Bloody" Morgan, to finance Soviet spy operations in America. Bond and his American counterpart, Felix Leiter, escape the clutches of Mr Big in New York with the aid of the latter's mind-reading employee, Solitaire, who supports Bond's cover story. Solitaire then escapes from her employer, and she, Bond, and Leiter have more run-ins with Mr Big's organisation in Florida before Bond continues his mission in Jamaica, from where he swims out to Mr Big's island to destroy his smuggling operations. Bond is captured and reunited with Solitaire, and, in a parody of Bloody Morgan's cruelty, Mr Big plans to tow them behind his boat to be dragged over the reef and eaten by sharks. They survive when the bomb Bond had earlier planted destroys Mr Big's boat.

In *Dr No* Bond is sent on "a bit of a holiday"⁸ to Jamaica to investigate the sudden disappearance of Commander Strangways, the local representative of the British Secret Service in the Caribbean, and his number two, Mary Trueblood. In Jamaica Bond discovers that Strangways had been investigating the activities of the reclusive Chinese-German Dr Julius No, who operates a guano mine on nearby Crab Key. He soon realises that his movements are being monitored, and, after surviving two attempts on his life, decides to find out if there is a connection between Dr No and Strangways's disappearance. Bond and his old friend Quarrel secretly travel to Crab Key, where they meet Honeychile Rider, who is there to collect valuable shells. After Quarrel is burnt to death by Dr No's mechanical dragon, Bond and Honey are captured and taken to Dr No's extraordinary underground facility from where he plans to sabotage American missile tests. Bond survives the gruesome trial of pain and endurance Dr No has set for him, buries Dr No alive under a mound of guano, and escapes with Honey. The battle over, Bond is free to turn his attention to sexual adventure, the "bit of a holiday" earlier promised by M (and more broadly by island tourist discourses), before he must return to London.

In *Thunderball* the criminal organisation SPECTRE, headed by regular Bond villain Ernst Stavro Blofeld, hijacks a Royal Air Force plane and steals two atomic bombs. When SPECTRE attempts to blackmail the Western Powers for their safe return, Bond is sent to the Bahamas to search for the missing weapons. He soon suspects that Emilio Largo, seemingly a rich playboy in the West Indies to hunt for treasure, is a member of SPECTRE, and has the stolen bombs. With the aid of his old CIA friend Felix Leiter, and Largo's mistress, Domino, Bond has to find a way to eliminate Largo and rescue the atomic devices before they can be deployed against a major Western property or city. Largo and his men are attacked as they try to plant the first atomic bomb, and Domino rescues Bond (in something of a reversal of the usual ending where Bond saves the girl, but without undercutting his heroism).

All Fleming's Bond novels and stories were written at Goldeneye, the house he built outside the small town of Oracabessa on Jamaica's north coast, where he spent two months every year. Apart from providing the setting for three Bond novels and one short story, the Caribbean island of Jamaica permeates the books in other ways, directly and indirectly. In *Casino Royale* (1953) Bond signs into the Hotel Splendide as "James Bond, Port Maria, Jamaica," and passes himself off as "a Jamaican plantocrat whose father had made his pile in tobacco and sugar and whose son chose to play it away on the stock markets and in casinos."[9] In *You Only Live Twice* (1964) there is a reference back to an earlier assignment in Jamaica.[10] And two notable Bond girls, Solitaire in *Live and Let Die* and Domino in *Thunderball*, are named after rare Jamaican birds.[11] In his biography of Fleming, Andrew Lycett explains that while *Casino Royale* had been set in and around Fleming's "old gambling haunts in Europe," his next book "was to be a study of organized crime in his new domain of the Caribbean and North America."[12] In a handwritten note inside the front cover of his own copy of *Live and Let Die* Fleming is very specific about the settings in the novel, including the model for Mr Big's lair, the Isle of Surprise: "All the settings are based on personal experience [...] the undertaker chapters are based on Cabritta Island, Port Maria, Jamaica, where Bloody Morgan careened his ships & which is still supposed to contain his treasure."[13] Fleming's marginalia clearly emphasises the verisimilitude of his "satellite islands."[14] However, while the reader expects geographical verisimilitude in those parts of the novel that take place on the charted island of Jamaica (though Fleming does not always accurately name island locations), geographical verisimilitude is less important for those sections that occur on the renamed and thus uncharted Isle of Surprise and Crab Key. While Jamaica in the Bond series is, for the most part, a realistic representation of that island, the Isle of Surprise is not Cabritta (or Cabarita) Island. As with Christie's Soldier Island and Smugglers' Island, the Isle of Surprise and Crab Key are places that can be topographically stage-managed to serve the action of the novels in a way that Jamaica (or the Bahamas) cannot. They are unknown and dangerous locales into which Bond must venture to restore both local and global order. And they are the bounded geographical spaces where Bond's heroic masculinity is performatively enacted.

Although the Caribbean is the setting for only the final third of *Live and Let Die*, the potential menace of the islands permeates the whole novel. The prospect of pursuing the case to "the Caribbean. Jamaica,"[15] is on the agenda from the outset: "Station C has been interested in a Diesel yacht, the *Secatur*, which has been running from a small island on the North Coast of Jamaica through the Florida Keys into the Gulf of Mexico, to a place called St Petersburg."[16] As M briefs Bond on the case, he provides a brief history of the pirate Bloody Morgan and his treasure trove, "one of the most valuable treasure-troves in history,"[17] which he believes Mr Big has found in Jamaica. M's speculation about Bloody Morgan's treasure and his references to the activities of the pirate Blackbeard remind the reader of the wider history of buccaneering along the Spanish Main, and, of course, the tradition of pirate adventure fiction set in the Caribbean, including Robert Louis Stevenson's nineteenth-century classic, *Treasure Island* (1883) and Rafael Sabatini's *Captain Blood* (1922), and continued by such contemporary adventure fictions as Michael Crichton's *Pirate Latitudes* (2009). Parker is right to suggest that, "with its lost pirate treasure, sharks and killer centipedes and black magic, [*Live and Let Die*] is really an old-fashioned *Boy's Own* adventure story."[18] In the best adventure tradition the reader is drawn in from the outset by "the steady pull of [Fleming's] storytelling."[19] Jeremy Black argues that once Bond is in Jamaica "the book becomes an adventure story, shorn of politics."[20] However, while it is true that the explicit geopolitics of the post-World-War-Two era give way to adventure in the final section of the book, the islands of the Caribbean are always representations of the British Empire, outposts that must be protected if the centre (Britain, but also America) is to hold—even though, as Fleming acknowledges in *Dr No*, it cannot hold forever: "One day Queen's Club will have its windows smashed and perhaps be burned to the ground, but for the time being it is a useful place to find in a sub-tropical island."[21] Thus the islands of the West Indies consistently function in the Bond fictions as "contact zones" where the battles for global supremacy take place against the backdrop of a fading Empire. For Mary Louise Pratt, who introduced the term in her path-defining book *Imperial Eyes*, contact zones are most often trading posts or border towns, places where Western cultures encounter, and engage with, the other. In Fleming's Bond fiction contact zones are often islands or other peripheral spaces, where

Bond encounters, and engages with, the villain; in other words, they intersect with Bondspace.

The sense of islands and island customs is gradually built up in *Live and Let Die* in various ways well before the action of the novel shifts to Jamaica. In preparation for the case, and on M's recommendation, Bond reads Patrick Leigh Fermor's 1950 book *The Traveller's Tree: A Journey Through the Caribbean Islands*, from which Fleming rather obtrusively quotes two lengthy passages (running to five pages) on Haitian Voodoo.[22] There are also early references to the "cargoes of queen conchs and other shells from Jamaica and also highly prized varieties of tropical fish"[23] brought to Florida by the *Secatur*. Along with the mystery of Voodoo—not widely integrated into, or distorted by, Western popular culture in the 1950s, though Voodoo had featured prominently in Dennis Wheatley's occult thriller *Strange Conflict* (1941)—these details promote the islands as both exotic and dangerous. This sense of the dangerous exotic is further enhanced when Bond's flight from Florida to Jamaica stops in Nassau, "the richest island in the world, the sandy patch where a thousand million pounds of frightened sterling lies buried beneath the Canasta tables,"[24] a passage which consciously draws a link between the gambling industry of the novel's present and the piracy of the past.

In Jamaica, Strangways, "the Chief Secret Service agent for the Caribbean,"[25] continues M's story about Bloody Morgan, focusing on Shark Bay, which "[t]he great buccaneer had made [...] his headquarters," and the Isle of Surprise, "a precipitous lump of coral and limestone that surges straight up out of the centre of the bay and is surmounted by a jungly plateau of about an acre."[26] The Isle of Surprise is now in the hands of Mr Big, who, using Morgan's old anchorage, is ostensibly shipping tropical fish and rare shells to Florida. Following the thunderous beating of Voodoo drums and the death of a local fisherman, the Isle of Surprise had become obeah, and even during the day the locals no longer ventured near the vicinity. Meanwhile, Strangways's unsuccessful attempts to penetrate the island had resulted only in the deaths of the two men he sent to make an underwater survey of the island. Thus, at the very outset of the Jamaican section of the novel Fleming employs the device of a villain whose base is a seemingly impregnable island fortress—now a common trope in spy and adventure thrillers, including John O'Donnell's *Modesty Blaise* (1965) and Clive Cussler's *Dragon* (1990)—that is protected by sharks and barracudas, and the nocturnal beating of the Voodoo drums. Here, Mr Big relies on superstition to create a sense of fear that keeps the locals at bay, so that he can go about his heinous activities without interference.

In *Live and Let Die* Fleming provides his readers with a narrative map of the island of Jamaica—its topography and its flora and fauna—as Bond and

Quarrel, specifically introduced (and defined) as a Cayman Islander, travel from Kingston, across the back of the island, to the north coast. If the geography of the island is encapsulated in the descriptions of the landscape they pass through, the *genius loci* of the island is captured when Bond comments on the number of people Quarrel greets along the way. Quarrel responds that "I been travelling this road twice a week. Everyone know you in Jamaica. They got good eyes,"[27] a remark that encapsulates the character of small islands where, as John Enright puts it in his Samoan mystery, *Fire Knife Dancing* (2013), "Within the enclosed and entangled world of island society no one was given the freedom of being a stranger."[28] Once on the north coast, having "passed through Port Maria and branched off along the little parochial road that runs down to Shark Bay,"[29] they look out over the ocean, and the reader is now offered a narrative map of the satellite island:

> In the centre of the crescent, the Isle of Surprise rose a hundred feet sheer out of the water, small waves creaming against its easterly base, calm waters in its lee.
> It was nearly round, and it looked like a tall grey cake topped with green icing on a blue china plate.
> [...] they were level with the flat green top of the island, half a mile away.[30]

This careful description of Mr Big's insular hideout and the sea which surrounds it is important not only in terms of establishing the setting but also in terms of directing the action—the way Bond approaches the island and how he goes about destroying Mr Big's clandestine operations. As Bond observes in *The Man With the Golden Gun*, also set in Jamaica, "The first law for a secret agent is to get his geography right, his means of access and exit."[31] The geography of islands and the action of island thrillers are inextricably linked.

Another iconic island trope Fleming employs in *Live and Let Die* is the postcard image of the tropical beach. Near the western tip of the island Bond looks out over Manatee Bay[32] and "the most beautiful beach he had ever seen, five miles of white sand sloping easily into the breakers and, behind, the palm trees marching in graceful disarray to the horizon."[33] The only element missing to complete this tourist brochure representation of the Caribbean is a girl. In this novel that comes obliquely in the final scene, when paradise is regained on the island and Bond and Solitaire are free to enjoy a "passionate holiday [...] in a house on stilts with palm trees and five miles of golden sand."[34]

Throughout *Dr No* Fleming again insists on the boundedness of his principal island settings—the "sub-tropical island"[35] of Jamaica and "an island called Crab Key between Jamaica and Cuba"[36] (which Black suggests is based on Inagua in the southern Bahamas[37])—and the significance of their proximity within the Antilles archipelago. Throughout genre fiction protagonists frequently arrive and depart islands by sea rather than by air, which serves to emphasise the insular geography and to stress the difficulty of arrivals and departures dependent on tides and weather. Here, though, Bond arrives in Jamaica by air, diminishing the sense of isolation, while also offering an opportunity to draw a narrative map of "the prosperous, peaceful island,"[38] which can be seen as a whole from the air in a way it cannot from the sea:

> Bond watched the big green turtle-backed island grow on the horizon and the water below him turn from the dark blue of the Cuba Deep to the azure and milk of the inshore shoals. Then they were over the North Shore, over its rash of millionaire hotels, and crossing the high mountains of the interior. The scattered dice of small-holdings showed on the slopes and in clearings in the jungle, and the setting sun flashed gold on the bright worms of tumbling rivers and streams. "Xaymaca" the Arawak Indians had called it—"The Land of Hills and Rivers". Bond's heart lifted with the beauty of one of the most fertile islands in the world.[39]

This arrival by air also firmly establishes Bond as on outsider. Moreover, Quarrel, who meets him at the airport is again described as "the Cayman Islander,"[40] linking him specifically to those islands; he is both an outsider, a non-Jamaican, and an insider, a West Indian, whom Bond needs to mediate the island: Quarrel "was a passport into the lower strata of coloured life which would otherwise be closed to Bond."[41] It is Quarrel who facilitates Bond's "more privileged access than the average tourist" might have to the islands and provides him with "access to the non-Western cultures and therefore give[s] him the strength to defeat the villain on his home territory."[42] Bond is able to go where others cannot because of the intimate connection he establishes (through Quarrel) with the islands.

While many thrillers—from Alistair MacLean's *Bear Island* (1971) to Sharon Bolton's Falkland Islands novel, *Little Black Lies* (2015)—include paratextual maps of their island locations, and many more employ narrative maps to portray their island settings, Fleming brings the two together when he describes Crab Key with reference to an ordnance survey map of the island that Bond studies in the library of the Jamaica Institute:

> The overall area of the island was about fifty square miles. Three-quarters of this, to the east, was swamp and shallow lake. From the lake a flat river meandered down to the sea and came out halfway along the south coast into a small sandy bay. [...] To the west, the island rose steeply to a hill stated to be five hundred feet high and ended abruptly with what appeared to be a sheer drop to the sea. [...]
> There was no sign of a road, or even a track on the island, and no sign of a house. The relief map showed that the island looked rather like a swimming water rat—a flat spine rising sharply to the head—heading west. [...]

Little else could be gleaned from the map. Crab Key was surrounded by shoal water except below the western cliff where the nearest marking was five hundred fathoms. After that came the plunge into the Cuba Deep.[43]

While the earlier descriptions of Jamaica establish its island identity, its accessibility, and its beauty, this cartographic, bird's-eye description of Crab Key emphasises its bounded nature, while the obviously phallic outline of the island anticipates both the masculine contest between hero and villain, and the appearance of the naked girl on the beach. As Bond looks down on the map "spread out on the table in front of him,"[44] in a "monarch-of-all-I-survey" moment (a term used by both Pratt in *Imperial Eyes* and Weaver-Hightower in *Empire Islands*), "he marks the boundaries of the island with his gaze,"[45] initiating a connection with the island that allows him to imagine wresting command of the space from Dr No.

Like Surprise Island in *Live and Let Die*, Crab Key in *Dr No* is a doubly islanded, or doubly peripheral, space. While Fleming's representation of Jamaica (or the Bahamas in *Thunderball*) is geographically and pejoratively insular in relation to the larger landmasses of the North and South American continents (and politically, too, in its colonial ties to Britain), in turn Fleming's smaller islands are geographically and pejoratively insular in relation to the larger islands of the Greater Antilles. Thus the satellite island of Crab Key is a secretive, fortress-like place that no one ever leaves, or as Quarrel somewhat euphemistically puts it, "Dat a bad luck place."[46] This is further emphasised as Bond and Quarrel approach the island by boat: "Soon there was a thickening of the darkness ahead. The low shadow slowly took on the shape of a huge swimming rat. A pale moon rose slowly behind them. Now the island showed distinctly, a couple of miles away, and there was the distant grumble of surf."[47] Again the descriptors are all negative: the land is shadowy and shaped like a rat, while the surf which encapsulates it "grumbles."

The islands in this and other Bond novels are either feminised spaces to be enjoyed by Bond (Jamaica) or malevolently male spaces to be conquered by the hero (Crab Key); in each instance they serve to emphasise the superior masculinity of the British secret agent and offer a stage on which masculine heterosexual fantasies can be played out. This is nowhere more apparent than in *Dr No*, the novel in which the girl-on-the-beach trope reaches its zenith.

When Bond awakens on Crab Key and peers out from his hiding place onto the beach, his heart misses a beat:

> It was a naked girl, with her back to him. She was not quite naked. She wore a broad leather belt round her waist with a hunting knife in a leather sheath at her right hip. The belt made her nakedness extraordinarily erotic. She stood not more than five yards away on the tideline looking down at something in her

hand. She stood in the classical relaxed pose of the nude, all the weight on the right leg and the left knee bent and turning slightly inwards, the head to one side as she examined the things in her hand.

It was a beautiful back. The skin was a very light uniform *café au lait* with the sheen of dull satin. The gentle curve of the backbone was deeply indented, suggesting more powerful muscles than is usual in a woman, and the behind was almost as firm and rounded as a boy's. The legs were straight and beautiful and no pinkness showed under the slightly lifted heel. She was not a coloured girl.

Her hair was ash blonde. It was cut to the shoulders and hung there and along the side of her bent cheek in thick wet strands. A green diving mask was pushed back above her forehead, and the green rubber thong bound her hair at the back.

The whole scene, the empty beach, the green and blue sea, the naked girl with strands of fair hair, reminded Bond of something, He searched his mind. Yes, she was Botticelli's Venus, seen from behind.[48]

In this remarkable passage the eroticism of islands is personified in the body of Honeychile Rider, the contours of her body standing in for the contours of the island and vice versa. Her pose perfectly matches that of Botticelli's Venus (with her weight on her right, rather than her left, leg—though seen from behind the symmetry of the image is maintained), and whereas in Botticelli's painting Venus emerges from the sea in a shell (widely interpreted as a metaphor for the vulva), Honey emerges from the sea with a handful of shells.

In this scene (which links voyeurism and tourism) the menace of the island is temporarily displaced by the dreamlike image of a girl on an island beach, alone, and apparently waiting to be claimed by the spy hero—a reward he will be entitled to claim only when he has demonstrated his masculinity by eradicating the evil on the island, or, as Tony Bennett and Janet Woollacott would have it, "he has reacquired his phallic authority."[49] As a creole, Honey stands for a feminised Caribbean desired by the white male imperialist, who must prove himself by defeating the racialised enemy other, in this case the Chinese-German Dr No and the "Chigroes," the Chinese-negro foot soldiers who work for him. Honeychile is an innocent, child-like as her name suggests, who needs to be coached to adulthood by Bond in what is at once a parent–child, coloniser–colonised relationship. She is the Caribbean, part of what Denning (borrowing from Louis Turner and John Ash) would term "the pleasure periphery,"[50] and dependent on Bond/Britain.

This passage is translated memorably in an iconic scene in the 1962 film adaptation of the novel (the first Bond film) in which Ursula Andress portrays Honey Ryder (her name shortened and the spelling changed).[51] She emerges from the sea, glistening and with the sun shining on her wet blonde hair, wearing a white bikini and a white webbing belt around her waist, with a large diving knife on her left hip, and carrying a large conch shell in each hand.[52]

The scene with Honeychile in the novel is also significant for its explicit allusions to *Robinson Crusoe* and the history of islands in adventure fiction: when Honeychile returns to the beach after dressing she "looked like a principal girl dressed as Man Friday,"[53] and later, after they have been captured by Dr No's henchmen, "She stood and fiddled at the hem of her Man Friday skirt."[54] There is a degree of irony in this casting of Honey as Man Friday when, as Sam Bourne (aka Jonathan Freedland) notes in his introduction to the 2012 Vintage edition of the novel, the loyal Cayman Islander, Quarrel, is clearly typecast as "Man Friday to Bond's Robinson Crusoe."[55] The line from thrillers back to the classic adventure fiction is enhanced when Bond explains to Honey what he is doing on the island: "Bond told the story in simple terms, with good men and bad men, like an adventure story out of a book."[56] And later, in a self-reflexive moment in the novel, Dr No accuses Bond of "reading too many novels of suspense."[57] As Bourne/Freedland points out, Fleming is aware that Bond is "the latest in a long line of British imperial adventurers to have alighted upon Jamaica or places like it,"[58] most noticeably when he has Bond walk in the footsteps of Bloody Morgan: "Bond almost smelled the dung of the mule trains in which he would have been riding over from Port Royal to visit the garrison at Morgan's Harbour in 1750."[59]

Here again Fleming emphasises the idea of the island as a contained or containing space, quickly apparent once Bond and Honey have been captured and taken to Dr No's highly technical lair. "Nobody who comes to this island has ever left it,"[60] Dr No tells Bond. It is "a secure base,"[61] that offers him safety and privacy, where he deliberately quarantines his community of workers in a way that mirrors the stereotypical isolation that usually already exists in small island communities.

Pirate-island conventions are again employed in *Thunderball*, with the location shifted from Jamaica to the nearby Bahamas archipelago:

> The Bahamas, the string of a thousand islands that straggle five hundred miles south-east from just east of 27° down to latitude 21°, were, for most of three hundred years the haunt of every famous pirate of the Western Atlantic, and today tourism makes full use of the romantic mythology.[62]

In playing with pirate conventions, Fleming is deliberately exploiting island genre expectations, and self-consciously enlisting the geo-poetic conventions of familiar cultural texts—like tourism brochures, and ordnance survey maps—to manage the hero's itinerary and to motor the reader through the text at the efficient pace the thriller genre demands. Largo makes full use of the pirate/island nexus in his cover as a "rich Nassau playboy"[63] in search of treasure troves buried in sunken ships around islands of the Southern Bahamas including Crooked Island, Mayaguana, and the Caicos Islands (the

Turks Islands feature in *Dr No*). The mention of these islands, and several others—Bimini, where the hi-jacked Vindicator is ditched in the sea, Dog Island, under which the stolen bombs are hidden, Athol Island, North-West Cay, the Berry Islands, Grand Bahama, and New Providence, "the island containing Nassau, the capital of the Bahamas, [...] a drab sandy slab of land fringed with some of the most beautiful beaches in the world"[64]—all serve to emphasise the immense oceanic reach of the archipelago, and thus the difficulty of finding the bombs, or, indeed, the pirate treasure troves which have remained buried on the ocean floor for several centuries, and now provide the perfect cover for the activities of Largo's boat, the *Disco Volante*. The sum and the bounded nature of "the group of islands, many of them uninhabited, surrounded mostly by shoal water over sand," as well as their proximity to the United States—"the nearest of the Bahama group is only 200 miles [...] from the American coastline"[65]—persuades M (who is also manipulating island genre expectations) to send Bond there to search for the stolen atomic bombs. His cover in the Bahamas, that of "a rich young man looking for some property in the islands,"[66] further exploits their image as a paradise playground for the wealthy.

Robinson Crusoe is again invoked in *Thunderball* when Bond makes his way to the secluded beach for his assignation with the novel's sexual object, Domino Vitali, the consummation of which takes place in a "beach hut [that] was a Robinson Crusoe affair of plaited bamboo and screwpine with a palm thatch whose wide eaves threw black shadows."[67] This scene also functions as another version of the touristic discourse of islands, dominated by beaches and bikini-clad girls, so memorably exploited in *Dr No*, which clearly associates the island with sun, sand, sea, and sex. The island is represented in *Thunderball*, as in *Dr No*, as an uncomplicated locale for what Denning refers to as "Fleming's fantasies of male power"—for Bond's mission "to re-establish order in the world of gender."[68]

Fleming also extends the metaphor which links islands and crime in this novel when he lists among the members of the council of SPECTRE "three Sicilians from the top echelon of the Unione Siciliano, the Mafia" and "three Corsican Frenchmen from the Union Corse, the secret society, contemporary with and similar to the Mafia, that runs nearly all organized crime in France."[69] The reputation of these islands as sites of crime is further developed when Blofeld reminds his fellow SPECTRE members of an earlier operation involving the abduction of a young heiress in Monte Carlo, who was "taken by sea to Corsica,"[70] and then proceeds to execute the Corsican who raped the girl before she was returned to her family, despite assurances they had been given that she would be returned undamaged on payment of a ransom. (Corsica's reputation for lawlessness is again harnessed in *On Her Majesty's Secret Service* [1963] in which Teresa, the girl Bond marries at the end of the novel, is the daughter of a Corsican brigand and an English woman he had raped then married.)

In both *Live and Let Die* and *Dr No* the bounded nature and contained size of the principal island locations—the Isle of Surprise and Crab Key—are exploited to intensify the action of the novels. In contrast, in *Thunderball* the extensive scale of the Bahamas archipelago is exploited to propel the hunt for the missing nuclear bombs. The islands in *Live and Let Die* and *Dr No* are already known; in *Thunderball* the islands must be discovered before they can be known.

Islands are always touristic locales in Fleming's Bond novels, but they are never incidental settings. They are used to contain and confuse; they are hideaways; they are sites of danger; they are isolated places where the nefarious activities of the villains can be conducted beyond the ken of prying eyes. They are thrilling, exotic spaces, and bounded settings for the showdown between the masculine hero and the arch villain. Islands are the epitome of Bondspace, the setting in which James Bond's hyperbolic heroic masculinity is forged.

NOTES

1. Meaghan Morris, "Transnational Imagination in Action Cinema: Hong Kong and the Making of a Global Popular Culture," *Inter-Asia Cultural Studies* 5, no. 2 (2004): 192.

2. Michael Denning, *Cover Stories: Narrative and Ideology in the British Spy Thriller* (London: Routledge and Kegan Paul, 1987), p. 104.

3. Tony Bennett and Janet Woollacott, *Bond and Beyond: The Popular Career of a Popular Hero* (London: Macmillan, 1987), 26–27.

4. Vivian Halloran, "Tropical Bond," in *Ian Fleming and James Bond: The Cultural Politics of 007*, ed. Edward P. Comentale, Stephen Watt, and Skip Willman (Bloomington: Indiana University Press, 2005), 159.

5. Ian Fleming, *Goldfinger* (1959; repr., London: Vintage, 2015), 27.

6. Rebecca Weaver-Hightower, *Empire Islands: Castaways, Cannibals, and Fantasies of Conquest* (Minneapolis: University of Minnesota Press, 2007), p. xx.

7. Matthew Parker, *Goldeneye: Where James Bond Was Born: Ian Fleming's Jamaica* (London: Hutchinson, 2014), 153.

8. Ian Fleming, *Dr No* (1958; repr., London: Vintage, 2012), 30.

9. Ian Fleming, *Casino Royale* (1953; repr., London: Vintage, 2012), 26.

10. Ian Fleming, *You Only Live Twice* (1964; repr., London: Vintage, 2012), 24.

11. Parker, *Goldeneye,* 153, 263.

12. Andrew Lycett, *Ian Fleming* (New York: St Martin's Press, 1995), 237.

13. Halloran, "Tropical Bond," 175.

14. Halloran, "Tropical Bond," 176.

15. Ian Fleming, *Live and Let Die* (1954; repr., London: Vintage, 2012), 10.
16. Fleming, *Live and Let Die*, 20.
17. Fleming, *Live and Let Die*, 20.
18. Parker, *Goldeneye*, 153.
19. Andrew Taylor, introduction to *Live and Let Die*, by Ian Fleming (London: Vintage, 2012), ix.
20. Jeremy Black, *The Politics of James Bond: From Fleming's Novels to the Big Screen* (2000; repr., Lincoln: University of Nebraska Press, 2005), 14.
21. Fleming, *Dr No*, 2.
22. Fleming, *Live and Let Die*, 31–36.
23. Fleming, *Live and Let Die*, 43.
24. Fleming, *Live and Let Die*, 212.
25. Fleming, *Live and Let Die*, 214.
26. Fleming, *Live and Let Die*, 216.
27. Fleming, *Live and Let Die*, 227.
28. John Enright, *Fire Knife Dancing* (Las Vegas: Thomas and Mercer, 2013), 44.
29. Fleming, *Live and Let Die*, 227.
30. Fleming, *Live and Let Die*, 227–28.
31. Ian Fleming, *The Man With the Golden Gun* (1965; repr., London: Vintage, 2012), 85.
32. This is an example of Fleming's geographical licence. The Bay is Long Bay, not Manatee Bay. See John Griswold, *Ian Fleming's James Bond: Annotations and Chronologies for Ian Fleming's Bond Stories* (Bloomington: AuthorHouse, 2006), 89.
33. Fleming, *Live and Let Die*, 229.
34. Fleming, *Live and Let Die*, 307.
35. Fleming, *Dr No*, 2.
36. Fleming, *Dr No*, 38.
37. Black, *The Politics of James Bond*, 34.
38. Fleming, *Dr No*, 78.
39. Fleming, *Dr No*, 44.
40. Fleming, *Dr No*, 46.
41. Fleming, *Dr No*, 49.
42. Denning, *Cover Stories*, p. 105.
43. Fleming, *Dr No*, 82–83.
44. Fleming, *Dr No*, 82.
45. Weaver-Hightower, *Empire Islands*, p. xix.
46. Fleming, *Dr No*, 55.
47. Fleming, *Dr No*, 108.
48. Fleming, *Dr No*, 111–12.
49. Fleming, *Dr No*, 137.
50. Denning, *Cover Stories*, 104–105. See Louis Turner and John Ash, *The Golden Hordes: International Tourism and the Pleasure Periphery* (London: Constable, 1975). Turner and Ash describe the emergence of the "pleasure periphery" in the Caribbean, the Mediterranean, and the South Pacific following the advent of mass tourism.

51. *Dr No*, directed by Terence Young (United Artists, 1962), DVD (Twentieth Century Fox, 2006).

52. Fleming includes a mention of Ursula Andress in the novel *On Her Majesty's Secret Service* (1963): "that beautiful girl with the long fair hair at the big table, that is Ursula Andress, the film star. What a wonderful tan she has!" (1963; repr., London: Vintage, 2012), 155.

53. Fleming, *Dr No*, 118.

54. Fleming, *Dr No*, 198.

55. Sam Bourne aka Jonathan Freedland, introduction to *Dr No*, by Ian Fleming (London: Vintage, 2012), xii.

56. Fleming, *Dr No*, 157.

57. Fleming, *Dr No*, 245.

58. Bourne, Introduction, xii.

59. Fleming, *Dr No*, 97.

60. Fleming, *Dr No*, 226.

61. Fleming, *Dr No*, 228.

62. Ian Fleming, *Thunderball* (1961; repr., London: Vintage, 2012), 160.

63. Fleming, *Thunderball*, 136.

64. Fleming, *Thunderball*, 169.

65. Fleming, *Thunderball*, 108.

66. Fleming, *Thunderball*, 109.

67. Fleming, *Thunderball*, 274.

68. Michael Denning, "Licensed to Look: James Bond and the Heroism of Consumption," in *The James Bond Phenomenon: A Critical Reader*, ed. Christoph Lindner (2nd ed., 2006; repr., Manchester: Manchester University Press, 2014), 69.

69. Fleming, *Thunderball*, 68.

70. Fleming, *Thunderball*, 74.

Chapter Six

The Proximity of Islands
Dirk Pitt's Insular Adventures

The cover of the 1978 Bantam Books edition of *The Mediterranean Caper* (1973) shows a male swimmer largely submerged in the sea, with what appears to be a military ship looming in the distance (figure 6.1). In this over-under image, the swimmer's masked head breaking the surface of the water both anticipates a fantastic adventure story and uncannily resembles an island; similarly, the nebulous contours of the distant grey vessel suggest a landmass. Several of the twenty-three thrillers in Clive Cussler's Dirk Pitt Adventure series feature islands, including the three which are the focus of this chapter: *The Mediterranean Caper*, *Dragon* (1990), and *Shock Wave* (1996). Both *Dragon* and *Shock Wave* include paratextual maps of islands. The opening page of *Dragon* is faced by a small-scale map showing the locations of several islands that are referenced in the novel, while part 3, "Ajima Island," is prefaced by detailed cross-section topographic maps of the subterranean Edo City and the adjoining Soseki Island, the principal island location in the novel. A third map at the beginning of part 4 shows the proximity of Dennings' Demons' crashed B-29 to Soseki Island. Similarly, three sections of *Shock Wave* are prefaced by maps: at the beginning of part 1 there is a map of the "Course of the Polar Queen," between Seymour Island and the Danger Islands off the Antarctic Peninsula; part 2 opens with a map showing the deathly "Acoustic Convergence" that emanates from islands in the four corners of the Pacific Ocean to come together in the Hawaiian archipelago (figure 6.2); and part 4 includes a detailed map of the fictional "Gladiator Island," the location of the novel's climax. Cussler's adventure thrillers are remarkable not only for their extravagant plotting and fast-paced action but also for their rich description of natural and built places. In examining Cussler's attention to topographical and cartographical detail in these three novels, this chapter will show that genre islands can

Chapter Six

Figure 6.1. Front cover. Clive Cussler, *Mediterranean Caper* (New York: Bantam Books, 1978).

be both stages for masculine melodrama and anchored in an awareness of geographical reality.

In Cussler's first Dirk Pitt Adventure, *The Mediterranean Caper*, Pitt and his sidekick Al Giordino have been sent to help investigate a series of incidents aboard the NUMA (National Underwater Marine Agency) research vessel, *First Attempt*. They pick up a mayday call from the Brady Air Force Base on the Greek island of Thasos, indicating that it is under attack by a World-War-I biplane. Pitt responds, and after a spectacular dogfight his World-War-II-era PBY Catalina flying boat, armed only with a pair of rifles, gets the better of the World-War-I fighter. After seducing Teri von Till and being invited to her uncle's villa for dinner, Pitt soon suspects Bruno von Till was involved in the attack on the airfield. When he confronts von Till he is forced at gunpoint into the Pit of Hades, a labyrinth from which, against all odds, he manages to escape. After discovering that von Till is attempting to smuggle a massive shipment of heroin into the United States aboard his fleet of cargo ships, Pitt works out how von Till has managed the operation, and bests the old German in his underwater lair.

Dragon, Dirk Pitt's tenth outing, begins with an historical prologue: in 1945 a B-29 bomber carrying a third atomic bomb is shot down by a Japanese fighter and crashes into the sea, sinking to the bottom of the ocean with its deadly cargo. The story then moves forward to the present where a huge explosion destroys three ships and causes massive damage to "Soggy Acres," NUMA's top-secret underwater research facility, and incapacitates *Old Gert*, an underwater vehicle which had been operating from the British survey ship destroyed in the blast. Pitt, who had been living in NUMA's underwater facility, rescues the crew of *Old Gert* and manages to get them and the NUMA team to the surface. Pitt and Giordino are then whisked to Washington where they join a MAIT (Multi-Agency Investigative Team) to foil the Japanese criminal cartel, headed by arch-villain Hideki Suma, which is planning to use an arsenal of mini atomic bombs—one of which exploded prematurely—to blackmail the Western world into complete economic submission. From here it is a race against time for Pitt and his accomplices to prevent the Japanese plan. Pitt manages to penetrate Suma's high-tech island headquarters, run by robots, and rescue his girlfriend, Congresswoman Loren Smith, and Senator Mike Diaz, who have been abducted by Suma, but fails in his bid to destroy the facility. Pitt is then sent back to the sea bed with a submersible DSMV (Deep Sea Mining Vehicle) to locate the B-29 bomber and detonate its fifty-year-old bomb in order to trigger an earthquake and tsunami that will finally destroy Suma's "Dragon Center."

Shock Wave, the thirteenth Dirk Pitt Adventure, begins with a lengthy prologue, a castaway narrative set in the mid-nineteenth century. Fast-forwarding to the present, a group of tourists from the cruise ship the *Polar Queen*, stranded on Seymour Island, are rescued by Pitt and Giordino, who are in the area investigating the deaths of large numbers of marine animals. Our heroes locate the *Polar Queen* and Pitt manages to stop it being wrecked against the cliffs of the Danger Islands, which (in a wry self-reflexive moment which acknowledges the literary antecedents of the island adventure thriller) Pitt observes "sound like the setting for an adolescent pirate novel."[1] But apart from Deirdre Dorsett, the sister of Maeve Fletcher, the tour guide Pitt had earlier rescued, all aboard the ship are dead. Pitt suspects these deaths, like those of the marine animals, have been caused by intense sound waves emanating from the four corners of the Pacific, which he discovers are generated by the fiendish mining tycoon, Arthur Dorsett, who plans to destroy the world diamond trade and corner the market in coloured gemstones. Pitt, Giordino, and Maeve are caught and cast adrift in the middle of the Pacific. They are shipwrecked, but manage to build another small craft and sail to Dorsett's lair, Gladiator Island, from where they hope to rescue Maeve's twin sons who have been taken hostage by their grandfather. Meanwhile Admiral Sandecker, head of NUMA, manages to prevent the deadly acoustic waves from converging and killing the population of Honolulu by redirecting them to Gladiator Island. Giordino escapes by helicopter with the boys and returns to rescue the badly injured Pitt.

Like Fleming's Bond novels, Cussler's Pitt adventures all follow a similar pattern which draws on the nineteenth-century idea of the "Great Game" that Kipling popularised in *Kim* (1901), the world of spying and international intrigue taken up by John Buchan in his Richard Hannay stories—from *The Thirty-Nine Steps* (1915) to *The Island of Sheep* (1936). And like Bond's, Pitt's domain can be described as Bondspace, the rarefied space in which the high-stakes games of the various novels are played out. For Pitt, these spaces are always extreme environments, and islands offer bounded geographical settings that may readily be manipulated by Cussler to provide the perfect stage for Pitt's performance of his heroic deeds. This is the case, for example, in *Shock Wave*, where at a point early in the novel Pitt and Giordino appear to be lured towards the Danger Islands by the tip of Moody Point which beckons like the bony finger of the Grim Reaper. The topographical view of the islands as they approach by air is menacing:

> The peaks of the three Danger Islands came into view, their rock escarpments rising out of a sea that writhed and thrashed around their base. They rose so steeply that even seabirds couldn't get a foothold on their sheer walls. They thrust angrily from the sea in contempt of the waves that broke against the unyielding rock in rapid explosions of foam and spray. The basalt formation was so hard that a million years of onslaught by a maddened sea produced little weathering. Their polished walls ran up to vertical peaks that possessed no flat spaces wider than a good-sized coffee table.[2]

The descriptive lexicon—"writhed," "thrashed," "thrust angrily," "maddened"—depicts the islands as malevolent; the anthropomorphisation only gestured towards in this passage is made explicit as Pitt and Giordino drop towards the third, outermost island:

> This one looked dark and evil, and it took surprisingly little imagination to see that the peak was shaped in the likeness of an upturned face, much like that of the devil, with slitty eyes, small rock protrusions for horns and a sharp beard below smirking lips.[3]

But if the personification of the island as malevolent is made manifest in this second passage, so too is the islands' indifference to the fate of the humans who venture too close to their rugged cliffs. The "evil" that Pitt must face is not the islands themselves. Instead, the islands that populate this novel are the dangerous environments where Pitt must test himself against the human villains—Arthur Dorsett and his daughters, one of which, ironically, he is about to save from being dashed against the basalt formations of the Danger Islands.

The representations of the island are relatively straightforward in *The Mediterranean Caper*, and similar to countless approach-by-plane scenes (such as those in several of Fleming's Bond novels, for example). Cussler's stylistic choice of geographical realism over metaphor in this early Dirk Pitt novel conceals the degree to which it relies on standard island tropes. The plot of *The Mediterranean Caper* is dependent on the stereotypical view of islands as bounded and contained rather than connected to other islands or to continents. Thus the circumscribed topography of Thasos is accentuated early in the novel:

> The island was separated from the Greek Macedonia mainland by sixteen miles of water, appropriately called the Thasos Strait. The Thasos land mass consisted of one hundred and seventy square miles of rock, timber and remnants from classical history dating back to 1000 B.C.[4]

And as Pitt and Giordino approach the island from the air the enclosed geography of the island is again highlighted by their bird's-eye view:

> Both men stared at the approaching mound rising out of the sea. The beaches bordering the surf were yellow and barren, but the round sloping hills were green with trees. The colors danced in the heat waves and vividly contrasted against the encircling blue of the Aegean.[5]

The narrative map drawn in these two early descriptions of Thasos emphasise the boundedness of the island. It is *separated* from the mainland, *bordered* by beaches and *encircled* by the sea. The lack of metaphor serves here to stabilise the island setting.

Cussler achieves further spatial verisimilitude through regular references to and shorthand descriptions of the island's scenery: the breath-taking view from von Till's villa above the village of Liminas, "the bare peak of Hypsarion, the highest point on the island,"[6] a "stretch of rugged cliffline that intrigued Pitt,"[7] and so on.

The island is quickly established as a place of danger and intrigue. The bright yellow World-War-I biplane that attacks Brady Field comes from "inland over the island,"[8] "sneaking in through a pass in the island mountain range."[9] Similarly, when Pitt discovers that the broken cable connected to the *First Attempt*'s decompression chamber has been sabotaged, he returns to Thasos to look for clues, and later he is convinced that the island holds the key to both the attack on the airfield and the menace threatening the research vessel: "The solution lies [...] either near the island, or on it, or maybe both."[10]

Cussler also exploits the iconic tourist brochure image of the Greek islands, as an escape location or a part of the pleasure periphery, in *The Mediterranean Caper*: sand, sea, and a bikini-clad woman whom Pitt wastes no time in seducing. Claiming to be half Greek, Teri von Till becomes, albeit briefly, a metonym for the island, and her submission to Pitt signals his heterosexual masculinity both in terms of his own menace (consuming the woman/ island) and the promise that he will be able to successfully combat the threat the island contains. And there are other self-conscious postcard images of the island scattered through the novel: "a harbor full of flat-beamed fishing boats offered a picturesque travel folder scene,"[11] while the emptiness of a narrow beach on the western tip of the island "possessed all the mystic allure and romantic charm so often pictured in South Seas travel posters. It was indeed a fragment of paradise."[12] By so clearly locating the island on the pleasure periphery, Cussler codes the island as the contested territory over which Pitt and Bruno von Till must compete. The physical descriptions of the island also provide a geographical reality against which this competition is waged. Thus Thasos functions in the novel as both Bondspace and as a recognisable geographical island. Here, as in the other novels we discuss in this chapter, Cussler embraces the narrative opportunities provided by the geographical conditions of islands (real or fictional) if their defining qualities are accepted as isolation and boundedness, rather than if their accessibility and openness is emphasised.

Islands are again pivotal settings in *Dragon*, and as such clearly play a significant role in Pitt's adventure, as well as providing a structural link that gives the novel continuity. The prologue, set in 1945, almost fifty years before the 1993 present of the novel, begins and ends with islands: from Shemya Island in the Aleutian Islands archipelago where Dennings' Demons take off with their lethal cargo, to the crash site off the coast of the Japanese island of Honshu near an unnamed small island, with "Sheer rock walls" and "No sign of a beach anywhere," which "Looks like a hot dog sticking out of the water," and "Doesn't even show on the map."[13] In this short prologue, the shift from real to fictional geography, from Shemya Island to an unmapped imagined rock needle, takes readers to what will be the principal setting of the main story, Soseki Island, the location of Suma's Dragon Center.

It is some hundreds of pages before Cussler's novel reaches its climax on Soseki Island, but along the way both the main plot and the numerous subplots are punctuated by island references: the explosion aboard the *Divine Star* which destroys several ships as well as NUMA's underwater research facility, Soggy Acres, occurs nine-hundred kilometres northeast of

Midway Island; naval units from both Midway Island and Guam respond to the blast; Admiral Sandecker rendezvous with the junk *Shanghai Shelly* off the Hawaiian Islands, and later the NUMA and British Survey teams rescued from Soggy Acres and *Old Gert* are taken to Oahu; a Japanese cache of World-War-Two loot is hidden on Corregidor Island at the entrance to Manila Bay in the Philippines; Japan's northern island of Hokkaido contributes to Frank Mancuso's background story; Koror Island in the Republic of Palau is used as a field operations site by the MAIT; and Wake Island in the western Pacific Ocean is identified as the nearest pick-up point to Soseki Island.

The references to the immense treasure hoard hidden in "over a hundred different sites in and around the island of Luzon"[14] by the Japanese during World War II, like the references to Bloody Morgan in Ian Fleming's *Live and Let Die*, provide a link back to nineteenth-century adventure fiction, with its rich tradition of Pacific island pirate romances, including Robert Michael Ballantyne's *The Coral Island* (1857) and *Gascoyne, the Sandal-Wood Trader: A Tale of the Pacific* (1864). And like the islands of the West Indies in Fleming's Bond novels, the islands of the Pacific function in Cussler's fiction as contact zones where Pitt must test himself against the enemies of the Western world. The numerous islands named in *Dragon* also function to move Pitt inexorably towards the key island location: Soseki Island, formerly known as Ajima Island.

The island that in 1945 Dennings' Demons had spotted from the air minutes before they were shot down is now the nerve centre of Suma's fiendish Kaiten Project, but before Pitt and his associates can begin to neutralise the threat facing the world, they must first determine the location of Ajima, an island that they believe exists, but is not down on any map. When the tangled subplots eventually lead Pitt to the painting of Ajima Island by Masaki Shimzu that Suma has unsuccessfully searched for, it offers a portrait of a forbidding island:

> Pitt's eyes traveled over the picture Shimzu had painted four hundred and fifty years ago of an island then called Ajima. It would never make a tourist paradise. Steep volcanic rock cliffs towering above pounding surf, no sign of a beach, and almost total absence of vegetation. It looked barren and forbidding, grim and impregnable. There was no way to approach and make a landing from sea or air without detection. A natural fortress, Suma would have it heavily defended against assault.[15]

Once NUMA have matched the painting to the island now known as Soseki, sixty kilometres off the coast of the fictional Edo City (borrowed from an old name for Tokyo), Pitt's mission becomes to gain access to Suma's island hideout.

The hostile geography of the island and the menace that awaits Pitt and Giordino there are signalled in their first, bird's-eye view of the island: "a purple-shadowed blemish between seas and sky, more imagined than real. Almost imperceptibly it became a hard tangible island, its jagged cliffs rising vertically from the rolling swells that crashed into their base."[16] The island is "hard," the cliffs "jagged," the swells "crash," and the whole is a "blemish" on the horizon.

The fictional terrain is familiar to readers of Fleming's *Dr No*: like Crab Key in that novel, it "is going to be damn near impossible" to get onto the island without being detected, and "Whoever tries it will surely die."[17] And the links to *Dr No* do not end there: Suma's unquenchable thirst for power makes him a villain in the mould of Dr No: the luxurious suite in which Loren Smith is imprisoned, with "no inside handle to the door and no windows"[18] mirrors the accommodation provided for Bond and Honeychile Rider; Pitt's first view of Soseki Island from the air stands in for Bond's first view of Crab Key from the sea; the dinner invitation Suma extends to Pitt and his fellow hostages repeats Dr No's invitation to Bond and Honey; and Pitt's test as Kamatori's quarry in the human hunt parallels the obstacle course Bond must run on Crab Key.

Soseki Island, like Crab Key, is "an impregnable island,"[19] a prison from which there is no hope of escape. As their robot guards inform Pitt and Girodino: "You cannot flee the island and there is no place to hide."[20] The geography of the island is again emphasised when Kamatori informs Pitt, before the manhunt begins, that "The island is small. No one has eluded me for more than eight hours."[21] However, Pitt has a significant advantage over Kamatori's earlier prey—a knowledge of the island's geography: "Thanks to Penner's detailed model of the island, Pitt was familiar with the general landscape. He recalled in his mind the dimensions and heights with exacting clarity, knowing precisely where he had to go."[22] This knowledge is power, and allows Pitt to plan a way to outwit Kamatori, and ultimately to win the deadly contest he must play.

The reader, too, is equipped with knowledge of Soseki Island through the inclusion of a pair of cross-section, labelled diagrams depicting the fictional Edo City and the adjacent Soseki Island. These diagrams clearly present the bounded nature of the island, but more importantly, they provide the reader with a degree of spatial specificity that, together with the correlative descriptive passages that track the characters' movements, enables them to follow the progress of the MAIT team once they enter Suma's island fortress.

The novel concludes with a gaunt Pitt, who by this time is believed to be dead by all except Giordino, emerging from the ocean in his DSMV onto the "satiny milk-white sands"[23] of Marcus Island, 1,125 kilometres south east of Japan. Following the successful destruction of Suma's island, Pitt's dramatic arrival on the beach of an invented "luxury resort"[24] on a real island shifts the novel's representation of islands from hostile and threatening to the iconic tourist brochure image of the island as "a select destination,"[25] an "exotic and faraway"[26] location, "a playground for romance and a mecca for honeymooners."[27] Here Cussler begins by playing with the tropes of both resort tourism and romance, before turning briefly to horror, when the tourists on the beach—"Australians, New Zealanders, Taiwanese, and Koreans"[28]—are alarmed by "some *thing* or some sea creature […] moving through the reef towards the lagoon."[29] But the "great shapeless thing covered with green and brown slime"[30] that "crawled into view"[31] is not a monster, but Pitt's submersible. This short scene reminds the reader that the island is a paradoxical space, that can be co-opted for any genre: thriller, romance, horror, fantasy, and so on. From the perspective of popular fiction, the island is a pliable and open space that simultaneously produces and is a product of multiple and seemingly incompatible genres.

Shock Wave opens with a two-part prologue in the form of a castaway narrative and its aftermath, set in 1856 and 1876, respectively, that again highlights the continuum between nineteenth-century adventure fiction and contemporary island thrillers. In his back story of the raft of the *Gladiator*, Cussler deliberately draws on key island adventure tropes—from direct references to "the *Bounty* mutineers on Pitcairn Island"[32] to allusions to Ballantyne's *The Coral Island* in, for example, the shark attack in the lagoon surrounded by a coral reef—to whet his readers' appetites for the Dirk Pitt adventure which follows. After fifteen days at sea, eight survivors from the storm-wrecked *Gladiator* find sanctuary on a large island in the Tasman Sea (see figure 6.2), which also provides the setting for the climax of the novel:

> It was shaped like a fishhook, five miles in length and a little less than one wide. Two massive volcanic peaks, each about twelve to fifteen hundred feet high, stood at the extreme ends. The lagoon measured about three quarters of a mile long and was sheltered by a thick reef to seaward. The rest of the island was buttressed by high cliffs.[33]

Here the island is presented as a literal as well as metaphorical hook, a setting which draws the reader in with its promise of fast-paced adventure and thrilling action.

In the novel proper, Dirk Pitt's adventure begins on Seymour Island, an Antarctic offshore island—"a singularly ugly place, inhabited only by a few varieties of lichen and a rookery of Adélie penguins"[34]—where Maeve Fletcher and her group of cruise-line passengers are marooned following the unexplained disappearance of their ship, the *Polar Queen*. Those that survive the unexplained shock wave that hits the island are fortuitously rescued by Pitt, who stumbles across Maeve in a blizzard. Thus in the opening three chapters (twenty-five pages), a second island castaway adventure is performed, mirroring that of the prologue, and providing a segue between the prologue and the main narrative, in terms of both event and character (Maeve Fletcher is a descendent of Jess Dorsett and Betsy Fletcher who were cast up on Gladiator Island in 1856).

Islands continue to be key settings throughout the novel: the rescued tourists from the *Polar Queen* are taken to King George Island; Pitt and Giordino skirt Dundee Island before Pitt prevents the *Polar Queen* from being smashed against the rugged cliffs of the Danger Islands; South Orkney Island and Chirikof Island (in the Gulf of Alaska) are, like Seymour Island, sites of mass animal killings; the *Mentewai*, en route from the Hawaiian Islands to the island of New Guinea, passes the junk *Tz'u-hsi* close to Howland Island, and the salvage crew plan to take it to Apia in the Samoan Islands, before an explosion aboard sinks the ship; the junk beaches a month later on Cooper Island in the Palmyra Atoll chain; the destructive sound waves that give the book its title stem from four island locations in the Pacific (Gladiator Island, the Komandorskie Islands off the Kamchatka Peninsula, the Kunghit Island in the Queen Charlotte Islands [Haida Gwaii] off British Columbia, and the Isla de Pascau, or Easter Island); Baffin Island, Moresby Island, and Campbell Island are all referenced while Pitt is investigating the north-east source of the acoustic waves; "the maze of islands"[35] around Wellington and New Zealand's South Island are referenced when the action shifts south; first Tasmania, then "Stewart Island, just below the South Island […] the Snares, the Auckland Islands, and […] the Macquaries"[36] are all considered as possible landfalls by Pitt, Giordino, and Fletcher after they have been cast adrift in the southern ocean; Oahu is identified as the convergence point for the four acoustic waves; when they discover an old Bermuda ketch after being wrecked on the Tits, "a pair of legendary islands south of the Tasman Sea,"[37] Maeve recalls "island-hop[ping]"[38] in a similar vessel on Saint Croix, in the US Virgin Islands; Molokai and "the big island of Hawaii" are key sites as the NUMA team battle to prevent a catastrophic convergence of the sound waves; and Tasmania is the final island setting in the novel, where Pitt recuperates before travelling back to the United States—impossibly, on a direct United Airlines flight from Hobart to Washington's Dulles International Airport.

Importantly, Cussler does not imagine these islands as part of the main in this novel, but as islands connected to each other, as the map of the acoustic convergence (figure 6.2) chillingly reveals. As Epeli Hau'ofa so clearly articulates in his enormously influential essay "Our Sea of Islands," "There is a gulf of difference between viewing the Pacific as 'islands in a far sea' and as 'a sea of islands.'"[39] Here (and to a lesser extent in *Dragon*, too) Cussler, like Hau'ofa, conceptualises the Pacific as "'a sea of islands,' rather than 'islands in the sea,'"[40] bounded but not separated, simultaneously contained and

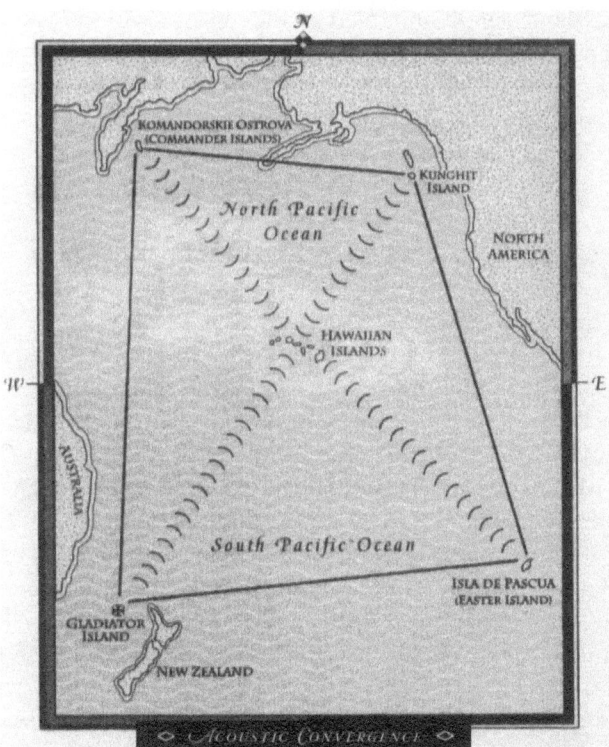

Figure 6.2. "Acoustic Convergence." Clive Cussler, *Shock Wave* (1996; repr., New York: Pocket Books, 2008), p. 158.

connected. The geography of the novel is a geography of islands. Thus, for example, as Pitt and Giordino fly off the *Ice Hunter* bound for Washington, Giordino stares ahead "at the restless sea as the islands north of Cape Horn grew in the distance"[41]: geography is controlled by references to islands, to the archipelago, rather than to the better-known southernmost headland of Hornos Island alone. This is reflected, too, in the several chapter headings used to locate the setting, which in both this novel and in *Dragon* mostly reference islands: Seymour Island, Howland Island, Gladiator Island, Hawaii; Shemya Island, Ajima Island, Marcus Island.

The map of the "Acoustic Convergence" (figure 6.2) clearly shows the sources of the shock waves in the four corners of the Pacific—the fictional Gladiator Island in the Tasman Sea, Easter Island, Kunghit Island, one of the Haida Gwaii (the Queen Charlotte Islands) in Canada, and the Komandorskie islands in the Bering Sea—connected by a grisly trapezium, with the Hawaiian Islands at its centre. In this unusual literary map the continental mains are pushed to the periphery, while island networks, the proximity and extent of the islands, are highlighted by the four sides of the trapezium which join the islands and emphasise, in Hau'ofa's words, "the totality of their relationships."[42] At the same time Cussler manufactures the geographical danger of islands: the threat in this novel emanates exclusively from a series of islands, rather than from continental mainlands. It is thus possible to use the bounded nature of islands to isolate, contain, and ultimately counteract the danger.

To use geography to control events, Pitt must reach Gladiator Island, the headquarters of Arthur Dorsett's family empire, which, like similar island hideouts in numerous thrillers, is presented as contained and impregnable. He is aided in his mission by the map Maeve Fletcher draws of her family's private island, which equips Pitt with the geographical knowledge he needs to penetrate the island, while the map included at the beginning of part 4 similarly provides the spatial specificity that enables the reader to track the movements of Pitt, Giordino, and Fletcher once the trio have landed.

The islands in Cussler's fiction are more than just exotic locations within which Dirk Pitt tests himself against a series of memorable villains. Rather, like all thrillers, Cussler's novels exploit the associations between setting and plot to achieve a particular type of narrative. Specifically, the island settings in Cussler's fiction both influence the nature of events and limit the possible interactions of the hero and villain. Ultimately, knowledge of setting, of the island, is a key factor in the hero's ability to complete his mission—to save the world, or a part of it, from the threat posed by the villain(s).

NOTES

1. Clive Cussler, *Shock Wave* (1996; repr., New York: Pocket Star Books, 2008), 114.
2. Cussler, *Shock Wave*, 115–16.
3. Cussler, *Shock Wave*, 116–17.
4. Clive Cussler, *The Mediterranean Caper* (1973; repr., New York: Berkley Books, 2008), 3.
5. Cussler, *The Mediterranean Caper*, 11.
6. Cussler, *The Mediterranean Caper*, 187.
7. Cussler, *The Mediterranean Caper*, 245.
8. Cussler, *The Mediterranean Caper*, 5.
9. Cussler, *The Mediterranean Caper*, 75.
10. Cussler, *The Mediterranean Caper*, 154.
11. Cussler, *The Mediterranean Caper*, 126.
12. Cussler, *The Mediterranean Caper*, 244–45.
13. Clive Cussler, *Dragon* (1990; repr., New York: Pocket Books, 2006), 12.
14. Cussler, *Dragon*, 99.

15. Cussler, *Dragon*, 317.
16. Cussler, *Dragon*, 370.
17. Cussler, *Dragon*, 317.
18. Cussler, *Dragon*, 352.
19. Cussler, *Dragon*, 360.
20. Cussler, *Dragon*, 388.
21. Cussler, *Dragon*, 414.
22. Cussler, *Dragon*, 416.
23. Cussler, *Dragon*, 599.
24. Cussler, *Dragon*, 598.
25. Cussler, *Dragon*, 598.
26. Cussler, *Dragon*, 598.
27. Cussler, *Dragon*, 599.
28. Cussler, *Dragon*, 599.
29. Cussler, *Dragon*, 600.
30. Cussler, *Dragon*, 601.
31. Cussler, *Dragon*, 601.
32. Cussler, *Shock Wave*, 46.
33. Cussler, *Shock Wave*, 45.
34. Cussler, *Shock Wave*, 61.
35. Cussler, *Shock Wave*, 356.
36. Cussler, *Shock Wave*, 430.
37. Cussler, *Shock Wave*, 476.
38. Cussler, *Shock Wave*, 475.
39. Epeli Hau'ofa, "Our Sea of Islands," in *A New Oceania: Rediscovering Our Sea of Islands*, ed. Eric Waddell, Vijay Naidu, and Epeli Hau'ofa (Suva: University of the South Pacific, 1993), 7.
40. Hau'ofa, "Our Sea of Islands," 7.
41. Cussler, *Shock Wave*, 187.
42. Hau'ofa, "Our Sea of Islands," 7.

Part III

ISLAND ROMANCE, ROMANCE ISLANDS

Chapter Seven

I ♥ Islands

The Emotional Geography of Popular Romance

In her guide for aspiring romance writers, Valerie Parv advises that thinking about the genre's "more common plot situations" can spark ideas for new stories.[1] She provides a list of "old ideas" that have been used countless times:

- ♥ Man and woman stranded together on an island.
- ♥ Arranged or forced marriage.
- ♥ Pretending to be engaged or married.
- ♥ Woman or man seeking revenge on the other.
- ♥ Woman assumes another identity (e.g., twins).
- ♥ Unequal balance of power (e.g., a new boss).
- ♥ Tutor or nanny to hero's child.
- ♥ Secretary to an author.
- ♥ Hired to have his child (or she wants him to father hers).
- ♥ Secret baby—hero is unaware he's fathered a child.
- ♥ Royalty and commoner.[2]

It is telling that islands are at the top of this list. In short, "island romance," signifies as a genre classification more immediately than "island crime," "island thriller," or "island fantasy." Importantly, all of the other "common plot situations" in Parv's list are often used by romance writers in combination with what she later terms the "desert island theme."[3] For instance, Robyn Donald's New Zealand romance *Island of Secrets* (2013) adapts the tried and tested marriage-of-convenience plot: the hero is forced by his stepfather's will to spend "six months in the company" of the heroine on fictional Rotumea Island, "a very small dot in a very empty ocean, a long way from anywhere."[4] Unequal power is the main point of contention in

Susan Stephens's *Bought: One Island, One Bride* (2011) in which the billionaire hero battles with the heroine, a local tour guide and "environmental warrior," when he adds the "beautiful and unspoiled" Greek island of Lefkis "to his property portfolio."[5] In an unusual variation on the nanny plot, the young hero of Tracey Garvis Graves's *On the Island* (2011) is stranded for three-and-a-half years on a remote island in the Indian Ocean with his much older tutor when the seaplane in which they are the only passengers crashes en route to Malé. These are only three recent examples from the enormous number and variety of island romances; we mention many more throughout this chapter, but to consider this topic in exhaustive detail would take an entire book, if not more.

The sea of island romances only becomes wider and deeper if we accept Parv's observation that the "desert island theme can be emotional as well as physical."[6] She offers the example of Anne Mather's *Leopard in the Snow* (1974) in which the damaged hero offers the heroine shelter; the snowbound romance remains a genre stalwart. Island romances often explicitly link one or both protagonists' emotional isolation with their retreat to a remote island. In Zoë Archer's *Skies of Gold* (2013), a steampunk romance set on the fictional Eilean Comhachag in the Outer Hebrides, both the hero and heroine are survivors of a catastrophic battle which has left Liverpool in ruins and each wants nothing more than to be "left alone," or so they think: "They could share this island without actually sharing it—couldn't they?"[7] In *Canyons of Night* (2011), by Jayne Ann Krentz writing as Jayne Castle, and set on the planet of Harmony, the hero retreats to remote Rainshadow Island in the Amber Sea, leaving the Federal Bureau of Psi Investigation (FBPI) to work as the island's police chief in the belief that his paranormal "talent" is waning. Both novels highlight the narrative potential which ensues when two characters "happen to find themselves stranded together on an island,"[8] and so invite readers to expect the romance and adventure of classic castaway tales. This potential is even clearer in historical romance novels in which the couple is literally marooned on an island, such as Laura Kinsale's *Seize the Fire* (1989), Candice Proctor's *Beyond Sunrise* (2003), or Darlene Marshall's *Castaway Dreams* (2012).

The vast majority of scholarship about popular romance focuses, perhaps unsurprisingly, on character and plot, but this misses that the "scenery is clearly more than a backdrop to the action."[9] Lynne Pearce argues for greater attention to the key elements of "early romances" which endure in contemporary manifestations of the genre, "especially the exotic (that is, stereotypically 'romantic') *locations* of romantic fiction."[10] For Pearce, who is interested in both literary and popular manifestations of the genre, "romantic stories cannot do without their romantic locations."[11] The genre's "investment in exotic locations" is, in these terms, one of its defining features. In fact, Pearce goes so far as to suggest that the setting "is often the *only* significant variable" in popular romance novels.[12] (Curiously, however, she offers virtually no close analysis to substantiate her generalisations about popular romance.) She finds in the genre's "unerring recourse to exotic/strange/'other' locations" evidence that the goal of the romance narrative is for the protagonist (typically the heroine) to "will herself into an alternative future."[13]

Pearce uses Ernest Bloch's 1959 book, *The Principle of Hope*, as her launch pad for considering the meaning and significance of "romantic locations," in particular the section of his book called "Beautiful Foreign Lands," in which he "links the subject's desire for travel 'into the unknown' (real or imaginary) to his/her anticipatory consciousness."[14] In Pearce's analysis "romantic locations" in contemporary popular fiction—and the island may well be the romantic location *par excellence*—are more than vehicles for propelling the necessary forward trajectory of the love plot. Whereas, she argues, in the classic romance, romantic locations offered both stages on which the lovers could fall in love and metaphors for their desires, popular romance "tends to make them into a lifestyle statement which is (in part) the undisguised *object* of romance."[15] For Pearce, that is, setting is the primary variable in the lifestyle "branding" offered by romance novels.

The Romance Writers of America (RWA) offers a definition of the genre which has become a shared reference point for writers, publishers, readers, and scholars:

> Two basic elements comprise every romance novel: a central love story and an emotionally satisfying and optimistic ending.
>
> **A Central Love Story**: The main plot centers around individuals falling in love and struggling to make the relationship work. A writer can include as many subplots as he/she wants as long as the love story is the main focus of the novel.
>
> **An Emotionally Satisfying and Optimistic Ending**: In a romance, the lovers who risk and struggle for each other and their relationship are rewarded with emotional justice and unconditional love.
>
> Romance novels may have any tone or style, be set in any place or time, and have varying levels of sensuality—ranging from sweet to extremely hot. These settings and distinctions of plot create specific subgenres within romance fiction.[16]

One way to gloss the RWA definition is to say a romance novel offers readers a fundamentally linear narrative: a chronological sequence of events with a predetermined ending or conclusion that may "be set in any place or time." When simplified in this way, the principal axis of romance narratives is a temporal one. It encompasses both the point in narrative time when the protagonists' mutual love and commitment appears incontrovertible and the indeterminate period of their imagined future. As the Australian romance writer Anne Gracie explains, the happy-ever-after ending (typically referred to in genre communities as the HEA) must convince the reader that the couple "will go on into the future, and live a happy life, and remain committed to each other."[17] However, the conventional narrative arc of the popular romance novel is also an inherently spatialised formation. This is apparent in the frequency with which writers of the genre describe both the protagonists' tale and the experience of reading it as a "journey." Michelle Douglas, who writes category romance novels for Harlequin Mills & Boon, sees "the journey to the happy ending" as the key to writers' efforts to "deliver a story that will delight [...] readers."[18] Similarly, historical romance author Stephanie Laurens describes the "hurdles along the journey from first meeting to forever-and-always commitment" as the "essence of a romance."[19] For paranormal romance author Nalini Singh, readers go with her on "journeys" through imagined worlds.[20] The many subgenres of romance are unified by their commitment to the romantic "journey" and its felicitous destination, or, in the words of the scholar and romance writer Catherine M. Roach, to the imperative, "Find your one true love and live happily ever after."[21]

In the world of popular romance—which Roach explains readers and writers playfully name "Romancelandia"[22]—countless heroes and heroines have found their "one true love" on an island. For many of these couples their declaration of mutual love goes hand in hand with a shared commitment to live together on the island into the future; for others, the island, as the site of shared experiences and as an emblem of intimacy, is the principal enabler of their courtship; and for some, the island is one stage of a journey with multiple "romantic locations."

The opening pages of island romances almost always orient the reader in relation to the circumscribed geographical and social context where the main events of the novel take place, often from the perspective of a character en route to or recently arrived on a small island, either as a new resident or a tourist. Terri Osburn's *Meant to Be* (2013) opens with a question swirling in the mind of the novel's heroine, Beth Chandler: *"Why did this godforsaken island have to be in the middle of the damn water?"*[23] Beth, who has a deep phobia of travelling by boat, is alone in her car on a ferry bound for Anchor Island, a tourist resort in the Outer Banks, North Carolina, to meet her future parents-in-law. When a handsome stranger comes to her rescue ("If it makes you feel any better, I've ridden this ferry a thousand times with no problem"[24]), Beth's apprehension begins to feel like desire and a close correspondence is anticipated between her geographical and emotional destinations. In *Three Sisters* (2013) by Susan Mallery, recently jilted Andi Gordon drives to the "highest point on Blackberry Island" and stares at the run-down house she has just bought to "escape" her life in Seattle.[25] From the novel's first chapter, we know that the house's renovation will parallel both Andi's love story and her transition from newcomer to local: "This was right, she thought happily. She belonged here. Or she would belong, with time."[26] The first scene of Suzanne Elizabeth Phillips' *Heroes Are My Weakness* (2014) depicts the heroine, Annie Hewitt, driving through the "swirling chaos of [a] winter blizzard" on "bleak, hostile" Peregrine Island off the New England coast. Annie's perilous journey takes her to the isolated cottage that will be her home for the next six weeks, within sight of menacing Harp House and its owner, her childhood-sweetheart-cum-reclusive-horror-writer, Will Shaw.[27] Anne Marsh's *Pleasing Her SEAL* (2016) opens with a blog entry by the heroine, Maddie Holmes: "Ladies, it's Saturday and I'm surrounded by honeymooners. [...] Any tips for where to look for a good guy? Because this wedding blogger is feeling lonely in paradise."[28] The next page introduces us to the "good guy," Mason Black, a Navy SEAL on an undercover operation on Fantasy Island. Kresley Cole's *The Price of Pleasure* begins with a journal entry by the shipwrecked heroine, Victoria Ann Dearbourne, from 17 January 1850, written on a "deserted isle somewhere in south Oceania."[29] Reading with the grain of the genre, for all of these characters arrival on a small island—voluntary, accidental, or enforced—is the first in a chain of events which will change their lives for the better. Falling in love and finding one's place are mutually defining objectives across the romance genre, a confluence which makes islands highly valued settings.

For Australian fantasy writer Kim Wilkins, "islands are perfect settings" for stories in which characters need "to stay in conflict." She points out that whereas "in real life, people try to avoid conflict," locating characters on an island typically "restricts them geographically" thus enhancing opportunities for intimacy and opposition.[30] Wilkins also writes commercial women's fiction as Kimberley Freeman, including the 2013 romance *Ember Island*, set on an invented island based on Moreton Island and St. Helena Island off the coast of Queensland, Australia. The spatial logic of the generic romance narrative requires that key characters meet and are mutually attracted, then continue to come into close proximity despite a barrier between them. Islands—especially small islands with few inhabitants—may be so common in the genre in part because they are a pragmatic choice for writers bound by a fairly strictly defined set of narrative conventions.

The narrative efficiency of small island settings is especially relevant to analysing the treatment of geography in category romances, short novels written to publisher guidelines and released in numbered series or lines. The category romance, "essentially a love story written to a particular pattern,"[31] is typified by the novels published by Harlequin Mills & Boon, names which have "long been synonymous with romance."[32] Pearce argues that twentieth-century category romance fiction associated with the brands Mills & Boon, Harlequin, and, to a lesser extent, Silhouette produced the "template" which "has become the twenty-first-century's base-line definition of romance."[33] In the introduction to her book, *For Love and Money: The Literary Art of the Harlequin Mills & Boon Romance*, Laura Vivanco follows Pearce's lead when she justifies her decision to avoid the problem of the polysemy of the label "romance," by taking category fiction as "defining."[34]

Mather's 2014 Harlequin Mills & Boon novel, *Stay Through the Night*, begins with the heroine, Rosa Chantry, waiting to board a ferry to "totally unknown territory," the invented island of Kilfoil, in the Outer Hebrides.[35] She is thus an avatar for the romance reader, about to be transported to what Linda Barlow and Jayne Ann Krentz term the "landscape of romance."[36] Unlike the novel's intended readers, however, Rosa is a naïve visitor to the fictional world Mather depicts, "a familiar world in which the roads are well-traveled and the rules are clear."[37] Following a common trope in romance fiction, Kilfoil is owned by the novel's hero, Liam Jameson, a world-famous horror writer who lives reclusively in the island's castle, which he has restored from ruins. From the novel's opening pages, Liam's strong association with the remote Scottish island is key to his characterisation as a worthy romantic hero for Rosa, a lonely English teacher who lives in a "shabby" flat in a small market town in North Yorkshire.[38] Rosa is apprehensive when she boards the ferry from Skye to Kilfoil, "taking tourists and backpackers to islands further afield": "Dear God, she thought, it sounded so remote, so inaccessible."[39] Remoteness and inaccessibility are also Liam's most remarkable qualities: he describes himself as a "reclusive soul" and Rosa eventually learns that he retreated from society after he was nearly killed by a crazed, knife-wielding fan.[40] Liam is the opposite of Rosa's unfaithful ex-husband Colin, who had used her teacher's salary to "afford the frequent trips to the continent that he so enjoyed."[41] Rosa is en route to the island to search for her much younger wayward and untrustworthy sister, Sophie, who is also a devoted reader of Liam's vampire novels. Rosa learns very quickly that Sophie has never been on the island, but—like countless other heroines before her—Rosa is stranded on the island by a storm and so kept within the hero's narrow orbit. Liam's "islandness" is also intensified by his aversion to the city: the island is "his retreat, his sanctuary," the "one place where he can escape the rat race of his life in London."[42] Of course, the hero's lifestyle is also made possible by his enormous wealth; he owns the island, lives in a staffed castle with fifty-three rooms, and has a helicopter for exigencies. Pearce argues that "in many instances it is the *lifestyle* implicit in the location, rather than the hero himself, that the heroine desires." The "location and the hero" are mutually defining, "intertwined in a nexus of wealth and status."[43] Accordingly, *Stay Through the Night* (the imperative "stay" is an apt one for this novel and for its type) concludes with an epigraph six months after the main events when Liam and Rosa are married and living happily on their island. Rosa, who only intended to stay on Kilfoil for a few days, now feels "as if she'd always lived there. Like Liam she had no desire to live anywhere else. This was their home."[44]

Island romances are not peculiar for their equation of falling in love with finding one's home, or, more accurately, with committing to sharing one's home. Rather, category romances such as *Stay Though the Night* or, indeed, many of Mather's numerous other island-set novels, reveal the extent to which "home" is a loaded word throughout the genre, by intensifying the characters' investment in belonging to a clearly defined place and a community. We would go so far as to say that, next to "love," "home" is the key concept of island romance; it is certainly one of the most frequently used words in all of the romances we have read during our research for this book. The final lines of two recent novels are exemplary, *Three Sisters*, and Virginia Kantra's *Carolina Home* (2012): "She'd found home, and that had turned out to be the very best thing that had happened to her"; "'You are my home,' he said. 'My parents taught me that. Everything else is just a house.'"[45]

The romance writer Kathleen Gilles Seidel argues that the "first function of the setting of a romance novel is to be Other, to transport the reader to somewhere else."[46] This is difficult to dispute, and highly relevant to reading the island settings of romance. For instance, the promise of an imaginary escape to a foreign or exotic elsewhere is immediately apparent in: Violet Winspear's *Beloved Castaway* (1971) in which the heroine is shipwrecked on the remote Brazilian island of Janezera; Jayne Ann Krentz's *A Coral Kiss* (1989) where hero and heroine travel to the "unspoiled tropic paradise" of Orleana Island in the Pacific; Linda Lael Miller's *Pirates* (1995) when the heroine answers a dubious advertisement offering a free vacation on Paradise Island in the Caribbean; and Kira Sinclair's invention of the adults-only Caribbean resort of Escape Island for three novels, *Bring It On* (2012), *Rub It In* (2012), and *Set It Down* (2012). However, as William Gleason explains, critics' emphasis on the association of romance with exotic locations has obscured the extent to which "domestic interiors (and the houses that make them possible) often matter profoundly [...] in popular romance fiction."[47] Island geographies are routinely deployed in romance as ciphers for both the characters' desire to escape the mundaneness of everyday life and their yearning for the safety and comfort of home. The romance island is therefore best thought of as a paradoxical space: it is at once a venue for excitement and (often erotic) adventure and a secure environment where the protagonists learn to live together and frequently settle. The genre island of romance is both holiday resort and home.

The underlying push-pull between the allure of the exotic and the yearning for a place to truly belong does not, however, mean that the narratives of island romances are inherently contradictory. For the most part, across its various subgenres, romance fiction handles the paradox of the genre island by casting one of the protagonists as a newcomer—through choice, foul play, or misadventure—and the other as a native islander or long-term resident. The opening chapter of Parv's *The Monarch's Son* (2000) is exemplary. Australian tourist Allie Carter washes up on the beach of Celeste, the main island of the fictional kingdom of Carramer, at the feet of its monarch, Lorne de Marigny. He chides her for swimming in the dangerous waters of Saphir Beach: "You Australians would call it a rip."[48] Allie retorts (somewhat confusingly) that the "only warning signs were in Carramer language," but by the novel's conclusion, she is Lorne's wife and a princess, and learning to speak Carramer: "From now on my heart and my kingdom are yours to command."[49]

Our focus is on romance novels in which islands are the primary setting, but actual and invented islands and archipelagos also feature as incidental settings throughout the genre, typically as devices to prompt or expedite the protagonists' sexual relationship. For instance, in the opening chapter of Stephanie Laurens's historical romance, *The Brazen Bride* (2010), Linnet Trevission nurses Major Logan Monteith back to health when he is found barely alive on the beach near her Guernsey home. Logan is "startlingly, heartbreakingly, breathtakingly beautiful" and when Linnet lies with him to warm his body, she feels as though they are submerged together in a "pleasurable sea."[50] The "long, rolling swells of pleasure" are so powerful, in fact, that Linnet and Logan's passion is consummated when he is still unconscious and her lust "hit[s] her in a crashing wave."[51] The castaway lover is a genre staple. In her study of the history of castaway fiction, Britta Hartmann analyses a selection of twentieth- and twenty-first-century romance novels to contend that the genre has taken up the "imperial island" of the Robinsonade and transformed [it] into a locale of love and sexuality."[52] In novels such as Winspear's *Beloved Castaway*, Julie Tetel Andresen's *Swept Away* (1989), Penelope Neri's *No Sweeter Paradise* (1993), Ginna Gray's *Always* (1994), Kandy Shepherd's *The Castaway Bride* (2011), and many others, "[s]etting makes the romance [...] possible."[53] For instance, Hartmann explains that Margery Hilton's *Girl Crusoe*, published by Mills & Boon in 1969, knowingly exploits the typical plot, setting, and themes of *Robinson Crusoe* and its long literary legacy. In the heroine's words, the island creates "propinquity": "We were forced into each other's company, all day and every day, where we would probably have met and passed on at any other time or place."[54] Numerous contemporary romances openly play with the narrative tropes and motifs of the Robinsonade and terms such as "stranded," "castaway," and, of course, "deserted island" are ubiquitous in titles. For example, in Nicola Marsh's *Deserted Island, Dreamy*

Ex (2010), Kristi Wilde is reunited with ex-lover Jared Malone when she agrees to spend a week alone with a stranger for a reality television show called *Stranded*: "Two people, placed on an island, with limited resources, for a week."⁵⁵ Similarly, shark expert Sean Carmichael and his ex-wife conservation biologist Daniela Flores must work together to survive in Jill Sorenson's *Stranded with Her Ex* (2011), when a killer strikes a research expedition to the Farallon Islands, an environment which, "inhospitable and extreme," mirrors the state of their relationship. "Man and woman stranded together on an island," begins to emerge as the ur-plot for popular romance fiction.

The appeal and significance of the island castaway plot became a hot topic for discussion and debate among commentators on the genre with the runaway success in 2011 of Graves's, *On the Island*, a self-published contemporary romance about a thirty-one-year-old teacher, Anna, and her sixteen-year-old student, T.J., marooned on a small island in the Maldives.⁵⁶ The novel opens in June 2001, with Anna and T.J. en route to join his parents on a family vacation; T.J. is in remission from Hodgkin's lymphoma and his family has employed Anna to help him catch up with school work. They are the only two passengers on a sea plane that crashes into the ocean when the pilot suffers a heart attack and dies. After drifting all night, T.J. cradling his unconscious teacher in his arms, they find themselves on the beach of a small island. They survive on breadfruit, coconuts, fish, and the occasional crab until the December 2004 tsunami destroys their tiny settlement and sweeps them out to sea, where they are spotted by search helicopters and finally rescued. Graves has said in an interview that the story was partly inspired by her love for the 1980 film *The Blue Lagoon*, and by her disappointment that Chuck Noland (Tom Hanks) is stranded alone, with only a volleyball for company, in *Cast Away* (2000).⁵⁷ "Man stranded alone on an island," represents a lost opportunity from the perspective of the romance genre. In Graves's novel, Anna and T.J. fall in love very slowly, and their relationship is not consummated until just before the boy's nineteenth birthday. After returning to Chicago, they separate when family and friends are unable to accept their relationship and media coverage prevents Anna from finding work as a teacher. T.J., however, is adamant that their mutual love is more important than their age difference and they reunite and are married. The novel concludes with an epilogue set three years later, when they are the parents of twins, Anna is pregnant, and they are living in a house built by T.J. in rural Illinois:

> I [Anna] often think about the island. When the kids are older, we'll have quite a story to tell them. We'll edit, of course. We'll also tell them that this house, and the property that surrounds it, is our island. And that T.J. and I are finally home.⁵⁸

On the Island was followed in 2013 by a sequel, *Uncharted*, which reinforces the metaphoric chain running from island to heterosexual couple to nuclear family unit to home. At issue also in *On the Island* is the tension between unreality and reality which is a key question for the genre as a whole, but which is heightened when the hero and heroine represent a taboo pairing. Anna cautions T.J. against imagining a life together off the island: "Because I'm thirteen years older than you are. This might be our world, but it isn't the real world."[59] The island is, in effect, a stage for a love story that would be implausible almost anywhere else.

As Hartmann points out, the island experience is frequently transformative for the protagonists of romance fiction—facilitating their meeting and mutual attraction, revealing the obstacles between them, and creating the conditions for their "betrothal"—even when their time on the island is short. The relative "unreality" of island geographies enables the truncated courtships of many island romances as readers are invited to accept the guiding assumption that life proceeds differently on an island, or, in simpler terms, that fantasies which are impossible in the "real world" can come true there. Ellie O'Neill's *The Enchanted Island* (2015) is partly inspired by the long history of Brasil Island or Hy Brasil, a "phantom island" off the coast of Ireland.[60] This novel is an excellent example of the romance genre's capacity to simultaneously deploy and interrogate normative ideas about the topographical and social qualities of islands. Maeve O'Brien is one of the few single people in a Dublin law firm and so "the most obvious choice for an assignment on a remote island."[61] Her mission is to travel to Hy Brasil, the "smallest and remotest island off the coast of Clare,"[62] and to obtain the signature of an islander, Sean Fitzpatrick, granting permission for the use of his land to erect a bridge to the mainland. Like many fictional visitors to islands, Maeve perceives Hy Brasil as both an anachronism and outside of historical time: "With no cars and only the sounds of birds chirping, the place felt otherworldly, like I'd jumped a hundred years into the past."[63] Her response to the islanders is also typical, as is their response to her. On this tiny island where everybody knows everybody, Maeve feels very aware of her status as an outsider; the island's policeman rebukes her for venturing off the narrow tourist trail and "trespassing" on Fitzpatrick's property: "Island matters are for island people."[64] As she spends more time on the island, Maeve comes to realise that the local opposition to the bridge is genuinely a life-and-death issue for the old island families. Nevertheless, the conventions of the genre romance mean that Maeve will come to feel a powerful affinity with the island and there are early clues that her status as an outsider is temporary. On her fourth day on Hy Brasil, Maeve climbs its highest peak, Mount Cullan. Nearing the summit, she is surprised to see a house with a plaque on the gate: "Abhaile, the Irish word for home; a comforting word for something that looked the complete opposite."⁶⁵ Maeve's response to the view from the top anticipates her conversion from city-dwelling outsider to islander and her recognition of Hy Brasil as her ideal home:

> The entire island was mapped out and I could see everything, every little nook and cranny, every tin roof and winding pathway, the island's coastline and the sea biting into it, the immense vast world of the ocean surrounding this tiny place. It shook me, I'll admit it. The starkness, the beauty; I would never have expected nature to pull at me. But it did. I was impressed.⁶⁶

On Hy Brasil, however, island clichés are material realities. Maeve learns that the island does change its inhabitants. A few days after climbing Mount Cullan, she again feels the draw of the island when she visits the beach that is the site of the proposed bridge. Maeve's reverie is broken when she is struck on the back of the head and hears someone shout, "Get off our island!" just before she passes out.⁶⁷

Maeve's struggle to adjust to life on the island hinges on a simple opposition between the centrality of face-to-face interaction in the close-knit island community and the constant, but artificial connectedness of social media that was her way of life in Dublin. When she tells Killian McCarthy, the island's school teacher, that she finds it difficult "living in a caravan in the pouring rain on a godforsaken island with nothing going on," he replies, "You'll be here long enough to fall in love with this place."⁶⁸ Killian's rightness for Maeve is signalled when he asks her out, the first time she's "been asked out on a date in person" rather than by text or instant messaging.⁶⁹ The familiar set of binaries in this episode (traditional/modern; natural/technological; real/artificial) are intensified as the islanders' resistance to visitors and their reluctance to adopt the trappings of urban life (the internet; mobile phones) are gradually revealed to be deliberate strategies to keep the island's secret. Hy Brasil has "healing properties" and keeps its inhabitants safe from disease and death by natural causes.⁷⁰ In a strange variation on the island-as-laboratory trope, Hy Brasil is a "little utopian society that has evolved independently under a microclimate."⁷¹ To put the book's message bluntly: the island gives Maeve back her life. She falls in love with Killian and Hy Brasil and the plan for a bridge is quashed. By the end of novel, Maeve and Killian understand "that the island wants you to be happy. The island gives you your heart's desire."⁷²

Romantic mysteries by late twentieth-century writers such as Phyllis A. Whitney, Victoria Holt, Barbara Michaels, and Mary Stewart were enormously popular and they all made use of remote island settings for atmosphere and storytelling. The degree to which islands represent the actualisation of the protagonist's "heart's desire," typically the heroine's, is highlighted when characters dream of the island before going there. Whitney's *Lost Island* (1971) begins with the heroine's return in a nightmare to a fictional island based on St Simons Island, Georgia: "In my dream I ran along the gray sands of Hampton Island."[73] It ends with her in the hero's embrace, the sound of the ocean coming through their bedroom window and her knowledge that "The island was not lost to [her] anymore."[74] Holt's *Lord of the Far Island* (1975) opens with the heroine's account of her recurring dream of a room with a "picture of a storm at sea" over the fireplace.[75] The novel's title foreshadows where she will find this room, on Far Island, off the coast of Cornwall. In histories of romance fiction, Whitney and Holt vie for the titles "Queen of Gothic Romance" and "Queen of Romantic Suspense." The back cover blurb of Michaels's *The Sea King's Daughter* (1975) offers a snapshot of the cluster of meanings attached to islands by the merging of the genre conventions of crime, horror, and romance:

> Since Sandy Frederick first set foot on the volcanic Greek isle of Thera, this breathtaking place of ancient myth and mystery has haunted her dreams. Joining her estranged, obsessed father on a dive to find astonishing secrets from the ocean's floor, she cannot shake the feeling that she was meant to be here; that some ancient, inscrutable power is calling to her. But there are others who have been eagerly waiting for her arrival to drag her into a tangled and terrifying web of secrets, dark superstition, betrayal, blood, and death. And suddenly Sandy's heritage and her destiny could be her doom.[76]

Nora Roberts's *Sanctuary* (1997) speaks back to the gothic island topography mapped by writers such as those listed above from its economical and evocative first sentence: "She dreamed of Sanctuary."[77] This novel both gestures back to past cartographies of romance and is an early example of what is for us one of the most curious developments in popular romance of the early twenty-first century: the creation of a romantic archipelago stretching the length of the American east coast in romance series including Lisa Kleypas's Friday Harbor, Terri Osburn's Anchor Island, Susan Mallery's Blackberry Island, and Marie Force's Gansett Island.

The romance genre, as the next two chapters illustrate is fascinated by the dynamic relations between social and intimate space. The itinerary of a romance novel is thus peculiarly suited to small islands. Not only does the genre relish the storytelling opportunities of a newcomer disembarking the morning ferry or of an islander returning home after many years away, the islands also afford the type of close social proximity which invites the possibility of intimacy.

NOTES

1. Valerie Parv, *The Art of Romance Writing: Practical Advice from an International Bestselling Romance Writer*, rev. ed. (Crows Nest, NSW: Allen & Unwin, 2004), Kindle, location 2195.
2. Parv, *The Art of Romance Writing*, location 2195.
3. Parv, *The Art of Romance Writing*, location 2222.
4. Robyn Donald, *Island of Secrets*, Sexy eBooks (Chatswood, NSW: Harlequin Mills & Boon, 2013), Kindle, location 39, location 619.
5. Susan Stephens, *Bought: One Island, One Bride*, Greek Tycoons (Toronto: Mills & Boon, 2011), Kindle, location 96, location 37, location 50.
6. Parv, *The Art of Romance Writing*, location 2222.
7. Zöe Archer, *Skies of Gold*, The Ether Chronicles (Sydney: Avon Impulse—HarperCollins, 2013), Kindle, location 435.
8. Krentz, *Canyons of the Night*, location 1129.
9. Pearce, "Another Time, Another Place," 101.
10. Lynne Pearce, *Romance Writing* (Cambridge: Polity, 2007), 16.
11. Lynne Pearce, "Popular Romance and Its Readers," in *A Companion to Romance: From Classical to Contemporary*, ed. Corinne Saunders (Malden, MA: Blackwell, 2004), 532.
12. Pearce, "Popular Romance and Its Readers," 531; see also Lynne Pearce, "Another Time, Another Place: The Chronotope of Romantic Love in Contemporary Feminist Fiction," in *Fatal Attractions: Re-Scripting Romance in Contemporary Literature and Film*, ed. Pearce and Gina Wisker (London: Pluto Press, 1998), 101.
13. Pearce, "Popular Romance and Its Readers," 531.
14. Pearce, "Popular Romance and Its Readers," 531.
15. Pearce, "Popular Romance and Its Readers," 533.
16. "About the Romance Genre," *Romance Writers of America*, accessed 1 May 2016, https://www.rwa.org/p/cm/ld/fid=578.
17. Anne Gracie, interviewed by Lisa Fletcher, "Writing the Happy Ever After: An Interview with Anne Gracie," *Journal of Popular Romance Studies*, 4, no. 2 (October 2014), accessed 9 March 2016, http://jprstudies.org/2014/10/writing-the-happy-ever-after-an-interview-with-anne-gracieby-lisa-fletcher/.
18. Michelle Douglas, e-mail message to Lisa Fletcher, 7 March 2014.
19. Stephanie Laurens, interviewed by Pamela Clare, *Happy Ever After—USA Today*, 9 February 2012, accessed 18 October 2012, http://happyeverafter.usatoday.com/.
20. Nalini Singh, "Imagining a World," (interview) *The Popular Romance Project*, 1 May 2016, accessed 5 April 2016, http://popularromanceproject.org/imagining-world/.
21. Catherine M. Roach, *Happily Ever After: The Romance Story in Popular Culture* (Bloomington: Indiana University Press, 2016), Kindle, location 128.
22. Roach. *Happily Ever After*, location 125.
23. Terri Osburn, *Meant to Be*, An Anchor Island Novel (Las Vegas: Montlake Romance, 2013), Kindle, location 28.

24. Osburn, *Meant to Be*, location 86.
25. Susan Mallery, *Three Sisters*, Blackberry Island Book 2 (Chatswood, NSW: Harlequin MIRA, 2013), Kindle, location 64, 87.
26. Mallery, *Three Sisters*, location 95.
27. Susan Elizabeth, Phillips, *Heroes Are My Weakness* (Sydney: William Morrow-HarperCollins, 2014), Kindle, location 43, 49.
28. Anne Marsh, *Pleasing Her SEAL* (2 Great Reads edition with Lisa Childs, *Red Hot*), Blaze (Sydney: Harlequin Mills & Boon, 2016), 7.
29. Kresley Cole, *The Price of Pleasure* (New York: Pocket Books, 2004), Kindle, location 89.
30. Kim Wilkins, email to Lisa Fletcher, 1 April 2016.
31. Kristin Ramsdell, *Romance Fiction: A Guide to the Genre,* 2nd ed. (Santa Barbara: Libraries Unlimited, 2012), Kindle, location 1619.
32. Ken Gelder, *Popular Fiction: The Logics and Practices of a Literary Field* (London: Routledge, 2004), 44.
33. Pearce, "Popular Romance and Its Readers," 521.
34. Laura Vivanco, *For Love and Money: The Literary Art of the Harlequin Mills & Boon Romance* (Penrith: HEB Humanities-Ebooks, 2011), Kindle, location 114.
35. Anne Mather, *Stay Through the Night, in Dark Seductions*, By Request (North Sydney: Harlequin Mills & Boon, 2014), Kindle, location 36.
36. Linda Barlow and Jayne Ann Krentz, "Beneath the Surface: The Hidden Codes of Romance," in *Dangerous Men and Adventurous Women: Romance Writers on the Appeal of the Romance* (Philadelphia: University of Pennsylvania Press, 1992), 16.
37. Barlow and Krentz, "Beneath the Surface," 16.
38. Barlow and Krentz, "Beneath the Surface," 1536.
39. Mather, *Stay Through the Night*, location 67.
40. Mather, *Stay Through the Night*, location 562.
41. Mather, *Stay Through the Night*, location 57.
42. Mather, *Stay Through the Night*, location 353.
43. Pearce, "Another Time, Another Place," 101.
44. Mather, *Stay Through the Night*, location 2172.
45. Mallery, *Three Sisters*, location 4608; Virginia Kantra, *Carolina Home* (New York: Berkley Sensation, 2012), Kindle, location 3765.
46. Kathleen Gilles Seidel, "Judge Me by the Joy I Bring," in Krentz, 165.
47. William Gleason, "The Inside Story: Jennifer Crusie and the Architecture of Love," in *Popular Fiction and Spatiality: Reading Genre Settings*, ed. Lisa Fletcher (New York: Palgrave Macmillan, 2016), 80.
48. Valerie Parv, *The Monarch's Son*, The Carramer Crown, Book 1, Sweet Romance (Chatswood, NSW: Harlequin Mills & Boon, 2000), 9.
49. Parv, *The Monarch's Son*, 9, 179.
50. Stephanie Laurens, *The Brazen Bride*, The Black Cobra Quartet (New York: HarperCollins e-books, 2010), Kindle, location 208, 393.
51. Laurens, *The Brazen Bride*, location 393, 428.
52. Britta Hartmann, "Island Fictions: Castaways and Imperialism" (PhD diss., University of Tasmania, 2014), 196.

53. Hartmann, "Island Fictions," 205.
54. Margery Hilton, *Girl Crusoe*, quoted in Hartmann, "Island Fictions," 205–206.
55. Nicola Marsh, *Deserted Island, Dreamy Ex*, Sexy (2011; repr., North Sydney: Harlequin Mills & Boon, 2015), Kindle, location 78.
56. *On the Island* was republished by Penguin in 2012. For a discussion of the book's fascinating publishing history, see "82. An Interview with Tracey Garvis Graves, Author of *On the Island*," *Smart Podcast, Trashy Books*, 14 March 2014, accessed 2 May 2016, http://smartbitchestrashybooks.com/podcast/82-an-interview-with-tracey-garvis-graves-author-of-on-the-island/.
57. "82. An Interview with Tracey Garvis Graves."
58. Graves, *On the Island*, location 3990–3992.
59. Graves, *On the Island*, location 2101–2102.
60. Barbara Freitag, "The Gaelicization of Brasil Island: From Cartographic Error to Celtic Elysium," in *Shipwreck and Island Motifs in Literature and the Arts*, ed. Brigitte le Juez and Olga Springer (Leiden: Brill Rodopi, 2015), 123.
61. Ellie O'Neill, *The Enchanted Island* (London: Simon & Schuster, 2015), 9.
62. O'Neill, *The Enchanted Island*, 2.
63. O'Neill, *The Enchanted Island*, 70.
64. O'Neill, *The Enchanted Island*, 112.
65. O'Neill, *The Enchanted Island*, 105.
66. O'Neill, *The Enchanted Island*, 105–6.
67. O'Neill, *The Enchanted Island*, 107.
68. O'Neill, *The Enchanted Island*, 151, 154.
69. O'Neill, *The Enchanted Island*, 268.
70. O'Neill, *The Enchanted Island*, 292.
71. O'Neill, *The Enchanted Island*, 369.
72. O'Neill, *The Enchanted Island*, 411.
73. Phyllis A. Whitney, *Lost Island* (1971; repr., London: Pan Books in association with Heinemann, 1980), 9.
74. Victoria Holt, *Lord of the Far Island* (1975; repr. New York: St Martin's Griffin, n.d.), 3.
75. Holt, *Lord of the Far Island*, 224.
76. Barbara Michaels [Elizabeth Peters], *The Sea King's Daughter* (1975; repr., New York: HarperTorch, 2005), back cover.
77. Nora Roberts, *Sanctuary* (1997; repr., London: Hachette Digital, 2008), Kindle, location 67.

Chapter Eight

Love on the Isle of Man
Margaret Evan Porter's The Islanders Series

Kissing a Stranger (1998), the first book in Margaret Evans Porter's historical romance series, The Islanders, was given a three-star rating (out of a possible five) on the website *RT Book Reviews*; the second book, *The Seducer* (1999), also garnered a three-star *RT* rating, and the third and final book, *Improper Advances* (2000), was rated a four-star historical romance.[1] Founded in 1981 by Kathryn Falk as a twenty-four-page newsletter, *Romantic Times*, or *RT*, evolved to become "Romance's premiere genre magazine,"[2] and now hosts a sophisticated book review website, which offers romance readers—referred to as "fiction lovers"—a powerful search engine to find reviews, interviews, articles, novel excerpts, and more, tailored to their particular reading interests. Dedicated romance readers classify and seek books according to preferred plot elements, character types, or settings. On an episode of the romance fiction podcast *Dear Bitches, Smart Authors* (*DBSA*) romance bloggers and reviewers Sarah Wendell and Kat Mayo identify "forced proximity" as one of their "favorite tropes": "romances where the hero and heroine are snowbound," or trapped by natural disaster, or on a "deserted island."[3] Wendell and Candy Tan explain that when a reader writes to their romance website Smart Bitches, Trashy Books "for help finding books that she may like, more often than not her preference is based on plot twist and setting, and not on character."[4] Similarly, readers can "Power Search" the review database on the website All About Romance by "Locale Setting." All About Romance also maintains reader-driven bibliographies, which sort novels by theme (Disabilities in Romance; War), structure or style (Point of View), character type (Bluestockings & Feminists; Rakes & Rogues), plot device (Shotgun Weddings), or setting (Big City Contemporary Romance; Cabin & Road Romances). The "Special Settings" list includes romances set in: Antarctica, Asia, Australia, and New

 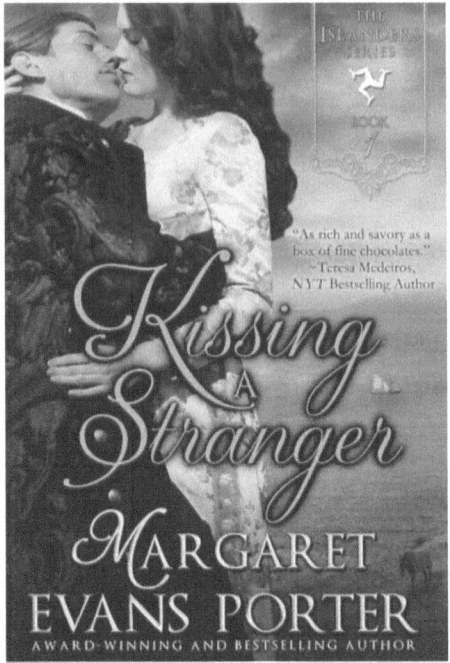

Figure 8.1. Front cover of *Kissing a Stranger*. 1998 Avon Books paperback edition.

Figure 8.2. Front cover of *Kissing a Stranger*. 2012 self-published ebook edition.

Zealand; Canada, Mexico, Hawaii, and Alaska; Europe; the Middle East and Africa; Miscellaneous Island; Russia; and Central and South America. Porter's series focuses on such a "Special Setting" or "Miscellaneous Island": the Isle of Man.

The series, first published as mass market paperbacks by Avon Books (1998–2000), was re-released by the author in significantly revised e-book editions in 2012. The new covers are the first indication that Porter's revisions amplify the import of the Isle of Man (figure 8.1 and figure 8.2). There is no reference to the island on the covers of the first editions. Instead, the cover blurbs subsume the specificities of the island setting under broad location categories: Lady Lavinia Cashin, the heroine of *Kissing a Stranger*, "arrives in Regency London with one purpose—to find a wealthy husband"; Kerron Cashin, "one of London's most notorious rakes," is "suddenly called to his country home" in *The Seducer*, where he meets "pretty Ellin Fayle" and "whisks her away from her sheltered home"; Oriana Julian conceals her scandalous London identity as the songbird Ana St Albans by masquerading as a "respectable widow on holiday in the countryside" in *Improper Advances*, but finds that the "secluded hamlet" is home to "handsome and intriguing"

Darius Corlett.[5] While close comparison of the first and revised editions is not our objective in this chapter—which offers close readings of the later e-book editions—it is nevertheless worth noting that some of the textual changes enhance the focus on Manx geography, history, and folklore, and intensify the use of island metaphors for characterisation and plot development. For instance, whereas Ellin in the first edition of *The Seducer* thinks that her beloved Kerron, Lord Garvain, is "too far above her touch," in the revised edition he is, like the island's famous peak, Snaefell, "too lofty and remote."[6]

The Author's Note included in each book, together with the Historical Note on the Isle of Man in *The Seducer*, anchors the series in Porter's "personal connection" to the island as well as in its distinctive history, culture, and geography: "In centuries past, my ancestors conquered the island. Some years ago, curiosity prompted my first visit, and the island conquered *me*."[7] The novels clearly engage, to varying degrees, with the island's history, language, and folklore, but this genuine interest in the uniqueness of a particular island is overlaid by a commitment to the conventions of the popular romance genre and, importantly, to those of historical romance fiction. In her *RT* review of the first edition of *Kissing a Stranger*, Michell Phifer describes a "light, fluffy plot that spirits off on tangents."[8] For Jill Brager, the "backdrop" of linen manufacturing on the Isle of Man "adds an interesting aside to this sweet, predictable tale."[9] Blythe Barnhill, reviewing *Improper Advances* for All About Romance, recommends the novel for "readers who like unusual settings and historical detail," but complains that Porter "goes overboard in her zeal" for the Isle of Man.[10] Comparison of the paratext of the two editions certainly suggests that Avon Books saw less value in the Isle of Man as a hook to attract readers than Porter later did. Accordingly, her personal author website includes a page about the Isle of Man with a map showing the locations used in the series, photographs of various sites and buildings depicted in the novels, and a Manx recipe for "Scallops Marsala for Two."[11]

Porter conducted significant research on the Isle of Man to write this series, and there are numerous references to the places, people, and folklore of the island in the 1790s. For instance, a key plot element in *Kissing a Stranger* is based on the history of customs tariffs imposed by England on imports from the Isle of Man, and the heroine's father is arrested and imprisoned when he is unable to pay the duty on a shipment of wool cloth. Manx proverbs appear as chapter epigraphs in *The Seducer*, in which a key secondary character is a member of the Teare family, "famous as Manx charmers, dispensing their folk medicines and magic until well into the twentieth century."[12] *The Seducer* also includes a glossary of Manx words and phrases. The heroine of *Improper Advances*, which begins in May 1799, learns of the island from John Feltham's 1798 *A Tour Through the Island of Mann, in 1797 and 1798*, which she borrows from a circulating library in Liverpool.[13] The author's note to this novel explains that almost all of the secondary characters from on and off the island were "real people," including the hero's friend Thomas "Buck" Whaley who lived on the Isle of Man from the late 1780s until his death in 1800.[14] As these examples suggest, *The Islanders* is about the Isle of Man.

In broad terms, historical fiction is defined by a contradiction between the priorities of history and the objectives of fiction. This contradiction is intensified in popular historical romance novels.[15] In short, the priorities of the romance genre trump the author's interest in the place and period of her story's setting: the rocky courtships of the heroes and heroines are the prime concern. To use the words of bestselling historical romance writer Anne Gracie, the "tension in romance between predictability and freshness" is one explanation for the appeal of islands to writers in this genre. The island setting is thus a device for writers like Porter who must "walk a bit of a tightrope" between "pleas[ing] readers who love the genre" with "predictable elements" and making every novel "fresh and unique." As Gracie explains, "Tweaking the predictable plot to surprise the reader: that's the game, really."[16] Further, close analysis of The Islanders Series through the lens of island studies reveals the tension between acknowledging (the appeal of) island universalities and claims for the particularity of individual islands.

For Pete Hay, each and every island is characterised by an "irreducible uniqueness."[17] In his 2013 article, "What the Sea Portends: A Reconsideration of Contested Island Tropes," Hay takes issue with Lisa Fletcher's argument for a greater sensitivity to and engagement with literature and literary theory in island studies. In particular, he rejects her proposal of a theory of "performative geographies" as "an approach to studying the island as a space of cultural production which privileges neither geography nor literature (in their narrow senses) but insists on their interconnection."[18] The aspect of Fletcher's argument with which Hay most takes issue is her contention that the claims of island studies to interdisciplinarity are hampered to the extent that scholars in the field fail to balance a commitment to "real islands" with a recognition that "human encounters with physical space are always already managed by our position in linguistic and cultural systems of representation."[19] Hay seeks island literature that "articulates particularity," which insists that islands "are real, that they are particular and that they are significant—the site of vital happenings."[20] Whereas Hay stresses a "bewildering diversity" that, for him, "renders each island radically particular,"[21] our emphasis on performativity does suggest that no island is entire of itself but exists in a complex of geographical, social, and cultural relations. Clearly, as the title of this book indicates, we see value in appreciating the non-phenomenological ways in which meanings are attached to islands. Our aim is not to deny or discount the meanings produced through direct engagement with islands but rather to show that the conceptualisations and representations of islands do not need to be restricted to "real islands." The Isle of Man, for example, is both a "real island" and a "genre island"; the latter formulation does not undermine or claim priority over the former.

This chapter argues that, far from closing down meaning, reading literature—in its broad sense—opens new avenues for exploring islands, and, to reverse direction, thinking deeply about islands can open up new ways of reading literature.[22] The "Listopia" feature on the social networking site, Goodreads, provides evidence that the question of generic versus distinctive spatial settings is not tangential to romance and, importantly for us, that island geographies have a special resonance in the genre.[23] Island-focused "Listopia" pages include "Romance in Mexico/Caribbean islands (and/or) Mexican/Caribbean Heroes and Heroines," "Gay Romance that Takes Place on an Island," "Pacific islanders in Romance Novels," and "Islands (historical romance)."[24] While such crowd-sourced bibliographies do not claim to be comprehensive, they are an invaluable barometer of the interests and predilections of genre readers. The instructions for voting on the "Island (historical romance)" list, for example, indicate the immediate familiarity of the island as a stock setting for love stories set in the past:

> Being shipwrecked on an island might also apply. But the main part of the story has to take part on the island.
> NOT to be confused with "island keepers."[25]

These instructions gesture also to the strong association of islands with the pleasure of romance reading in the genre's fan lexicon. All About Romance founder Laurie Gold lays claim to the now widely employed term "Desert Isle Keeper," which was first used on the site in the late 1990s to refer to the kind of book that you would want with you if your ship went down at sea.[26] In March 2016 the words "desert island books" returned 11 million results on a Google search; "desert island romance" returned 2.6 million. On the one hand, the idea of a "Desert Isle Keeper" in romance parlance is just a variation on the listing game popularised by the long-standing BBC radio programme *Desert Island Discs*, for which guests are asked to choose eight pieces of music, a book (to go with the Bible and the complete works of Shakespeare that are provided to every castaway), and a luxury item they would take with them to a "mythical desert island."[27] On the other hand, the easy association of islands with the pleasure of reading, and of reading romance in particular, marshals together many of the same ideas about islands that make them such a ubiquitous setting in the genre, not least that islands afford visitors adventure and sanctuary.

As Lynne Pearce points out, the "literary-historical origins of romance are [...] profoundly bound up with the *adventure* narrative."[28] This is no more apparent than in the subgenre of historical romance fiction, which routinely reaches back through literary history to deploy the character archetypes, plot elements, tropes, and motifs of earlier "romance" genres (late nineteenth-century and early twentieth-century adventure fiction; Victorian sensation novels; Gothic novels; eighteenth-century epistolary fiction; medieval romance). Indeed, historical romance novelists often display their engagement with literary ur-texts, both to enhance the text's verisimilitude (for example, characters read the most famous texts of their time) and to stake their claim in a genre with an esteemed history (epigraphs, character names, or plots are routinely borrowed from "classic" romances). As the previous chapter indicates, the literary heritage of late twentieth- and twenty-first-century popular romance fiction determines the treatment of setting, and this is especially apparent in island romances which invariably gesture back to ancient sagas of journey and peril in harsh terrains and climates and to swashbuckling tales of piracy, plunder, and treasure. Pearce argues for a "romantic love chronotope," which she presents as a variation on Bakhtin's "adventure chronotope." For Bakhtin, the ancient "adventure novel of ordeal," written between the second and sixth centuries, established the novelistic chronotope—or time-space—which "determined the development of the adventure novel up to the mid eighteenth century."[29] His summary of the "typical composite schema" of these ancient novels would, with minimal amendment, ring true in a study of popular romance fiction as we recognise the genre today:

> There is a boy and a girl of *marriageable* age. Their lineage is *unknown, mysterious* (but not always [...]). They are remarkable for their *exceptional beauty*. They are also exceptionally *chaste*. They meet each other *unexpectedly*, usually during some festive *holiday*. A *sudden* and *instantaneous* passion flares up between them that is as irresistible as fate, like an incurable disease. However, the marriage cannot take place straightway. They are confronted with obstacles that *retard* and delay their union. The lovers are *parted*, they seek one another, find one another; again they lose each other, again they find each other. There are the usual obstacle and adventures of lovers. [...] The novel ends happily with the lovers united in marriage.[30]

"Adventure-time," in Bakhtin's formulation, is essentially "empty time"; the series of encounters and events narrated between the meeting of the hero and heroine ("the arousal of passion") and the happy ending ("its satisfaction") are an "extratemporal hiatus that appears between two moments of a real time sequence."[31] Pearce defines the romantic chronotope as: "A spatio-temporal continuum which exists apart from the 'historical' lives of the characters, but into which all are likely to be swept as into a black whole."[32] In the space-time of romance, time "stands still"; Pearce sees a connection here between the chronotopic norms of romance and the spatiotemporal disconnection implicit in the idea of "falling in love." Furthermore, she uses the concept of the romantic chronotope to formulate an abbreviated schema of the love plot as the "transportation" of a lover-protagonist to " 'another time'/'another place'," from an "old world" to a "new world." The appeal of island settings to writers working within these storytelling parameters must be immediately apparent: in the popular imagination the chronotope of the island is another time/another place, a promised elsewhere in which one might escape the vicissitudes of chronological time.

David Lowenthal writes, "Islands are for lovers, it is often truly said."[33] In figurative terms, in popular island romance, it is also true to say lovers *are* islands. Porter's The Islanders Series delights in the genre's tendency to depict the hero and heroine, both individually and as a couple, through an intensely spatialised metaphorics. More particularly, as we argue below, descriptions of the titular islanders exemplify the related tendency to geomorphise key characters which unites the novels discussed in this section of the book. The titles—*Kissing a Stranger*, *The Seducer*, and *Improper Advances*—signal the series' preoccupation with the erotics of intimate space. All three titles, that is, evoke the frisson of a breach in the invisible boundaries which manage the dynamics of social and personal relations, but the happy resolution of each novel requires its title's inversion: strangers become lovers, the seducer finds himself entranced, and an unacceptable liaison is made entirely proper.

The first sentence of the prologue to *Kissing a Stranger* introduces one of the key words in this series: "Time to go home, Lavinia Cashin decided." The opening paragraphs depict Lavinia as both of and like the island: she collects sprigs of native plants for her buttonhole, and brushes a stray blossom from her "mud-brown skirt, woven from the fleeces of native Loghtan sheep."[34] The prologue reveals that "home" is a fraught notion for Lavinia and her "close-knit family, bound together by their adversity and their poverty."[35] Lavinia's father is the Earl of Ballacraine—a peerage invented for the novel—but there is virtually no capital left in the estate: their tenant crofters pay rents irregularly, and the "ancestral home is in a ruinous state."[36] Lord Ballacraine has therefore determined, with Lavinia's full cooperation, to take her to London to find a wealthy husband who will rescue the family from destitution. The first stranger Lavinia encounters in London mistakes her for an Italian ("I well know how people of your country greet one another"); he "poke[s] his head under her hat brim to kiss each of her cheeks" and "[brush] his lips against her mouth." This "bold" and "handsome" stranger turns out to be the novel's hero, Lord Garrick Armitage.[37] By the end of the first chapter, Lavinia's vulnerability to such trespasses is linked unmistakably to her island identity: her father has been arrested for insolvency and she is "alone and unprotected in this vast and dangerous city,"[38] a proxy for her strange and remote island, which is simultaneously part of and separate from the British Isles. When Garrick kisses Lavinia later in the novel, she feels "as free as she did when roaming her island's rocky coastline or riding across its heathery hills."[39] And when the course of their romance falters (as it must), the conflict between them is exacerbated by their shared inability to recognise that the coordinates of their world have changed irreversibly: Lavinia flees "home, where I belong"; Garrick seeks out a gambling den, "exactly where he belonged."[40] By the novel's end, Lavinia understands that "home" is no longer her family's crumbling estate on the Isle of Man, the fictitious Castle Cashin near Maughold Head on the island's easternmost point, but the body of her hero. When Garrick declares his love, she allows herself to be pulled "into his embrace": "This was her homecoming, after a lengthy and arduous exile."[41] In the light of scenes such as this, it seems no accident that Garrick's surname, Armitage, shares its etymology with "hermitage." Similarly, Lavinia's triumph at acquiring her husband/private dwelling place is humorously anticipated by her own surname.

As we saw in the previous chapter, the protagonists' islophilia occasionally seems to exceed their passion for each other. Island settings intensify the genre's commitment to a utopian concept of home and magnify the connection romance draws between finding a place to "belong" and lasting happiness. It is in these terms that the affective and erotic unit of the heterosexual couple becomes, in effect, an island unto itself. In contrast to crime fiction (except in the hybrid genre of romantic suspense) and the thriller, the romance island is almost always a device for at least one key character to achieve a sense of identity, typically by discovering an affinity with the geography and/or the community of the island. Pearce argues that "it is absolutely necessary that the romantic hero/ine begins their adventure without a fix on time and space."[42] Whereas *Kissing a Stranger* begins with the heroine preparing to leave her beloved island home, *The Seducer* opens on a scene of classic adventure as the hero attempts to return to the island: Lavinia's brother, Kerron, Baron Garvain, is aboard a smuggler's boat in a fierce storm on the Irish Sea, certain that he will "perish [...] mere miles from home."[43] Kerron is returning in disgrace—at least in his own mind. He has failed in his efforts to become an educated and cosmopolitan gentleman, and his mission to secure a wealthy bride has left him with a reputation as a "rogue and a libertine."[44]

This novel underscores the degree to which the HEA required by popular romance fiction is a spatial construction. Unbeknownst to Kerr, his unhappy return to the Isle of Man will be made unhappier still by the news that his twin sister, Kitty, died a day earlier. The first chapter opens with Kitty's wake, where the novel's heroine, Kitty's friend and servant, Ellin Fayle, feels "out of place," despite her love for the Cashin family.[45] Similarly, Kerr's resolution that founding a new business scheme on the island is "his duty and his purpose in life" cannot conceal his ambivalence about returning to the island.[46] In figurative terms, both hero and heroine thus begin the novel at sea, so to speak, and according to the genre's logic, their chance meeting in the opening pages initiates their journey towards mutual happiness. The happy ending is thus a destination: for the conclusion of a romance novel to be "emotionally satisfying and optimistic," to quote the definition of the genre promoted by the Romance Writers of America, the protagonists must find their place.[47] Importantly, finding one's place is typically figured as both an arrival and a return in this genre, and *The Seducer* is no exception.

For experienced readers of popular historical romance novels, the early chapters offer numerous clues that Kerr's and Ellin's future together will be on the Isle of Man: Kerr may be hesitant to identify fully as a Manxman at the beginning, but Ellin is secure in her identity as an islander. Ellin, who has desired Kerr "from a distance" for years, believes that she has cast him as a hero in an impossible romantic fantasy about a nobleman and an illegitimate orphan: he is "too lofty and remote" to be anything other than a figure in her dreams.[48] However, the correspondence between Ellin's perspective on Kerr and her view of the island ("remote" with "lofty" peaks and, like Kerr's eyes, "stormy gray"[49]) is a coded promise to readers. In keeping with this metaphorics of place, when Kerr first kisses Ellin, she learns that "her love for him, flowing from her head and her heart, also dwelled in other parts of her body."[50] "Kerr" and "Kerr's island"[51] (the toponym *Isle of Man* resonates in obvious ways here) are conjoined objects of desire for Ellin. Her romantic epiphany—the moment when the hero/ine hears the cry "you and no other"[52]—occurs when she realises that central to her "ambition for herself" is to "dwell wherever [Kerr] dwells."[53] By the novel's end Kerr and Ellin are living on the island, married and expecting their first child. The final words of the epilogue restate the association of (an island) home and happiness: Ellin is "restore[d] [...] to her rightful place—here, within his arms."[54]

That islands—as generic geographies overloaded by connotations of singularity—are readily adaptable to the spatial logics of popular romance is especially apparent in *The Seducer*. Pearce stresses "exclusivity" as one of the "first principles" of romantic love: "it is precisely this irrational valuing of the beloved over all others on the grounds of his/her uniqueness that distinguishes romantic love from all other models of personal love."[55] She cites Roland Barthes's *A Lover's Discourse* to highlight the fundamental contradiction in popular narratives of falling in love: "I encounter millions of bodies in my life, I may desire some hundreds; but of these hundreds, I love only one."[56] The hero and heroine of this novel (as is widespread in the genre) recognise love as commonplace and general at the same time as they experience it as unique and particular; the intensity of the latter is enhanced by frequent descriptions of the Isle of Man, and its people, as "unique." Kerr's business venture—to manufacture linen on the island for export to the London market—reinforces the connection between the distinctiveness of the island and the uniqueness of the couple in love. The linen includes "Manx damask" woven with the island's famous triskelion coat of arms, "Manx toile" depicting "fishermen and crofting folk, and the mountains and the coast" and scenes from Manx folklore and English literature. Kerr introduces Ellin to London society in gowns made from samples of his new fabric. Like Lavinia in *Kissing a Stranger*, Ellin comes to embody the island in London. Importantly, however, the success of the Manx cloth depends on both its specialness and its reproducibility. The tension between the rareness or exclusivity of this island romance and its familiarity or derivativeness is also evident in the fabric designs, which come from Kitty's sketchbook: Kerr and Ellin, who each experience falling in love with the other as revelatory, appear over and again as the "heroes and heroines" of the printed scenes.[57] For these novels to succeed as romances, the characters' experiences must be represented as profoundly personal and be immediately comprehensible to readers of the genre as stages on the journey towards a generic HEA.

From early in the novel, both Kerr and Ellin imagine the other as the Isle of Man personified. For Ellin, Kerr is "the storm and the shelter both."[58] Similarly, Kerr feels "pulled towards her" as though by a "tide, strong and relentless."[59] The use of geographical and meteorological metaphors to describe the protagonists—both individually and in relation to each other—also supports the development of a central conflict between them that must be resolved by the novel's end: Ellin is not attuned to the distinction between private and public space which manages social and domestic life in England. In short, reading with the grain of the text, Ellin is too much an islander, and Kerr is too estranged from his Manx identity for their courtship to run smoothly. Kerr, who has, in part, returned to the island to escape scandal, is persuaded to marry Ellin after Finlo Standish (a wealthy islander, the tenant of Castle Cashin, and, unbeknownst to him or Ellin, Ellin's father) discovers them in *flagrante delicto*. After the wedding, they travel immediately to England to promote the Manx linen company. When Ellin meets Felicity Tunbull, the wealthy woman Kerr once hoped to marry, she is made painfully aware that her behaviour marks her as an "island rustic."[60] Felicity chastises Ellin, who is used to roaming the Manx countryside without restriction, for wandering alone in Hyde Park picking flowers for a Manx ritual: "have a care how you behave in a public place." In these terms, the "public" spaces of the island are re-imagined as "private" spaces—jointly owned by the islanders. The stereotype of islands as prisons is overturned in this novel: Ellin feels "trapped [...] in London," and Kerr fears that he is "holding her hostage" and wishes her "free and unfettered from seacoast to mountaintop."[61] When Kerr declares his love, Ellin's "joy" is like that she feels when she "stepped out of her tree-shaded glen into the full light of day, and found an expanse of glittering blue sea."[62] This (over-)identification with the island is made possible by a geo-literary paradox: the island is simultaneously bounded and open.

In popular romance, the island is a promissory setting, a paradoxical literary geography which supports the essential forward trajectory of the romantic text towards a point of closure that is celebrated as the achievement of freedom—especially for the heroine. The promissory function of the island is sustained by the entanglement of the characters' topophilia with their erotic desire for the body of their beloved. The opening question of *Improper Advances*—"You're leaving town?"[63]— initiates a plot anchored in the same set of island tropes which prevail in the first two volumes. As outlined in the previous chapter, the arrivals and departures of characters frequently provide the narrative momentum that drives the plot and directs the reader of island romances; in this sense, island romances have much in common with "small-town" romances, in which the arrival of a newcomer provides the narrative hook. The novel's heroine Mrs Oriana Julian (aka Ana St Albans, singing diva and London celebrity) leaves London to avoid a scandal and explains to her friend, Harriot, her fanciful plot to escape the city:

> Perhaps I should copy the heroine of that absurd play we saw at Covent Garden, the night all this trouble with Matthew started. If I escape to a quiet, remote village and live there under a different name. I might impress some dashing fellow with my gentility and air of mystery.[64]

This scant précis provides a schematic for the love story to follow. Oriana travels to Liverpool where she has been booked to perform, and when the show is postponed, she selects the Isle of Man as an ideal remote location to spend three weeks out of the public eye.

Improper Advances suggests an association between the series' use of the island as a vehicle for the telling of highly conventional love stories and this book's specific interest in the history of theatre. Pearce finds in Jeanette Winterson's literary romance, *The Powerbook*, an awareness of "love as a 'performance' that depends upon a changing backdrop to keep it fresh and new."[65] A similar self-consciousness is evident on nearly every page of this novel. As, too, is the reflection on romance as a kind of "emotional tourism" (the link between notions of love and "foreign lands") that Pearce identifies in Winterson's novel.[66] *Improper Advances* gestures to the history of the Isle of Man as a tourist destination, which puts another spin on the series' preoccupation with the tension between generic and unique places. At the outset, Oriana is an island tourist: she selects her destination from a guidebook and wants her experiences there to be both predictable and exciting, reassuring and memorable. Island tourism and island romance are linked here by their shared investment in safe dramas of contingency: things may (and will) go wrong along the way, but the destination is guaranteed to be a happy and pleasurable one.

In each volume of The Islanders series—and they are exemplary of the genre in this regard—an essential condition of the happy resolution for the hero and heroine is a shared home, with all of the affective baggage the concept of "home" carries in popular discourse. In the opening chapter of *Improper Advances*, Darius ("Dare") Corlett's cousin proposes that he name the grand new house he is building on the island, "Happiness."[67] Moments later, Oriana—whom Dare mistakes for a prostitute—arrives at his door, "breach[ing] his well-guarded privacy," to enquire about renting accommodation for three weeks.[68] As in *Kissing a Stranger* and *The Seducer*, the violability of personal space is a point of contention between the hero and heroine of *Improper Advances*; later in the novel, Oriana, sees Dare as the "invader of her privacy."[69] She resists his initial suggestion that she look for a suitable property in town: "I do *not* care to live in a town. I deliberately chose a remote region of this island."[70] He agrees to let her a cottage not far from his coal mines and, as chance would have it, before very long he becomes a frequent visitor. It comes as no surprise that the novel's first sex scene is in Dare's near-finished villa, which Oriana names "Skyhill House" and declares "the prettiest house on the whole island."[71] Dare is an amateur geologist, which provides the impetus for the intensified geoerotics in this novel: Dare's desire "roil[s] and burn[s] like lava"; he approaches Oriana's body with an "explorer's zeal"; she is "vulnerable slate" to his "molten granite."[72] Curiously, Oriana, the only heroine in the series who is not Manx, is the one who most comes to embody an ideal of "home" for the hero. This is made explicit in the novel's, and the series', penultimate passage: "Home," [Dare] murmured against her neck, "'has nothing to do with the house I occupy, Oriana. My residence of choice is your heart, and I rejoice that you invited me to live there.'"[73] In the final passage, they are serenaded by a mistle thrush and take "full advantage of their seclusion."[74]

Romance is a highly self-reflexive genre, which never stops evaluating the meanings it produces and reproduces. Scholars of popular romance fiction have largely ignored the significance of setting, but writers and readers of this genre are very aware that the "elsewhere" depicted in romance is a linchpin to its success. This series is no exception: The Islanders trilogy foregrounds its treatment of the island setting as a stage for the performance of conventional narratives. A stage, of course, is a public platform on which dramas unfold. A central dynamic in all three novels is the protagonists' anxiety about the permeable barrier between their public and private lives. The island setting is key to resolving this anxiety as the Isle of Man comes to enable and signify privacy, seclusion, and, of course, intimacy. The itineraries of the heroes and heroines are a key structuring element in each novel as the characters move around the Isle of Man and between the island and England, but the mode of literary cartography enacted by Porter is underpinned by an equation of happiness with an idealised notion of home as a companionate and familial haven.

NOTES

1. Michell Phifer, review of *Kissing a Stranger*, by Margaret Evans Porter, *RT Book Reviews*, accessed 3 March 2016, http://www.rtbookreviews.com/book-review/kissing-stranger; Jill Brager, review of *The Seducer*, by Margaret Evans Porter, *RT Book Reviews* accessed March 3 2016, http://www.rtbookreviews.com/book-review/seducer; Michell Phifer, review of *Improper Advances*, by Margaret Evans Porter, *RT Book Reviews*, accessed 3 March 2016, http://www.rtbookreviews.com/book-review/improper-advances.

2. Ken Gelder, *Popular Fiction: The Logics and Practices of a Literary Field* (London: Routledge, 204), 86.

3. SB Sarah [Sarah Wendell], "Podcast Interview 104: Another Interview with Kat Mayo," Smart Bitches, Trashy Books, 6 September 2014 (4:00 p.m.), accessed 3 March 2016, http://smartbitchestrashybooks.com/2014/09/podcast-transcript-104-another-interview-with-kat-mayo/.

4. Sarah Wendell and Candy Tan, *Beyond Heaving Bosoms: The Smart Bitches' Guide to Romance Novels* (New York: Fireside, 2009), 115.

5. Margaret Evans Porter, *Kissing a Stranger* (New York: Avon Books, 1998), back cover; Margaret Evans Porter, *The Seducer* (New York: Avon Books, 1999), back cover; Margaret Evans Porter, *Improper Advances* (New York: Avon Books, 2000), back cover.

6. Porter, *The Seducer*, 10; Margaret Evans Porter, "Author's Note and Acknowledgements," in *The Seducer,* rev. eBook ed. (Margaret Evans Porter, 2012), Kindle, location 162. Citations to follow are all to the Kindle editions of the series.

7. Porter, "Author's Note and Acknowledgements," location 4797.

8. Phifer.

9. Brager.

10. Blythe Barnhill, review of *Improper Advances*, by Margaret Evans Porter, *All About Romance*, accessed 3 March 2016, http://www.likesbooks.com/cgi-bin/bookReview.pl?BookReviewId=4246.

11. Margaret Evans Porter, "Isle of Man," Margaret Evans Porter, accessed 20 March 2016, http://margaretevansporter.com/iom.html.

12. Margaret Evans Porter, "Historical Note: The Isle of Man," in *The Seducer*, location 4844.

13. Margaret Evans Porter, *Improper Advances*, rev. eBook ed. (Margaret Evans Porter, 2012), Kindle, location 241. See also John Feltham, *A Tour through the Island of Man, in 1797 and 1798; Comprising Sketches of its Ancient and Modern History, Constitution, Laws, Commerce, Agriculture, Fishery, &c. Including Whatever is Remarkable in Each Parish, its Population, Inscriptions, Registers, &c.* (Bath: R. Cruttwell, 1798), 166–167, Google eBook, accessed 20 March 2016, https://books.google.com.au/books?id=MJY9AAAAYAAJ&source=gbs_navlinks_s.

14. Porter, *Improper Advances*, location 5003.

15. Lisa Fletcher, *Historical Romance Fiction: Heterosexuality and Performativity* (Aldershot, UK: Ashgate 2008).

16. Anne Gracie, interviewed by Lisa Fletcher, "Writing the Happy Ever After: An Interview with Anne Gracie," *Journal of Popular Romance Studies*, 4, no. 2 (October 2014), accessed 9 March 2016, http://jprstudies.org/2014/10/writing-the-happy-ever-after-an-interview-with-anne-gracieby-lisa-fletcher/.

17. Pete Hay, "What the Sea Portends: A Reconsideration of Contested Island Tropes," *Island Studies Journal* 8, no. 2 (2013): 212. Accessed 3 March 2015, http://www.islandstudies.ca/sites/islandstudies.ca/files/ISJ-8-2-2013-Hay.pdf.

18. Lisa Fletcher, "'… some distance to go': A Critical Survey of Island Studies," *New Literatures Review*, nos. 47–48 (2011): 17–34.

19. Fletcher, "'… some distance to go,'" 19.

20. Pete Hay, "The Poetics of Island Place: Articulating Particularity," *Local Environment* 8, no. 3 (2003): 554.

21. Hay, "What the Sea Portends," 209, 210.

22. See Ralph Crane, "Reading the Club as Colonial Island in E. M. Forster's *A Passage to India* and George Orwell's *Burmese* Days." *Island Studies Journal* 6, no. 1 (2011): 25, accessed 9 March 2016, http://www.islandstudies.ca/sites/islandstudies.ca/files/ISJ-6-1-2011-Crane_0.pdf.

23. "Listopia," Goodreads, accessed 3 March 2016, https://www.goodreads.com/list.

24. "Romance in Mexico/Caribbean islands (and/or) Mexican/Caribbean Heroes and Heroines," Goodreads ("Listopia"), list created 24 March 2014, accessed 3 March 2016, https://www.goodreads.com/list/show/72254.Romance_in_Mexico_Caribbean_Islands_and_or_Mexican_Caribbean_Heroes_and_Heroines; "Gay Romance that Takes Place on an Island," Goodreads ("Listopia"), list created 22 January 2014, accessed 3 March 2016, https://www.goodreads.com/list/show/61463._Gay_Romance_That_Takes_Place_on_an_Island; "Pacific islanders in Romance Novels," Goodreads ("Listopia"), list created 20 July 2015, accessed 3 March 2016, https://www.goodreads.com/list/show/90104.Pacific_Islanders_in_Romance_Novels_; "Islands (historical romance)," Goodreads ("Listopia"), list created 11 June 2012, accessed 3 March 2016, https://www.goodreads.com/list/show/21234.Islands_historical_romance_.

25. "Islands (historical romance)."

26. "Frequently Asked Questions," All About Romance, 2009, accessed 3 March 2016, http://www.likesbooks.com/faq.html#7. For a response to Laurie Gold's claim

in 2008 that the romance blog *DIK (Desert Isle Keepers)* (2008–2012) should attribute the term and acronym to All About Romance in their header, see Jane [Litte], "Once Upon a Desert Isle Keeper," Dear Author, 26 September 2008, accessed 3 March 2016, http://dearauthor.com/features/letters-of-opinion/once-upon-a-desert-isle-keeper/.

27. "Desert Island Discs," BBC Radio 4, accessed 3 March 2016, http://www.bbc.co.uk/programmes/b006qnmr.

28. Lynne Pearce, *Romance Writing* (Cambridge: Polity, 2007), 16.

29. M. M. Bakhtin, "Forms of Time and of the Chronotope in the Novel," in *The Dialogic Imagination: Four Essays by M. M. Bakhtin*, ed. Michael Holquist, trans. Caryl Emerson and Michael Holquist (Austin: University of Texas Press, 1981), 86.

30. Bakhtin, "Forms of Time and of the Chronotope in the Novel," 87.

31. Bakhtin, "Forms of Time and of the Chronotope in the Novel," 90–91.

32. Lynne Pearce, "Another Time, Another Place: The Chronotope of Romantic Love in Contemporary Feminist Fiction," in *Fatal Attractions: Re-Scripting Romance in Contemporary Literature and Film*, ed. Pearce and Gina Wisker (London: Pluto Press, 1998), 99.

33. David Lowenthal, "Islands, Lovers, and Others," *Geographical Review* 97, no. 2 (2007): 202.

34. Margaret Evans Porter, *Kissing a Stranger*, rev. eBook ed. (Margaret Evans Porter, 2012), Kindle, location 60.

35. Porter, *Kissing a Stranger*, location 113.

36. Porter, *Kissing a Stranger*, location 182.

37. Porter, *Kissing a Stranger*, location 145.

38. Porter, *Kissing a Stranger*, location 284.

39. Porter, *Kissing a Stranger*, location 872.

40. Porter, *Kissing a Stranger*, location 2758, location 2781.

41. Porter, *Kissing a Stranger*, location 3578.

42. Pearce, "Another Time, Another Place," 102–103.

43. Porter, *The Seducer*, location 75.

44. Porter, *The Seducer*, location 396.

45. Porter, *The Seducer*, location 112.

46. Porter, *The Seducer*, location 75.

47. "About the Romance Genre," RWA: Romance Writers of America, accessed 16 March 2016, https://www.rwa.org/Romance.

48. Porter, *The Seducer*, location 75.

49. Porter, *The Seducer*, location 146; see also location 2496.

50. Porter, *The Seducer*, location 797.

51. Porter, *The Seducer*, location 164.

52. Pearce, *Romance Writing*, 9.

53. Porter, *The Seducer*, location 4410.

54. Porter, *The Seducer*, location 4791.

55. Pearce, *Romance Writing*, 9.

56. Roland Barthes quoted in Lynne Pearce, "Popular Romance and its Readers," in *A Companion to Romance: From Classical to Contemporary*, ed. Corinne Saunders (Malden, MA: Blackwell, 2004): 522.

57. Porter, *The Seducer*, location 876.
58. Porter, *The Seducer* location 4548.
59. Porter, *The Seducer*, location 1353.
60. Porter, *The Seducer*, location 2228; location 2802–2808.
61. Porter, *The Seducer*, location 3552, location 3193–3195.
62. Porter, *The Seducer*, location 3216.
63. Porter, *Improper Advances,* location 63.
64. Porter, *Improper Advances*, location 127.
65. Pearce, "Popular Romance and its Readers," 532.
66. Pearce, "Popular Romance and its Readers," 532.
67. Porter, *Improper Advances*, location 159.
68. Porter, *Improper Advances*, location 187.
69. Porter, *Improper Advances*, location 693.
70. Porter, *Improper Advances*, location 229.
71. Porter, *Improper Advances*, location 1265.
72. Porter, *Improper Advances*, location 1748, location 2867, location 3573.
73. Porter, *Improper Advances*, location 4988.
74. Porter, *Improper Advances*, location 4990.

Chapter Nine

The Island Happy Ever After
Nora Roberts's Three Sisters Island Trilogy

Nora Roberts's Three Sisters Island lies off the coast of Massachusetts, a pleasant ferry ride from Boston. At roughly nine square miles and with a year-round population of just over 3,000, this "knuckle of land, bumpy and green"[1] is the largest of New England's offshore islands, or at least it would be if it existed. On the "book lovers" social network, Goodreads, one reader, Jennifer, posted, "I wish Three Sisters Island was a real place and I could go there."[2] Jennifer's message offers a distillation of the treatment of setting in Roberts's trilogy, in which the island's status as both a "wish" and a "real" place is crucial to the course of each book's romance and propels the paranormal plot which provides the series' overarching narrative. As Christina A. Valeo suggests, writing in series helps Roberts "maintain her incredible annual output; she writes three or more books, but she builds only one world."[3] The island setting is, as we have shown throughout this book, commercially expedient. One way to read this series is therefore as an example of the convenience of geographical stereotypes for writers of popular fiction, but the island in this trilogy is more than an expedient stock setting for Roberts's brand of popular romance. Almost all of the action takes place on the island, and when key characters do venture "off-island,"[4] they tend to do so reluctantly or by astral projection. In broad terms, the Three Sisters Island trilogy—*Dance Upon the Air* (2001), *Heaven and Earth* (2001), and *Face the Fire* (2002)—explores the relationship between generic storytelling and generic island geographies. More particularly, these novels, separately and together, are about the meaning and significance of islands for contemporary popular romance fiction and for the genre's commitment to happy heterosexuality. This chapter offers a spatially oriented response to Eric Murphy Selinger's question, "What would 'close-reading a romance' [...] look like in practice?"[5] By depicting characters who are aware that their island home is a fantastic projection—"torn away from the mainland"[6]—Roberts foregrounds the extent to which the chronotope of the island enables the kinds of bridges between fact and fiction that are so important to this genre. The Three Sisters Island trilogy reveals the meta-geographical potential of genre fictions as it both depicts and reflects on islands as performative geographies or spaces that make and unmake individual and social identities.

Three Sisters Island is named to signal its genre; both diegetically (within the fictional world) and extradiegetically Roberts's toponym explicitly associates islands with tales of magic and romance that are, in some fundamental way, bound up with the lives of women. The appeal of the island setting is related to the reliability of its symbolism and narrative terrain. This is even clearer in the naming of Roberts's 1997 romantic suspense, *Sanctuary*, which is set on the fictional island of "Lost Desire," off the coast of Georgia. The novels analysed in this chapter—as dedicated readers of the genre are well aware—comprise only one of many contemporary romance trilogies set on islands and centred on three sisters or friends. Three Sisters Island was brought into being by a spell cast by three witches in Salem in 1699. The first novel, *Dance Upon the Air*, opens with a prologue in which the sisters, Air, Earth, and Fire, conjure the island, so that they and their descendants might live in safety from persecution: "Carve rock, carve tree, carve hill and stream. Carry us with it on midsummer moonbeam. Out past the cliff and out past the shore to be severed from this land forever more. We take our island out to the sea. As we will, so mote it be."[7] Three Sisters was thus cut off from the mainland and flung out to sea by a fantastic speech act (an utterance that does not so much describe as perform an action). Created by magic, the island's existence is precarious. For nearly 300 years—since September 1702—Three Sisters Island has been under the protection of another spell, cast by the third sister, Fire, before she leapt to her death from a cliff at the island's highest point: "As she plunged toward the sea, she hurled her power around the island, where her children slept, like a silver net."[8] Fire's spell was made to last for a "hundred years times three" until a "circle of sisters joined in power [...] stand and face the darkest hour."[9]

The island's future, as landform and community, is dependent upon the direct descendants of its founders, three modern-day witches, Nell Channing, Ripley Todd, and Mia Devlin, and their ability to suture their individual and collective identities to the island or, as Nell puts it, their ability to "carve out [their] own space and stick."[10] Unless these twenty-first-century heroines learn from the tragic fates of their ancestors and come together to "turn back the dark," Three Sisters Island "will sink into the sea."[11] Of course, as this is a popular romance trilogy, the circle of key characters and their island are guaranteed a happy ending. The witches are haunted, in nightmares and hallucinatory visions, by images of their island toppling, tumbling, or falling into the swirling sea. But these images of a floating landmass "swallowed by the sea"[12] lack the force of true horror. Instead, the making of the island, rising "up toward the sky, circl[ing] madly toward the sea,"[13] rather than its destruction, provides the trilogy's narrative fulcrum as each of the romantic couples in turn (Nell and Zack Todd in *Dance Upon the Air*, Ripley and MacAllister Booke in *Heaven and Earth*, and Mia and Sam Logan in *Face the Fire*) become a metaphorical island-in-themselves, and the three couples unite to become an intimate familial and social circle.

By the final pages of the trilogy, the boundaries of the three couples' intimate social circle are exactly proximate with the roughly circular coastline of the island. The organising shape for relations among key characters, and the bounded topography of the island, in this series is the circle. This is clearest in the power invested in the witches—the "circle of three"[14]—and the centrality of making a circle in their spells and rituals. In this regard, Roberts draws heavily on prevailing tropes for the representation of witches as Mac, a professor of paranormal studies, acknowledges in *Heaven and Earth*: "Most rites of paranormal origin involve protective circles."[15] More importantly, the circles used in these rites make their mark on the island; they leave behind rings of energy, which Mac, "the Indiana Jones of the paranormal,"[16] hunts, records, and maps with a battery of witch-finding machines. So, on the one hand, the spatial motif of the "circle" might appear to be a mundane marker of genre, but examining the recurrence of this shape in the series highlights the assumptions of islandness that underpin Roberts's treatment of setting in these novels and in the genre more broadly. What is important here is the relationship between the social tropology of the circle and the romantic topology of the fictional island. The motif of the circle is multiplied throughout the trilogy as the protagonists increasingly figure their shared lives in relation to the island as a set of intersecting concentric circles. Each heroine occupies her own innermost circle, an intimate space, which is both a point on a circle connecting the three witches and which expands to embrace the hero as their personal love plot progresses. Furthermore, each couple co-inhabits an "invisible bubble"[17] within a larger circle containing and protecting the central group of characters; this core group is supported in the next band by their close friends and family, most importantly Lulu, Mia's childhood guardian. This shared social geometry is made explicit in their spells, especially in the casting of protective circles: "Circle within circle within circle protects all from cold and dark"[18]; "They were linked, a circle within a circle."[19]

For each protagonist, the island space affords them the outer perimeter of their social space. It functions, that is, as the measure of "social distance" as Edward T. Hall defines it: the boundary of the island is "the hidden band that *contains* the group."[20] The paranormal plot augments this sense of the containment by a band or barrier as the witches are able to *feel* when one of their number arrives on or leaves the island. For example, in the opening chapter of *Face the Fire* Mia knows that her first love and fellow witch, Sam, has arrived on the island "the instant" he steps ashore.[21] The strength of this romantic circuitry is confirmed when, near the novel's end, Sam is awakened by "the snapping of the connection"[22] the moment Mia leaves and feels a "light [go] on inside him"[23] when she returns. This "hidden band" also marks the perimeter of the territory policed by sibling sheriffs, Zack and Ripley Todd, members of a family who have lived "on the island for centuries."[24] Both Zack, the hero of the first book, and Ripley, heroine of the second, regard the island as their "turf." A seemingly incidental episode in the first novel highlights the importance of this invisible barrier or fortification to the series' version of islanded identities. Zack, who "has never spent more than three months at a time off-island,"[25] responds to a domestic violence incident involving a wealthy mainland tourist, Joe McCoy, who has clearly beaten his wife, Diane. Joe is unrepentant: "By the time my lawyer's done, I'm going to own this fucking island!"[26] And Diane pleads with Zack not to press charges: "I aggravated him. [...] The least I can do is leave him alone on his vacation."[27] Zack escorts the couple to the ferry and waits, "watching, until the jeep and the people inside it were no more than a dot on their way to the mainland."[28]

The primary relational figure of islandness throughout the trilogy is severance from the mainland: "carve," "sever," and "slice" are all terms used to describe the relation of Three Sisters Island to the North American continent and the wider world. Thus the island is perhaps less a "perfect little slice of the world"[29] than a little world unto itself. The island's isolation, the sense that it is cut off from the mainland, both connotes vulnerability and, true to the trilogy's conservative ideological register, is the basis for its salvation. Godfrey Baldacchino points to the "geography of excision" as one aspect of the "lure of the island": "In contrast, mainlands, with their sprawling hinterlands, with their vastness and unfathomable complexity, overwhelm and frighten."[30] In the terms of this series, islandness is not registered as connectedness across the space between landmasses but as the condition for enhancing connectedness within the island space; apart from a clumsy link to Ireland drawn to bolster the paranormal plot in the final volume, there are no references to other islands (real or imaginary) in this series. The utopian promise of Three Sisters Island, both within the narrative and in its address to readers, is based on a presumption of insularity as the basis for enhanced sociality. As Ripley tells Nell the first time they meet: "You live on an island, everybody's business is your business."[31] Archipelagic thinking is thus utterly foreign to the discourse of islands which informs this trilogy and, indeed, Roberts's other island romances, *Island of Flowers* (1982), *Treasures Lost, Treasures Found* (1986), *Risky Business* (1986), *The Welcoming* (1989), *Sanctuary*, and *The Search* (2010).

The first chapter of *Dance Upon the Air* and the main action of the series begins in June 2001—the year in which the first two books were published—with Nell's arrival by ferry "with one small bag of belongings, a rusted secondhand Buick, and $208 to her name."[32] Nell Channing is an alias for Helen Remington, a twenty-eight-year-old woman who has faked her own death to escape an abusive husband, the villain of the first book. Nell, who An Goris reads as a "metaphorical virgin,"[33] does not yet know that she is a witch or understand that her arrival on the island initiates a narrative "pattern" (a key word in the trilogy) into which her destiny is already woven. She is, however, powerfully aware—from the moment she disembarks the ferry—that she is unusually attracted to "this pretty little island" and associates its strange pull with her longing for a "home": "Wasn't that what she'd always wanted? A home, roots, family, friends."[34] The island feels like home to Nell so soon after her arrival because, according to a sentimental geography familiar to insular romances, she has finally arrived in the place where she has always belonged. Indeed, according to the geographical lexicon Roberts draws from, "island" is a synonym for "home," an idealised locale where one feels both safe and free. When she first arrives, Nell wanders the island's main settlement on foot and realises that "nothing [...] had ever called more truly to her soul than this little postcard village."[35] At the opening of the second chapter, Nell pictures a day when she "would be as much a part of the island as the narrow post office with its faded gray wood or the tourist center cobbled together by old clinker brinks, and the long, sturdy dock where fishermen brought their daily catch."[36] By chapter 3, alone in the "thick wedge of forest"[37] south of the village—the island zone with which Nell is most strongly identified—she is utterly convinced that she is home: "This was her place. She was as sure of that as she'd been of any single thing in all her life. She belonged here as she'd belonged nowhere else."[38] By chapter 7, she notices with pleasure that she can "spot a mainlander" and thinks of herself as an "islander."[39]

Nell's first walk through the island's village establishes the phenomenological approach to descriptions of place that prevails throughout the trilogy.

> Gardens were lovingly tended, as if weeds were illegal. Dogs barked behind picket fences and children rode bikes of cherry red and electric blue.
> The docks themselves were a study in industry. Boats and nets and ruddy-cheeked men in tall rubber boots. She could smell fish and sweat.[40]

The island's main zones—village, beach, forest, cliff—are seen, heard, smelled, and touched from the perspective of protagonists who come to associate the island with their individual and collective happiness. This is despite (or perhaps because of) their awareness that *"Geographically, topographically, there's nothing unusual about Three Sisters Island."*[41] In simple terms, the island is special because of the people who live there. More abstractly, the trilogy dwells on the fundamental co-dependence of character and setting, and the narrative gains its momentum from the assumed rule that agents of narrative events must be located in place. Stories, that is, are always spatial. The third chapter of *Dance Upon the Air* delivers this message with one of the series' pivotal images: a human body falling from the cliff-top and, through some magical gravitational pull, dragging the landmass behind her to be engulfed by the sea. Nell dreams of leaping from the rocks and plunging toward the water: "And the cliffs, the light, the trees all tumbled in after her."[42]

The witches' fears for their island—their sense its magical origins have led to an unstable geography—are balanced by the acknowledgement in almost every description of place, that the trio of Salem witches (like Roberts) created a generic island. When Nell first sees the island's lighthouse, "pure and white, […] on a craggy cliff," it looks, she thinks, "Just as it should."[43] Moments such as these are central to Roberts's self-conscious use of island topography as the stage for a popular romance fiction. Three Sisters Island is an imagined place for both its readers and its characters. When key characters first arrive by ferry, they recognise the island from their reading, from their dreams, and from a generalised sense of belonging or placial attraction. Both within the narrative and for readers, Three Sisters Island is defined both by its immediate legibility as a generic islandscape—it looks and feels "[j]ust as it should"—and by its uniqueness: characters are drawn inexorably to *this* island. The idea that Three Sisters Island looks "just as it should" is especially significant for the characterisation of Nell, whose identity as a powerful witch emerges as she realises that she has "dreamed of this place"[44] since childhood, and resonates as a gesture to the romance genre's pleasure in tropes that, from a high-literary perspective, might be dismissed as hackneyed.

Nell, a traumatised and terrified woman on the run, feels a moment of panic immediately after stepping ashore and calms herself by breathing deeply: "Salt air, water. Freedom."[45] This moment of free indirect speech (which is typical of Roberts and the dominant style of narration in the genre) draws a link between the island setting, the generic promise to readers that Nell's (love) story will end happily, and, more broadly, the issue of women's freedom. This association is underlined more boldly at the beginning of the second chapter: "For the first time, wandering the pretty streets with their quaint houses, breathing in the sea air, listening to the New England voices, she *felt* safe. And free."[46] Pamela Regis, in *A Natural History of the Romance Novel*, insists that both mainstream literary culture and most critics have missed the "virtues of the romance novel":

> The genre is not silly and empty-headed […]. Quite the contrary—the romance novel contains serious ideas. The genre is not about women's bondage, as the

literary critics would have it. The romance novel is, to the contrary, about women's freedom. The genre is popular because it conveys the pain, uplift, and joy that freedom brings."[47]

Similarly, Goris identifies the narrative goal of Roberts's romance fiction as the "emancipation of the heroine."[48] The argument that romance is about freedom chimes with the thematic and ideological agenda of this trilogy, in which the island setting provides the foundation for three entwined love stories. For each of the couples, achieving their happy-ever-after ending involves aligning their personal and social limits with the coastline of the island, so that they experience boundedness and containment as states of safety and liberation rather than danger and entrapment.

When Nell climbs the village's "curvy and whistle-clean"[49] cobblestone streets, she reads the signs of industry, "Fishing and tourism," in relation to the virtue of "courage."[50] Three Sisters Island "has stood against sea, storms, and time, surviving and flourishing at its own pace."[51] Nell, who has "taken too long" to find her own courage, hopes to find a job, so that she can stay on the island, and daydreams of a future in which she will no longer be a stranger: "In a few months, people would know her. They'd wave as she walked by, or call out her name."[52] Nell's fantasy—pictured in snapshot in the trilogy's first chapter—casts her as a surrogate romance reader within the text: her wish to join the island's community mirrors the genre expectations of experienced romance readers that are heightened by this opening chapter. The alignment of Nell, the "new mainlander,"[53] with the novel's implied readers is strengthened later in the chapter when she finds a warm welcome and her dream job at the local bookstore: "Café Book. Well, that was perfect."[54]

"Perfect" is a ubiquitous spatial adjective throughout the trilogy, for the island as a whole and its principal locations, including the bookstore, the beach, the hidden cave, Mia's cliff-top home, and her yellow cottage in the village. The idealisation of Three Sisters as the "perfect" scene for the enactment of a romance is supported and augmented by the narrative map of the island, which unfolds over the course of the trilogy beginning with Nell's arrival in the first chapter of *Dance Upon the Air*.

Nell disembarks the ferry and walks uphill along the steep cobbled High Street, past shops and restaurants. She pauses to study the "undeniably romantic"[55] hotel, The Magick Inn, then continues until she reaches the bookstore: "Not only the hotel was magic, Nell thought, the minute she crossed the threshold."[56] The bookstore's owner, Mia Devlin, is the most powerful witch of the three and the character most identified with the island. She owns the most property and lives alone at its highest point. She offers Nell a job and the tenancy of her yellow cottage, a short walk from the village: "You need a place, I have a place."[57] The cottage, on the boundary between town and forest and with a view of the water from its kitchen window, is a key transitional site in each volume of the trilogy. Mac Booke, a scholar on sabbatical, rents it in *Heaven and Earth*. The house becomes vacant again when he falls in love with Ripley Todd, and Sam Logan moves in at the beginning of *Face the Fire*. By the end of the series, Sam will make his home with Mia, at her house above craggy cliffs on the northeast coast. A "long and curving road"[58] runs from the village to the Devlin house, where Mia's lavish garden creates "juxtaposition between raw cliffs and lush fairyland."[59] Sam's family home lies at "nearly the precise opposite end of the island,"[60] so roughly south-southwest. This makes sense within the terms of the island's paranormal genealogy: Mia's element is fire, Sam's water. Accessible by a narrow shale road, the Logan house stands empty for much of the trilogy, until Mac recognises it as "Right for him": "It's a lonely spot, but it doesn't feel lonely. More like it's waiting. It's odd that it feels like it's waiting for me."[61] The Logan-cum-Booke house is the closest to one of the most highly charged sites on the island (as Mac's equipment confirms), the small cave where Fire discovered her selkie lover and where Mia and Sam first made love in their teens. If, as Robert T. Tally Jr. writes, "Narratives are, in a sense, mapping machines,"[62] these novels generate a detailed map of Three Sisters Island as a place saturated by the tropes and associated values of popular romance fiction. Tally explains that narrative maps are "always and already formed by the interpretations or by the interpretative frameworks in which we, as readers, situate them."[63] The popular romance genre provides the principal interpretative framework through which the island mapping of this trilogy can, to use another of Tally's phrases "make sense" to readers in relation to the "world in which we live."[64] This trilogy is all the more interesting because it foregrounds "literary cartography as a fundamental aspect of storytelling."[65]

At a crisis point in *Heaven and Earth*, Ripley feels powerless to fight back the dark force that threatens to engulf her home and family and demands that Mia answer her honestly: "What if I leave the island, if I pack up, get on the ferry and just don't come back? Could it break the chain?"[66] Mia says that Ripley "already know[s] the answer" but deflects the question to Mac, "as an academic, an observer, and someone who has done considerable research into such matters."[67] Mia and Mac work together throughout the trilogy as the experts on the island's history and mythology. This pairing is overstressed—she runs Café Book; his name is Dr Mac Booke—but its effect is to encourage scrutiny of the island setting and its contribution to this trilogy and the romance genre more broadly. Mac's reply to Ripley's urgent question gestures to the appeal of island settings to commercial storytellers: "The island itself has power. In a sort of holding pattern until it's stirred up or applied."[68] Three Sisters Island is thus explicitly a genre island. Characters see it as "storybook tidy,"[69] or like the "perfect" scene in a souvenir "snow globe."[70] Roberts's conscious deployment of tried-and-true island tropes is one of the main ways in which this trilogy nurtures and facilitates reflection upon the pleasure of familiarity valued by the romance genre. Categorically, from the perspective of popular romance it is not a failing that this set of novels gives us an island that fulfils expectations, both for the people in the books and those who are reading it. This is why scenes of arrival carry such emotional weight in each of the love stories. In the first book, Nell tells Mia that coming to the island "was like finally being allowed to come home."[71] Similarly, in book two, Mac tells Ripley, "I've been heading here all my life."[72] For both of these newcomers, their arrival is reframed as a happy return as they learn that they are both descendants of the three sisters. And, more important, both Nell and Mac fall in love with islanders who have never felt the desire to leave and can trace their origins back to the island's beginnings: "This nine square miles of rock and sand and soil was all the world [Ripley] needed"[73]; and Zack, who tried the mainland but "couldn't take it" has everything he wants on the island.[74] Sam's arrival at the beginning of the third and final book is a literal return. He left his island home to go to college and his first love, Mia, has never forgiven him nor, as it turns out, has she ever stopped loving him. Sam has ostensibly returned to take over the running of his family's hotel, The Magick Inn, but of course the main reason he is back is for Mia. Approaching the island on the ferry, Sam feels the "pull and tug" of the island, the "sheer simplicity of pleasure," and is "surprised" by his depth of feeling. Within moments of disembarking the ferry, he realises that "He'd come home and hadn't realized, not completely, what that meant to him until he'd gotten there."[75]

The island—while a site of romantic saturation—does not signify in a uniform way for the three heroines. Instead they are each, through their tie to one of the island's magical founders, strongly identified with a particular island region or zone and, by extension, each of the novels emphasises one variation on the genre island more than others.

Nell, for whom the island marks the end of Helen Remington's traumatic journey of escape and self-discovery and the beginning of her new life—"she was now and always Nell"[76]—feels a powerful association with the forest, "the heart of the Sisters."[77] And it is here that she finds the courage her ancestor lacked to defeat the enraged darkness that seeks the island's destruction and has possessed her husband. Nell's book, *Dance Upon the Air*, presents the island as sanctuary. Each morning, Nell stands at the kitchen window of the yellow cottage "dreaming into her woods" and imagines herself protected:

> Rains swept in, pounded the beaches, the cliffs, then swept out again until it seemed to her that the whole of the world sparkled like something under a glass dome.

> She was under that dome, Nell thought. Safe and secure away from the world that raged beyond sea and inlet.[78]

The key spatial binary in Nell's vision of the island—which the narrative endorses—is between distance and proximity. She is both reassured by the island's removal from the world "beyond sea and inlet" and aroused by the heightened proximal relations afforded by living on an island: "Nothing's really that far on an island this size."[79] Insularity here is revalued as the condition for greater intimacy.

Whereas Nell seeks the security and safety of the inland, "the soft floor of the forest,"[80] Deputy Ripley Todd, heads every morning to the island's "curving shore"[81] to run. She "love[s] the winter best"[82] when the beach holds "no footprints but her own."[83] Like her brother, Ripley is cast as an intensely territorial character: "The little clump of land off the coast of Massachusetts was hers, every hill, every street, every cliff and inlet."[84] The connotations of her association with the beach are clear: Ripley is motivated by a belief that "Three Sisters, its village, its residents, its well-being" are her "responsibility."[85] *Heaven and Earth* thus focuses on the island as a natural fortress. In her nightmares, Ripley stands "on the beach, where the waves rose like terror."[86] The violence of the sea, which pounds "black and bitter, on the shore,"[87] is emblematic of external threats to herself and home. Ripley, like her ancestor, Earth, three hundred years before her, struggles to harness her own rage, the power of which thrills her in "some deep and secret place."[88] *Heaven and Earth* thus plays most on the tension between interior and exterior as it enables the conflation of self and island. Together Nell and Ripley's narratives lay the groundwork for the figurative anthropomorphisation of the island and the concomitant geomorphisation of the heroine in the final novel, *Face the Fire*.

Mia is the trilogy's apex heroine. She lives at the island's highest vantage point and the symbolism of her cliff-top home is unmistakable from the trilogy's first chapter, when Nell looks from the ferry towards the stone house atop the island and sees "a widow's walk circling the top story."[89] Mia's love story is the subject of the final book, *Face the Fire*, and so her happy ending functions also as the happy ending for Three Sisters Island. The geographical codes mobilised in this trilogy are not meant to occlude meaning; in order to drive the romance forward, they must be readily decipherable. This final book brings to the surface a metaphor, which is implicit in the first two books: the island as self. Soon after Sam returns, Mia's sadness casts a gloom over the island, bringing "rain, a steady drumming splatter" and a wind that blows until the air is "raw with damp, the sea as unremittingly grey as the sky."[90] Much later in the novel, when they have sex in the shower, "She crested, an endless warm wave."[91] Soon after this they fall into bed and Mia "dreams of floating in a dark sea. [...] She drifted on her own pleasure, the water cool, the air sweet. In the distance, the shadows and shapes of her island rose out of the sea."[92] Mia's equanimity is disturbed—"Her world tilted"[93]—when Sam's father asks him to return to New York, confirmation that, while Mia and the island are coextensive, their joint destiny requires her to welcome Sam, the fourth witch, back into her innermost circle. This book thus underscores the trilogy's governing geopoetic emblem—the couple-as-island—and strengthens its endorsement of love as "an image of an expanded self."[94]

The first novel in Jude Deveraux's Nantucket Brides trilogy, *True Love* (2013), begins with Jared Kingsley planning to avoid meeting Alix Madsen: "I'll get someone to pick her up at the ferry."[95] It is immediately clear to the reader that the meeting of the hero and heroine is inevitable. Valeo terms this the "pleasure of the predictable": "We know which characters will end up together long (sometimes months or years, or hundreds of pages) before they realize it themselves." She writes, "Roberts has taken this game to wonderful extremes, where the drop of a name in some early chapter works like a wink to her experienced readers-in-the-know."[96] Valeo and Goris explain that the series form multiplies this strategy of reader engagement.[97] Close reading of island romance trilogies like Three Sisters Island show that the significance of setting to the "pleasure of the predictable" is not fully subsumed by the dyad of character and plot. Instead, setting matters more than romance scholars have hitherto realised because, to borrow a phrase from Hall, "space relates to everything."[98] In *Face the Fire* Mia learns that she has been misguided in imagining that she is an island-unto-herself—a lesson readers have understood since the opening chapters of *A Dance Upon the Air*. As a teenager, Sam—whose eyes are "the color of the sea"[99]—etched a declaration of eternal love in Gaelic on the wall of their cave: "My heart is your heart. Ever and always."[100] Mia carved a Celtic knot beneath his words: "A promise of unity."[101] The literal and figurative association of Mia and Sam with the cave points to the trilogy's investment in the symbolic potential of bounded spaces. When Mia interrupts a passionate moment between Mac and Ripley in the cave—*her* place—Mac's equipment begins to "shrill" and smoke.[102] This scene of inadvertent trespass on Mia's imagined private place is entirely consistent with the trilogy's overinvestment in the symbolism afforded by a stereotypical island setting to hyperbolise the conventional love plot and its stock characterisations.

The implicit link made throughout the trilogy between the island as bounded landform, intensified by the cave scenes, and what Lauren Berlant calls the "two-as-one intimacy of the couple form"[103] is made explicit in the sex scenes between each hero and heroine. One look from Nell does more to "warm [Zack's] blood than an ocean of hot water"[104] and when "at last he slipped inside her, the gentle rise and fall was like waves of silk."[105] Simultaneous orgasm severs the couple from the world: "Their hands joined, fingers linking as they slid off the world together."[106] After sex, they lay curled together, listening to the last of a storm pass over the island: "Her haven, Nell thought, was safe, as they were safe inside it."[107] Mac has similar thoughts after sex with Ripley. The wind begins to rise outside the yellow cottage, but he is untroubled: "It was as if they were the only two people on the island."[108]

At the time of writing, Roberts has released the first two books of her Guardians Trilogy set on Capri—*Stars of Fortune* (2015) and *Bay of Sighs* (2016). The similarities to the Three Sisters Island trilogy are striking. In a time long ago three goddesses created gifts for a new queen, a star of fire, a star of ice, and a star of water, but their wishes were foiled by a fourth dark sister. Three contemporary heroes and three heroines are drawn to Capri, which is here transformed into an American genre island through the telling of their interlinked love stories. This new series points to the continuing appeal of the pattern of romance islands utilised in Roberts' Three Sisters Island trilogy and embraced throughout the genre.

NOTES

1. Nora Roberts, *Dance Upon the Air*, Three Sisters Island Trilogy (New York: Jove Books, 2001), 5.
2. Message on Goodreads, 24 June 2009 (at 6:01 p.m.), accessed 4 May 2015, https://www.goodreads.com/review/show/29236469.
3. Christina A. Valeo, "The Power of Three: Nora Roberts and Serial Magic," in *New Approaches to Popular Romance Fiction: Critical Essays*, ed. Sarah S. G. Frantz and Eric Murphy Selinger (Jefferson, NC: McFarland, 2012), Kindle, location 4535.
4. Roberts, *Dance Upon the Air*, 136.
5. Eric Murphy Selinger, "How to Read a Romance Novel (and Fall in Love with Popular Romance," in *New Approaches to Popular Romance Fiction: Critical Essays*, ed. Sarah S. G. Frantz and Eric Murphy Selinger (Jefferson, NC: McFarland, 2012), Kindle, location 685.
6. Roberts, *Dance Upon the Air*, 93.
7. Roberts, *Dance Upon the Air*, 4.
8. Nora Roberts, *Face the Fire*, Three Sisters Island Trilogy (New York: Jove Books, 2002), 3.
9. Roberts, *Face the Fire*, 3.
10. Roberts, *Dance Upon the Air*, 224.
11. Roberts, *Face the Fire*, 3.
12. Roberts, *Heaven and Earth*, 129.
13. Roberts, *Dance Upon the Air*, 4.
14. Roberts, *Dance Upon the Air*, 201.
15. Roberts, *Heaven and Earth*, 84.
16. Roberts, *Heaven and Earth*, 92–93.
17. Edward T. Hall, *The Hidden Dimension* (1966; repr., New York: Anchor Books, 1990), 13.

18. Roberts, *Face the Fire*, 348.
19. Roberts, *Heaven and Earth*, 20.
20. Hall, *The Hidden Dimension*, 14.
21. Roberts, *Face the Fire*, 13.
22. Roberts, *Face the Fire*, 294.
23. Roberts, *Face the Fire*, 303.
24. Roberts, *Dance Upon the Air*, 35.
25. Roberts, *Dance Upon the Air*, 136.
26. Roberts, *Dance Upon the Air*, 165.
27. Roberts, *Dance Upon the Air*, 167.
28. Roberts, *Dance Upon the Air*, 169.
29. Roberts, *Heaven and Earth*, 153.
30. Godfrey Baldacchino, "The Lure of the Island: A Spatial Analysis of Power Relations," *Journal of Marine and Island Cultures* 1, no. 2 (2012): 57.
31. Roberts, *Dance Upon the Air*, 58.
32. Roberts, *Dance Upon the Air*, 8
33. An Goris, "From Romance to Roberts and Back Again: Genre, Authorship and the Construction of Textual Identity in Contemporary Popular Romance Novels" (PhD diss., University of Leuven, 2011), 351.
34. Roberts, *Dance Upon the Air*, 6.
35. Roberts, *Dance Upon the Air*, 8.
36. Roberts, *Dance Upon the Air*, 24.
37. Roberts, *Dance Upon the Air*, 6.
38. Roberts, *Dance Upon the Air*, 42.
39. Roberts, *Dance Upon the Air*, 120.
40. Roberts, *Dance Upon the Air*, 8.
41. Roberts, *Heaven and Earth*, 23.
42. Roberts, *Dance Upon the Air*, 61.
43. Roberts, *Dance Upon the Air*, 5.
44. Roberts, *Dance Upon the Air*, 151.
45. Roberts, *Dance Upon the Air*, 7.
46. Roberts, *Dance Upon the Air*, 24.
47. Pamela Regis, *A Natural History of the Romance Novel* (2003; repr., Philadelphia: University of Pennsylvania Press, 2007), xiii.
48. An Goris, "From Romance to Roberts and Back Again." Goris uses the phrase "emancipation of the heroine" throughout her thesis.
49. Roberts, *Dance Upon the Air*, 8.
50. Roberts, *Dance Upon the Air*, 9.
51. Roberts, *Dance Upon the Air*, 9.
52. Roberts, *Dance Upon the Air*, 9.
53. Roberts, *Dance Upon the Air*, 72.
54. Roberts, *Dance Upon the Air*, 11.
55. Roberts, *Dance Upon the Air*, 9.
56. Roberts, *Dance Upon the Air*, 11.
57. Roberts, *Dance Upon the Air*, 22.

58. Roberts, *Face the Fire*, 91.
59. Roberts, *Dance Upon the Air*, 109.
60. Roberts, *Heaven and Earth*, 166.
61. Roberts, *Heaven and Earth*, 166.
62. Robert T. Tally Jr., "Introduction: Mapping Narratives," in *Literary Cartographies: Spatiality, Representation, and Narrative,* Geocriticism and Spatial Literary Studies. ed. Robert T. Tally Jr. (New York: Palgrave Macmillan, 2014), 3.
63. Tally, "Introduction: Mapping Narratives," 3.
64. Tally, "Introduction: Mapping Narratives," 3.
65. Tally, "Introduction: Mapping Narratives," 3.
66. Roberts, *Heaven and Earth*, 228.
67. Roberts, *Heaven and Earth*, 228.
68. Roberts, *Heaven and Earth*, 228.
69. Roberts, *Heaven and Earth*, 24.
70. Roberts, *Heaven and Earth*, 38.
71. Roberts, *Dance Upon the Air*, 151.
72. Roberts, *Heaven and Earth*, 246.
73. Roberts, *Dance Upon the Air*, 55.
74. Roberts, *Dance Upon the Air*, 136.
75. Roberts, *Face the Fire*, 5.
76. Roberts, *Dance Upon the Air*, 364.
77. Roberts, *Heaven and Earth*, 84.
78. Roberts, *Dance Upon the Air*, 230.
79. Roberts, *Dance Upon the Air*, 64.
80. Roberts, *Dance Upon the Air*, 42.
81. Roberts, *Heaven and Earth*, 4.
82. Roberts, *Heaven and Earth*, 5.
83. Roberts, *Heaven and Earth*, 4.
84. Roberts, *Heaven and Earth*, 4–5.
85. Roberts, *Heaven and Earth*, 5.
86. Roberts, *Heaven and Earth*, 18.
87. Roberts, *Heaven and Earth*, 18.
88. Roberts, *Heaven and Earth*, 19.
89. Roberts, *Dance Upon the Air*, 5.
90. Roberts, *Face the Fire*, 57.
91. Roberts, *Face the Fire*, 192.
92. Roberts, *Face the Fire*, 214.
93. Roberts, *Face the Fire*, 223.
94. Lauren Berlant, *Desire/Love* (Brooklyn: Punctum Books, 2012), 6, Adobe PDF eBook.
95. Jude Deveraux, *True Love*, Nantucket Brides 1 (London: Headline Eternal, 2013), Kindle, location 107.
96. Valeo, "The Power of Three."
97. Valeo, "The Power of Three"; An Goris, "Happily Ever After ... and After: Serialization and the Popular Romance Novel," *Americana: The Journal of*

American Popular Culture 1900 to Present 12, no. 1 (Spring 2013), accessed 5 May 2015, http://www.americanpopularculture.com/journal/articles/spring_2013/goris.htm.

98. Hall, *The Hidden Dimension*, ix.
99. Roberts, *Face the Fire*, 7.
100. Roberts, *Face the Fire*, 56.
101. Roberts, *Face the Fire*, 56.
102. Roberts, *Heaven and Earth*, 170.
103. Berlant, *Desire/Love*, 6.
104. Roberts, *Dance Upon the Air*, 292.
105. Roberts, *Dance Upon the Air*, 294.
106. Roberts, *Dance Upon the Air*, 295.
107. Roberts, *Dance Upon the Air*, 295.
108. Roberts, *Heaven and Earth*, 235.

Part IV

ISLAND FANTASY, FANTASY ISLANDS

Chapter Ten

Islands of the World

The Archipelagic Geography of Fantasy Fiction

In a 1963 letter to a reader of *The Lord of the Rings*, J. R. R. Tolkien likens the appeal of his three-volume novel and its "imaginary world" to the lure of a remote island:

> Part of the attraction of The L.R. is, I think, due to the glimpses of a large history in the background: an attraction like that of viewing far off an unvisited island, or seeing the towers of a distant city gleaming in a sunlit mist. To go there is to destroy the magic, unless new unattainable vistas are again revealed.[1]

Tolkien thus compares readers who are drawn to the tales set in his vast story-world—Arda, of which Middle-earth is a part—to travellers or explorers venturing beyond their known world. The sense of wonder, or "magic," that Tolkien attaches to the view of a far-off island or towered city is, importantly, contingent on the distance between the reader/traveller and the new place on the horizon. In his book, *Here Be Dragons: Exploring Fantasy Maps and Settings*, Stefan Ekman accepts the assumption that fantasy fiction offers worlds that the "reader's mind can enter."[2] Similarly, in *Building Imaginary Worlds: The Theory and History of Subcreation*, Mark J. P. Wolf writes that books, television, film, video games, and other media "open portals" for access to other worlds, "inviting us to enter and tempting us to stay, as alive in our thoughts as our own memories of lived experience."[3] Tolkien, however, understood that the vistas offered readers by Middle-earth remain ever "unattainable." Both the worlds invented by the fantasy genre and readers' experiences and memories of visiting their shores are, of course, virtual constructions. Throughout popular culture, islands carry—some might say are burdened by—a powerful association with the "fantastic." This association, which locates small islands in relation to continental locales in terms of the related oppositions of fiction and fact, romance and realism, fantasy and truth, partly explains why islands, archipelagos, and the spaces and places between them are so central to the geography (the "earth-writing") of the fantastic. The atlas of twentieth- and twenty-first-century fantasy fiction is crowded with islands. From Terry Pratchett's Discworld to the "known world" of George R. R. Martin's A Song of Ice and Fire series, and from China Miéville's Bas-Lag to Scott Lynch's Therin Throne Empire, islands are essential to the world-building projects of fantasy writers, both as narrative elements and in the imaginary cartography of the detailed maps which are a treasured feature of the genre.

The late nineteenth-century writer, George MacDonald, a forerunner of and influence on Tolkien, used the preface to his 1893 book *The Light Princess, and Other Fairy Tales* to consider the necessary relationship between the writer's actual world and any world they may invent:

> The natural world has its laws, and no man must interfere with them in the way of presentment any more than in the way of use, but they themselves may suggest laws of other kinds, and man may, if he pleases, invent a little world of his own, with its own laws; for there is that in him which delights in calling up new forms—which is the nearest, perhaps, he can come to creation.[4]

The islands of fantasy are never so fantastic that the invented "little world" bears no meaningful relation to the author's "natural world." Tolkien, who read and admired MacDonald, introduced the terms "Primary World" and "Secondary World"—which we use throughout this and the following two chapters—to distinguish between our "real" world and the invented fantasy world; like MacDonald, Tolkien saw our world as the creation of God and so referred to the process of world-building as "sub-creation."[5] Further, John Clute explains that, for the most part, the settings of fantasy tales located entirely in secondary worlds fall into two main categories: "a Land, consisting of an assortment of countries which frequently surround a central inland sea; and a world-straddling oceanscape, featuring archipelagos."[6] Tolkien remains the most influential writer—and theorist—of fantasy fiction, and his secondary world of Arda includes a number of islands, some of which are located in Middle-earth. For example, the fourth part of *The Silmarillion* (1977), "Akallabêth," focusses on the rise and fall of the island kingdom of Númenor, while "The Valar dwelt originally on the Isle of Almaren, which lay in the Great Lake in the midst of the land,"[7] and is thus at the very heart of Middle-earth. In *The Hobbit* (1937) Bilbo first encounters Gollum, who "lived on a slimy island of rock in the middle of the lake,"[8] when he is lost deep inside the Misty Mountains. And the map of "Part of the Shire," included in *The Fellowship of the Ring* (1954), shows Girdley Island in the Brandywine River north of the Brandywine Bridge.[9] Islands, then, are a feature of both Tolkien's maps and his narrative cartography, part of the geography of his secondary world, although that world remains essentially a continental one. In other words, Tolkien's islands are an integral part his world, but they are not principal settings in their own right. Throughout the contemporary fantasy genre—a largely post-Tolkien cultural phenomenon—islands almost always feature as locales in the context of a larger world.

As Kim Wilkins explains, "[f]antasy novels are, in many ways, setting driven, a feature that marks them out as unique among popular genres."[10] Similarly, Ekman advocates what he calls "topofocal readings of fantasy," in recognition of the centrality of spatial settings to the conventions and the appeal of the genre.[11] For both Wilkins and Ekman, the genre's privileging of setting is immediately apparent in its affection for maps: literary maps, as Sally Bushell defines them, are routinely included in the front matter of novels; fan cartographers create new maps or elaborate on literary maps; and maps are key features of compendiums to bestselling fantasy series. A good example of the latter is Terry Pratchett's *The Compleat Discworld Atlas* (2015). In this author-driven atlas and gazetteer Pratchett offers what he calls "a most complete audit of our world."[12] It offers fans of Discworld colourful maps and information about geography and climate, agriculture and industry, culture and customs, and so on, for each region, including the Sumtri Archipelago, Krull and the Turnwise Ocean Islands, the islands off the Counterweight Continent, and the Foggy Islands and Purdeigh Island off the landmass of Fourdecks. "The Discworld Map," a large (1000 x 885 mm) full-colour, foldout map, shows the importance of the numerous islands dotted around the rim in Pratchett's secondary world.

In a blog for the science fiction and fantasy publisher Tor, Brian Staveley suggests that he "wrote three quarters of a million words of epic fantasy just so I could have my own damn map."[13] This statement is made only partly in jest. The blog entry includes a copy of the map from *The Last Mortal Bond* (2016), the final novel in Staveley's Chronicle of the Unhewn Throne series. It depicts the Annurian Empire, a sea-encircled landmass with two distinct halves joined by an isthmus labelled "The Neck," and connected to unmapped land beyond the map's southern boundary by another isthmus, "The Waist." Dotted and dashed lines across land and sea, through mountains, along rivers, and around islands anticipate a narrative structured by the journeys of characters, and the names of locations (such as The Ghost Sea, Blood Steppe, The Cursed Canal, an offshore island named The Skull) evoke the primary connection between place-making and storytelling which undergirds the genre.

Staveley defends the primacy of the fantasy map in terms which recall Tolkien's view that the attraction of *The Lord of Rings* is the expansiveness of its world:

> A map is more than a two-dimensional catalogue of locations. First, and most importantly, it is a promise. By mapping a world, or a continent, or even a city, a writer assures his/her readers that their imagination has ranged well beyond the boundaries of their particular story, that they have imagined, not just the room in which the scene takes place, but the street beyond that room, the political structure responsible for building those streets and maintaining them, the agricultural system on which that political structure rests, the natural resources that undergird that system, and all the rest.[14]

Staveley's depiction of writer as cartographer chimes with Nicola Humble's contention that fantasy, "by definition, takes place somewhere else, in a world that the writer has to imagine into being in every detail."[15] Robert T. Tally Jr. uses the term "literary cartography" for the process by which "a writer maps the social spaces of his or her world."[16] This chapter argues for an amendment to this claim to recognise the existence of fantasy's distinctive "genre cartography" and to gesture to the fact that maps in novels—whether graphic or narrative—are not genreless constructions. While fantasy writers invent worlds which become strongly attached to their author-brands (for example, Ursula K. Le Guin's Earthsea, Katharine Kerr's Deverry, or Raymond E. Feist's Midkemia), processes of "sub-creation," to use Tolkien's term, are anchored in the textual and industrial history of the genre. Thus, the mapping of new worlds in fantasy fiction deploys an archipelagic geography in which no island is entire of itself, both in relation to the text or series in which it appears, and through the multiple points of connections between fantasy worlds.

Clute, in his influential *Encyclopedia of Fantasy*, defines a fantasy text as "a self-coherent narrative," the unity and soundness of which is measured with reference to setting: "When set in this world, it tells a story which is impossible in the world as we perceive; when set in an otherworld, that otherworld will be impossible, though stories set there may be possible in its terms."[17] Like Wilkins and Ekman then, Clute defines fantasy as a setting-driven genre in which worlds and stories become coterminous; this is a fascinating entry point for thinking about where islands fit in the atlas of contemporary fantasy fiction.

Reading contemporary fantasy fiction through the lens of island studies shows that fantasy writers manipulate the workings of setting, "the big engine of the genre,"[18] in relation to the shared machinery of fantasy world-building. Further, the symbolic meanings and narrative roles attached to islands throughout fantasy fiction are not unique to the genre, but put a fantastic spin on the wider conventions of island conceptualisation and representation which we have traced in crime fiction, thrillers, and romance. In turning our attention to fantasy for this final section of the book, however, we hope to show that fantasy both exploits the habits of thinking about islands that prevail throughout popular fiction and—given the delight the genre takes in moving between the poles of the "real" and the "unreal"—goes further than the other genres we have considered in challenging default assumptions about landmasses encircled by water. Chapter 11 turns to Le Guin's Earthsea, the quintessential fantasy archipelago, to consider the formal and thematic significance of islands for a setting-driven genre that values what Pat Harrington and Noah Wardrip-Fruin call "vast narratives."[19] The opportunity fantasy affords us to think a world of islands anew is the focus of Chapter 12 which examines the degree to which Robin Hobb's Liveship Traders invites us to question "the marginalization of the maritime world,"[20] charted and challenged by scholars such as Phillip E. Steinberg and Kimberley Peters.

It is perhaps no surprise that Alberto Manguel and Gianni Guadalupi's *Dictionary of Imaginary Places* has more entries for islands than for any other type of place.[21] Islands also dominate Wolf's "Timeline of Imaginary Worlds," which begins in the ninth century BC with Homer's *The Odyssey*, and on which islands feature as self-contained imagined "worlds" (including Pytheas's Thule, Henry Neville's the Isle of Pines, and Daniel Defoe's Crusoe's Island), as parts of invented archipelagoes on our own and other worlds (for example, the Waq archipelago from *The One Thousand and One Nights*, Herman Melville's Mardi Archipelago, and Le Guin's Earthsea), and as offshore, lake, and/or oceanic islands in enormous, often transmedia, cartographic enterprises (such as the Star Wars expanded universe, the world Nirn of the *Elder Scrolls*, and Azeroth for the *World of Warcraft*). Wolf explains that until the twentieth century, world-building was principally a literary phenomenon, and, for the first half of the century books remained "the main place where imaginary worlds were conceived and incubated" including "uncharted islands, remote desert cities, lost worlds hidden away in mountains or jungles, underground realms, underwater worlds, future civilisations, and an increasing number of planets."[22] With the advent and rise of screen media and technologies, including film, television, video games, and the internet, the creation of imaginary worlds has become a multimedia and transmedia phenomenon with more "new" worlds being invented in the twentieth century than in all of the previous centuries combined.[23] Travelling beyond the pages of novels to consider the meaning and significance of imaginary islands in popular culture might take us to the isle of Catan in the bestselling board game, *The Settlers of Catan*, to the titular island of the video game *Myst*, or to the island at the centre of the television series, *Lost*. Importantly, however, study of these myriad insular or archipelagic worlds would need to be anchored in an appreciation of the influence of contemporary fiction genres—especially fantasy and science fiction—on our geographic imagination.

Fantasy fiction is marked by what Wilkins calls " 'magic-tower verisimilitude': the recurring imbrication of the supernatural (hence, magic) and the European (hence its iconic architectural feature, the tower)."[24] This layering of elements of the supernatural with the history and geography of Medieval Europe is regularly harnessed in the treatment of islands in fantasy. *The Tough Guide to Fantasyland*, by British fantasy writer Diana Wynne Jones, includes entries for islands and islanders, which playfully indicate the ubiquity of islands in fantasy and point to the intensification of the fantastic that the genre finds on islands: "ISLANDERS are always unusual in some way; this is the Rule."[25] Small islands—in seas or lakes—frequently appear in fantasy fiction as landscapes where magic is concentrated, as intensified fantastic sites within the secondary world. In Terry Brooks's *Magic Kingdom for Sale Sold!* (1986), the first book of his Magic Kingdom of Landover series, Ben Holiday, a lawyer struggling to come to terms with the death of his wife, finds an advertisement in a "Christmas catalogue of wishes and dreams"[26]:

MAGIC KINGDOM FOR SALE

> Landover—island of enchantment and adventure rescued from the mists of time, home of knights and knaves, of dragons and damsels, of wizards and warlocks. Magic mixes with iron, and chivalry is the code of life for the true hero. All of your fantasies become real in this kingdom from another world. Only one thread to this whole cloth is lacking—you, to rule over all as King and High Lord. Escape into your dreams and be born again.[27]

The Christmas Wishbook (which also includes a "week on a privately owned Caribbean Island," on its list of "exotic and strange" gifts[28]) lists Landover for sale for one million dollars. Surrounded by mists and the "ephemeral"[29] fairy world, Landover is an "island" in the sense that it stands apart from, but is accessible from, other secondary worlds as well as from our primary world. The crude literary map which precedes the novel anticipates the catalogue's claim for Landover's insularity (its location in a mystical archipelago). It comes as no surprise to readers that the kingdom's castle, Sterling Silver, stands on an "island in the middle of a lake"[30] adjacent to a region named "The Heart." When Holiday buys Landover, he is provided with a medallion by which he will be recognised as the King and High Lord of the land, "an aged, tarnished piece of metal, its face engraved with a mounted knight in battle harness advancing out of a morning sun that rose over a castle encircled by a lake."[31] The centrality of the island-within-an-island to Brooks's world-building is also evident in the existence of the Landsview, a silver lectern mounted on the guardrail of a viewing platform high in one of the castle's towers, which, with the aid of a parchment map, enables Holiday to magically traverse his kingdom.

Two of Katharine Kerr's fifteen-volume Celtic-infused fantasy series, the Deverry Cycle, are set in part on the Bardekian Archipelago which lies to the south of Deverry: *Dragonspell: The Southern Sea* (1990), the fourth and final volume of the first "act"[32] of the series, "Deverry," and *A Time of Omens* (1992), the second of the four-volume "Westlands" series. Bardek is set apart from Deverry by the Southern Sea, which is "impassable for many a long month"[33] each winter. And "Although most people in Deverry thought of Bardek as one single country like their own, in truth it was an archipelago."[34] The contained and bounded nature of the islands play a crucial role in the plot of *Dragonspell*. The sorcerers who practice dweomer (magic) in the series communicate with each other, and track their enemies by scrying, but "not even the greatest dweomer minds in the world could scry across large bodies of open water. The exhalations of elemental force, particularly over the ocean proper, quite simply obscured the images like fog."[35] Thus even the most powerful sorcerers like Nevyn can only discover what is happening on the islands by travelling to and between them. The islands of the Bardekian Archipelago, then, function in this series in much the same way as the island of Crab Key does in Ian Fleming's *Dr No*. Just as Bond must travel to Crab Key in order to best the evil Dr No, so Nevyn must travel to the island of Surtinna and enter the villain's lair in order to destroy Tondalo, the master of dark dweomer.

While the majority of the first book in Jacqueline Carey's Kushiel's Legacy series, *Kushiel's Dart* (2001), takes place in the fictional continental nation of Terre d'Ange, a key section of this erotic historical fantasy takes place on the island of Alba and on the Third of the Three Sisters Islands located in the middle of the Straits separating Alba from the continental landmass. The references to these islands (and to Eire and the island of Cythera), like islands in many fantasy series, are used to build verisimilitude for the larger fantasy world. And like the "forbidding, inhospitable" island of Morrowindi in Brooks's The Heritage of Shannara series,[36] the "almost uninhabitable" Isle of the Winds in David Eddings's The Belgariad,[37] and the Bardekian Archipelago in Kerr's Deverry novels, they are represented as "elsewhere" in relation to the continent. Significantly, the only overt example of magic in this book is linked to the Three Sisters. The fleet carrying the novel's protagonist, Phèdre nó Delauney, and her contingent back across the Straits from Alba to Terre d'Ange is driven onto the islands by a storm summoned up by the Master of the Straits. As Clute recognises, fantasy is attracted to the long association between the "constricted and isolated territory of an island"[38] and magician figures such as Prospero in Shakespeare's *The Tempest*, the Merlin of Arthurian legend, or Homer's Circe. Like Odysseus, the characters in *Kushiel's Dart* must use their wits to escape the enchanted isle, which is only secured when Phèdre solves the riddle and her oldest friend, Hyacinthe, agrees to take the place of the magus-like Master of the Straits who has been bound to the island and "estranged from the world"[39] for eight hundred years. Dominique Beth Wilson explains that the first trilogy of the Kushiel's Legacy series, comprising *Kushiel's Dart*, *Kushiel's Chosen* (2002), and *Kushiel's Avatar* (2003), became a "publishing phenomenon, selling millions of copies and winning her a devoted following."[40] For Wilson, the popularity of the series is explained by the "imaginative richness of the world"[41]; reviewers compare her world-based series favourably to George R. R. Martin's A Song of Ice and Fire. Like Martin, Carey "blends familiar elements into a distinctive secondary world; her backdrop is recognisably Europe from late antiquity to the Renaissance but with a twist."[42] Also like Martin, Carey places islands at the periphery of her invented world and, like Martin's Bear Island and the Iron Isles of Westeros, the islands in the Kushiel's Legacy series are essential parts of Carey's literary cartography. La Serenissima, to where Phèdre travels in *Kushiel's Chosen*, is a "counter-historical equivalent of Venice,"[43] where religion is based on the goddess Asherat-of-the-Sea. Asherat is said to have conjured an island, La Dolorosa, off the coast of La Serenissima as a monument to her lost son. Phèdre is imprisoned on La Dolorosa, also referred to as "the black isle" and the "isle of sorrows,"[44] and after her escape spends time on the island of Kriti, a version of Crete.

From Tolkien to Martin, the overwhelming majority of invented islands in fantasy fiction draw on the history, geography, and mythology of medieval Europe. N. K. Jemisin's Inheritance trilogy—*The Hundred Thousand Kingdoms* (2010), *The Broken Kingdoms* (2010), and *The Kingdom of Gods* (2011)—is an exception. Her imaginary world, which contains the Islands, a vast volcanic archipelago east of High North and the largest continent, Semn, draws less on medieval Europe and more on the legacies of post-medieval empires. Helen Young notes that Jemisin's "Inheritance trilogy subverts many of the tropes of epic Fantasy, writing back into many of them in ways which both reveal and critique colonialist ideologies within them."[45] And while epic fantasies like Tolkien's *The Lord of the Rings* conclude with "good triumphing over evil and ushering in an implied sustained era of stability and peace under the rule of a single realm,"[46] Jemisin's trilogy "is situated millennia into such a regime, and demonstrates the oppression inherent in the imposition of imperial rule."[47] Wilkins identifies Australian fantasy writer Glenda Larke's Isles of Glory trilogy—*The Aware* (2003), *Gilfeather* (2003), and *The Tainted* (2004)—as another significant exception to the genre's prevailing medievalism. For Wilkins, Larke's characterisation, invented argot, and plotting gesture to the British isles, but her Glorian archipelago is also "reminiscent of the Pacific Islands."[48] While the climate, topography, flora, and fauna of the Isles of Glory, and the invented history of empire which frames the series, do indeed suggest the influence of the Pacific, Larke's more immediate inspiration came from the Indian Ocean and the South China Sea. The Isles of Glory are therefore "varied and unusual landscapes" in contemporary fantasy fiction.[49] Larke has said that the series was inspired in part by growing up in Western Australia, and, more broadly, by her experience of living in Malaysia for several decades, including some time in Borneo, where she worked as a field ornithologist and in nature conservation.[50] Nevertheless, Donna Maree Hanson points to the historical and political commentary on South East Asia woven through the series,[51] its invented imperial archive of maps and explorers' journals, and the oral histories of islanders that comprise the bulk of the texts.

Unusually, the series opens with four double-page maps of "a sea full of islands,"[52] which date the discovery, exploration, and survey of the Isles of Glory and indicate scale in nautical miles, statute miles, and island miles. The first map is of the archipelago as surveyed by the second Kellish exploration of 1782–1784 and shows the relationship between the Norther Isles, the Souther Isles, and the Middling Isles, which are depicted in greater historical and topographical detail in the maps to follow. For instance, the map of the Souther Isles, discovered by Sallavuard i. Rutho in 1781 and surveyed by the *R.V. Horn* during the second exploration from the distant continent of Kells in 1784, draws an intriguing contrast between Mekaté Island, the Stragglers, and the Spatts, each of which are busy with the names of individual islands, settlements, landmarks, and bays, and the Dustels, the southernmost group of islands. The latter is a ring of islands circling a central bay, roughly one-hundred nautical miles at its widest point, with a sharply jagged coastline and no named settlements. On the map, the Dustels are shaded dark grey to suggest a stark contrast from the other isles. The mystery of the Dustels is reinforced early in *The Aware*, which is presented as the translated transcripts of interviews conducted with the novel's heroine Blaze Halfbreed by Shor iso Fabold, President of the National Society for the Scientific, Anthropological and Ethnographical Study of non-Kellish Peoples.

> So you want to know what the Isles of Glory were like back then, eh? In the days before the Change, in the years before you people found us—and we found out that we weren't the only islands in the ocean. [...] [T]here wasn't much I didn't know about the Isles then, and much of it I remember better than what happened yesterday. I'd visited every islandom, except for the Dustels, before I was twenty-five, and the Dustels didn't exist then anyway.[53]

Blaze's story begins on Gorthan Spit "a middenheap for unwanted human garbage and the dregs of humanity"[54] in the Souther Isles and the only landfall in the archipelago where the "citizenless" can stay for any length of time. From the outset, the trilogy exemplifies the capacity of archipelagic settings to heighten the taxonomic—or even the racialising—impulse of fantasy fiction. The citizens of each islandom are hyper-distinguished by their looks, voices, and predilections: Calmenters are "invariably honey-eyed blondes"[55]; green eyes are the "exclusive property of the Fen Islanders"[56]; only the Cirkase Islands produce blue eyes, yellow hair, and golden skin; Blaze can pinpoint a Southerman's island group to the Stragglers by his accent or recognise Mekaté islanders by their clothing. As her surname announces, however, Blaze is a "halfbreed" and "would have done anything—almost anything at all—to have had a citizenship tattoo on her earlobe."[57] Instead, she has spent her life island-hopping. The compulsory tattoos and the ban on cross-island interbreeding are managed from the aptly named Keeper Isles, the centre of "sylvmagic." Blaze is one of the Awarefolk and so impervious to, yet able to see and smell the magic of both sylvs and their dark equivalents, dunmagickers. The Dustel Isles were sent beneath the waves generations ago by the novel's archvillain, Morthred, and the islanders who survived transformed into birds. Their descendants, Dustel Birds, are the archipelago's most mobile sentient inhabitants, rivalled only by the non-human ghemphs, elusive and gentle creatures with "large webbed feet" and "streamlined bodies"[58] who retreat into the ocean when the Kell ships first appear on the horizon. When Blaze's friend Gilfeather (his aquatic-avian name is significant) kills Morthred, the Dustel Birds resume their true human form, though many of those in the air fall to their deaths, and the islands rise up from the "boiling ocean."[59]

As the trilogy progresses, the imbalance caused by the opposed powers of sylv and dun emerges as the archipelago's greatest problem and Blaze works with her band of friends and lovers to cure her world of magic and achieve relative and long-lasting peace—at least until the arrival of the Kellish adventurers, scientists, and missionaries sketched in the frame tale. Gilfeather, with other key characters, discovers the secret to magic in the blood of slyvs and invents an antidote, but the water world itself rises up to cleanse the "tainted" islands. At the climax of *The Tainted* a tsunami engulfs the Hub, the heart of the Keeper Isles and of sylvmagic; from then on, "the world was a different place."[60] Archipelagic settings are well suited to epic narratives in which restoring or achieving social, cultural, and environmental equilibrium achieves the happy ending, or more accurately what Tolkien termed the "eucatastrophe," "the good catastrophe, the sudden joyous 'turn' (for there is no true end to any fairytale)."[61] We see this also in Le Guin's Earthsea Cycle and Hobb's The Liveship Traders.

A strong metafictional current runs through fantasy novels and series in which the narrative foregrounds the question of the secondary world's history and origins. Lynch's Gentleman Bastard Sequence begins in the island city of Camorr, a kind of Dickensian Venice in a world unconnected to our own, which was settled but not built by humans in "ages past."[62] In the novel's present, the people of Camorr are ever aware that they live in an alien-made city but know very little about the "older civilization,"[63] the Eldren, that planned its streets and constructed its bridges, tunnels, and towers. Camorr is an island city-state comprised of numerous islands connected by bridges, many made of the mysterious Elderglass left by the population's forebears. In its cluttered islandscape, individual islands function as socially and economically stratified neighbourhoods, but the binary of land to sea holds sway to unite its population as Camorri who survive in the "cramped confines of a hazard-rich city."[64] On summer nights a "bloodwarm fog [...] seep[s] up from Camorr's wet bones" and the city defies the "salty grasp of the Iron Sea" through its structures and management.[65] On the island-city's seaward side, iron gates shield every canal but one from intruders, a portent for characters and readers alike that Camorr is no self-contained world. Subsequent books in the series take readers landward to the continent and to equally fascinating islands, including the Ghostwind Isles in the Sea of Brass and the estuarine Karthain.

In Tim Lebbon's *The Island* (2009)—which blends elements of speculative fiction and the thriller—"the strange island"[66] that appears off the coast of Noreela following a huge storm is itself the "enemy" that must be fought to save the Noreelans. The initial view of the island, "painted green and lush with vegetation,"[67] gradually gives way to ever more menacing descriptions as the threat the island poses becomes apparent: "The island was ambiguous in the early morning mist. It looked as if it floated above the sea, a ghost island, an image thrown across the ocean by strange effects in the air."[68] And later "the jagged silhouette of that strange place took on sinister proportions."[69] The island is invested with such an unusual degree of agency that the reader is prompted to wonder whether the "island that moved itself"[70] is sentient. Later in the novel the inhabitants of the island, the Komadians, reveal that "their island has been doing this for a long time,"[71] though it is never clearly established how the island moves: whether it moves itself or, as legend has it, is moved by relic technologies "buried deep to shift the island"[72] by elders "many generations ago."[73] What is clear is that the island is predatory and that its "rugged geography" changes as it consumes other land, in this case the Noreelan village of Pavmouth Breaks.[74] Lebbon's novel is significant for the way it uses the island as a heightened trope for placial instability and incoherence. This island that shifts and appears suddenly off the coast of Noreela unsettles standard tropes of insularity, but the novel stops short of casting the island as self-motivated and aware.

Perhaps unsurprisingly, islands are rarely significant settings in the urban fantasy subgenre, "in which faerie and the modern world collide."[75] In *Turn Coat* (2009), the eleventh book of Jim Butcher's hard-boiled fantasy series,

The Dresden Files, the titular P. I. wizard, Harry Dresden, casts a "sanctum invocation" on an uncharted island, "a sullen and threatening presence" in the middle of Lake Michigan, which Chicago had "completely expunged" from its records at some point in the nineteenth century.[76] Whereas literature routinely grants human qualities to islands, it rarely depicts them behaving knowingly as characters. The "weird island"[77] in this series is, however, sentient, invested with a level of agency and affect usually only associated with character. Described as a "genius loci," the island "has a kind of spirit to it, an awareness"; it is "a brooding and dangerous thing that did not care for visitors"; it "holds a grudge"; and it feels "outrage" and "smug satisfaction."[78] During Harry's ritual of sanctum the island's spirit takes "material form" as a tall limping figure in a dark cloak with glowing green eyes[79]; its peculiar power is explained and its function as a character enhanced in later books in the series, especially *Cold Days* (2012) and *Skin Game* (2014). During the sanctum invocation in *Turn Coat*, Harry names the island "Demonreach" and from that point onwards they have a "sort of partnership or peerage" that is activated whenever Harry steps ashore.[80] The wizard and Demonreach's shared awareness is such that he senses when other beings arrive on the island, "the way you know it when an ant is crawling across your arm."[81]

Fantasy offers almost unlimited opportunity for re-conceptualising islands, both singularly and as part of larger invented worlds. While the genre has not rejected the tropes of insularity that define most genre islands, those tropes are only a part of the way islands are represented in fantasy where islands look, move, or speak in sometimes surprising ways.

NOTES

1. J. R. R. Tolkien, "To Colonel Worskett [A Letter to a Reader of *The Lord of the Rings*]," in *The Letters of J.R.R. Tolkien*, ed. Humphrey Carpenter with the assistance of Christopher Tolkien (1995; repr., Boston: Houghton Mifflin Company, 2000), 333.

2. Stefan Ekman, *Here Be Dragons: Exploring Fantasy Maps and Settings* (Middletown, CT: Wesleyan University Press, 2013), Kindle, location 288.

3. Mark J. P. Wolf, *Building Imaginary Worlds: The Theory and History of Subcreation* (New York: Routledge, 2013), 2, Adobe PDF eBook.

4. George MacDonald, Preface, in *The Light Princess, and Other Fairy Tales* (New York: G. P. Putnam's Sons, 1893), iv, accessed 26 April 2016, https://archive.org/details/lightprincessoth00macd.

5. J. R. R. Tolkien, "On Fairy-Stories," in *Tree and Leaf* (1964; repr., London: HarperCollins, 2012), Kindle, location 84–1040.

6. John Clute, "Archipelago," in *Encyclopedia of Fantasy*, ed. John Clute, June 1997, accessed 26 April 2016, http://sf-encyclopedia.uk/fe.php?nm=archipelago.

7. Karen Wynn Fonstad, *The Atlas of Middle-Earth*, rev. ed. (New York: Houghton Mifflin, 1991), 1.

8. J. R. R. Tolkien, *The Hobbit, or, There and Back Again* (1937; repr., London: Longmans, 1966), 66.

9. J. R. R. Tolkien, *The Fellowship of the Ring*, Lord of the Rings 1 (1954; repr., London: Allen & Unwin, 1978).

10. Kim Wilkins, "From Middle Earth to Westeros: Medievalism, Proliferation, and Paratextuality," in *New Directions in Popular Fiction: Genre, Distribution, Reproduction*, ed. Ken Gelder (London: Palgrave Macmillan, 2016), 202.

11. Ekman, *Here Be Dragons*, location 123.

12. Terry Pratchett [with the Discworld Emporium], *The Compleat Discworld Atlas* (London: Transworld, 2015), 5.

13. Brian Staveley, "Cartography and its Discontents," *Tor.com* (blog), 11 April 2016, accessed 22 April 2016, http://www.tor.com/2016/04/11/cartography-and-its-discontents/.

14. Staveley, "Cartography and its Discontents."

15. Nicola Humble, "The Reader of Popular Fiction," in *The Cambridge Companion to Popular Fiction*, ed. David Glover and Scott McCracken (Cambridge: Cambridge University Press, 2012), 97.

16. Robert T. Tally Jr., "Introduction: On Geocriticism," in *Geocritical Explorations: Space, Place, and Mapping in Literary and Cultural Studies*, ed. Tally Jr. (New York: Palgrave Macmillan, 2011), 1, Adobe PDF eBook.

17. John Clute, "Fantasy," in *Encyclopedia of Fantasy*, ed. Clute, June 1997, accessed 26 April 2016, http://sf-encyclopedia.uk/fe.php?nm=fantasy.

18. Wilkins, "From Middle Earth to Westeros," 201.

19. Pat Harrigan and Noah Wardrip-Fruin, eds. *Third Person: Authoring and Exploring Vast Narratives* (Cambridge, MA: MIT Press, 2009).

20. Jon Anderson and Kimberley Peters, "'A perfect and absolute blank': Human Geographies of Water Worlds," in *Water Worlds: Human Geographies of the Ocean*, ed. Anderson and Peters (Farnham: Ashgate, 2014), 4.

21. Alberto Manguel and Gianni Guadalupi, *Dictionary of Imaginary Places* (New York: Macmillan Publishing Co., 1980).

22. Wolf, *Building Imaginary Worlds*, 125.

23. Wolf, *Building Imaginary Worlds*, 111.

24. Kim Wilkins, "The Process of Genre: Authors, Readers, Institutions," *Text* 9, no. 2 (2005), accessed 27 July 2015, http://www.textjournal.com.au/oct05/wilkins.htm.

25. Diana Wynne Jones, *The Tough Guide to Fantasyland*, rev. ed. (New York: Firebird, 2006), 102.

26. Terry Brooks, *Magic Kingdom for Sale Sold!* (1986; repr., London: Orbit, 1991), 13.

27. Brooks, *Magic Kingdom for Sale Sold!*, 14.

28. Brooks, *Magic Kingdom for Sale Sold!*, 13.

29. Brooks, *Magic Kingdom for Sale Sold!*, 93.

30. Brooks, *Magic Kingdom for Sale Sold!*, 64.

31. Brooks, *Magic Kingdom for Sale Sold!*, 53.
32. "Deverry Cycle," accessed 15 May 2016, http://deverry.com/?page_id=22.
33. Katharine Kerr, *Dragonspell: The Southern Sea* (1990; repr., London: Grafton, 1998), 25.
34. Kerr, *Dragonspell*, 51.
35. Kerr, *Dragonspell*, 45.
36. Terry Brooks, *The Elf Queen of Shannara*, Heritage of Shannara 3 (1992; repr. London: Orbit, 2006), 60.
37. David and Leigh Eddings, *The Rivan Codex: Ancient Texts of the Belgariad and the Mallorean*, illust. Geoff Taylor (1998; repr., London: Voyager, 1999), 185; see David Eddings, *Castle of Wizardry*, Belgariad 4 (1984; repr., London: Corgi Books, 1987).
38. John Clute, "Islands," in *Encyclopedia of Fantasy*, ed. Clute, June 1997, accessed 26 April 2016, http://sf-encyclopedia.uk/fe.php?nm=islands.
39. Clute, "Islands."
40. Dominique Beth Wilson, "Myth and Re-Imagined Religion in *Kushiel's Legacy*," *Literature and Aesthetics* 19, no. 9 (2009): 248, accessed 19 May 2016, http://openjournals.library.usyd.edu.au/index.php/LA/article/view/5013.
41. Wilson, "Myth and Re-Imagined Religion in *Kushiel's Legacy*," 248.
42. Wilson, "Myth and Re-Imagined Religion in *Kushiel's Legacy*," 248.
43. Wilson, "Myth and Re-Imagined Religion in *Kushiel's Legacy*," 256.
44. Jacqueline Carey, *Kushiel's Chosen* (New York: Tor, 2002), 268, 333.
45. Helen Young, *Race and Popular Fantasy Literature: Habits of Whiteness* (New York: Routledge, 2016), 131.
46. Young, *Race and Popular Fantasy Literature*, 131.
47. Young, *Race and Popular Fantasy Literature*, 131.
48. Kim Wilkins, "Popular Genres and the Australian Literary Community: The Case of Fantasy Fiction," *Journal of Australian Studies* 32, no. 2 (2008): 276, accessed 13 January 2015, http://dx.doi.org/10.1080/14443050802056771.
49. Donna Maree Hanson, "Creating a Fantastical World Through Passion and Words," *Canberra Times*, 6 November 2004.
50. Glenda Larke, interviewed by Donna Maree Hanson. *Andromeda Spaceways Inflight Magazine* 13 (June/July 2004): 121–123.
51. Hanson, "Creating a Fantastical World Through Passion and Words," 20.
52. Glenda Larke, *The Aware*, Isles of Glory 1 (Sydney: Voyager, 2003), 8.
53. Larke, *The Aware*, 3.
54. Larke, *The Aware*, 5.
55. Larke, *The Aware*, 7.
56. Larke, *The Aware*, 7.
57. Larke, *The Aware*, 9.
58. Glenda Larke, *Gilfeather*. 2003. Isles of Glory 2. (Reprint, n.p.: Fablecroft Publishing, 2013), Kindle, location 5878.
59. Glenda Larke, *The Tainted*. 2003. Isles of Glory 2. (Reprint, n.p.: Fablecroft Publishing, 2013), Kindle, location 138.
60. Larke, *The Tainted*, location 7031.
61. Tolkien, "On Fairy-Stories," location 861.

62. Scott Lynch, *The Lies of Locke Lamora*, Gentleman Bastard Sequence 1 (2006; repr., London: Gollancz, 2007), 133.

63. Lynch, *The Lies of Locke Lamora*, 144.

64. Lynch, *The Lies of Locke Lamora*, 134.

65. Lynch, *The Lies of Locke Lamora*, 2, 5.

66. Tim Lebbon, *The Island* (2009; repr., London: Allison & Busby, 2010), 60.

67. Lebbon, *The Island*, 60.

68. Lebbon, *The Island*, 180.

69. Lebbon, *The Island*, 285.

70. Lebbon, *The Island*, 156.

71. Lebbon, *The Island*, 169–70.

72. Lebbon, *The Island*, 341.

73. Lebbon, *The Island*, 340.

74. Lebbon, *The Island*, 440.

75. Farah Mendlesohn and Edward James, *A Short History of Fantasy* (2009; rev. ed., Faringdon, UK: Libri Publishing, 2012), Kindle, location 361.

76. Jim Butcher, *Turn Coat*, Dresden Files 11 (London: Hachette Digital, 2009), Kindle, location 4955, location 5022.

77. Butcher, *Turn Coat*, location 5015.

78. Butcher, *Turn Coat*, location 5034, location 5083, location 5683, location 6390, location 6478.

79. Butcher, *Turn Coat*, location 5150.

80. Butcher, *Turn Coat*, location 5089.

81. Butcher, *Turn Coat*, location 5775.

Chapter Eleven

Putting Islands on the Fantasy Map

Ursula K. Le Guin's Earthsea

Jonathan Pugh argues that in a world of "island-island movements," a new key question arises for island studies: *"what does it mean to think with the archipelago?"*[1] For Pugh, "archipelagic thinking" both moves beyond a focus on the singular, bounded, isolated island and "denaturalizes the conceptual basis of space and place."[2] While this question is a relatively new one for island studies, fantasy fiction has been thinking with the archipelago for decades and in ways which unsettle prevailing assumptions about what Tolkien called our "primary world." Furthermore, as the previous chapter indicates, if we were to approach the modern fantasy genre as the most recent phase of a centuries-long record of secondary world-building in popular literature, creative and critical thinking with the archipelago in popular fiction has a long history.

Writing about the postcolonial histories and literatures of the Caribbean and Pacific, Elizabeth DeLoughrey advocates an analytical vocabulary and paradigm that rejects Euro-American island stereotypes: "no island is an isolated isle and [...] a system of archipelagraphy—that is, a historiography that considers chains of islands in fluctuating relationship to their surrounding seas, islands and continents—provides a more appropriate metaphor for reading island cultures."[3] There is no better place to begin an analysis of fantasy's "archipelagraphy," to adopt DeLoughrey's key concept, than with Ursula K. Le Guin's Earthsea. This chapter therefore provides what Stefan Ekman terms a "topofocal, or place-focused"[4] reading of Le Guin's six books set in Earthsea: *A Wizard of Earthsea* (1968), *The Tombs of Atuan* (1971), *The Farthest Shore* (1972), *Tehanu: The Last Book of Earthsea* (1990), *Tales from Earthsea* (2001), and *The Other Wind* (2001). By giving precedence to the conceptualisation rather than the narrative functions of islands, this chapter traces an alignment between the imagined geography of a world-embracing archipelago and the structural logic and related thematic preoccupations of fantasy fiction, or, more simply, it argues that the geography of the archipelago and the genre of fantasy are a good fit.

Millicent Lenz, in her analysis of the first four books of the series, asks what Earthsea "'offer[s] to today's readers?' (In addition, of course, to the sheer pleasure of the stories!)"[5] Her parenthetical remark is significant. As this chapter shows, the pleasures offered by Earthsea are archipelagraphic: from the toponymic title to the maps of the archipelago and individual islands, and in its plotting and characterisation, Le Guin presents the archipelago as a world of adventure, wonder, and joy for readers of all ages. It would be remiss of us to neglect the question of reading pleasure in a book about the appeal and significance of islands in popular fiction. While we do discuss the fun of reading island-set fiction in other chapters, especially in relation to the cross-genre tendency to depict protagonists enjoying experiences analogous to "escapist" reading, this chapter has much more to say about the pleasures afforded to genre writers and readers by islands. Peter Hunt explains that criticism of fantasy fiction underplays the importance of reading-for-pleasure and the same can be said of crime fiction, thrillers, and popular romance. From the perspective of most scholarship, "invented worlds cannot be 'merely' places of wonder or delight: they must mean something else (morally, rather than inevitably) if they are to be interesting or valuable."[6] As Hunt puts it, critics of Le Guin "concentrate on the *meaning* rather than the *fact* of her wonders."[7] Consequently, this chapter looks closely at what Le Guin calls the "fictional fact"[8] of Earthsea.

The Dictionary of Imaginary Places describes Earthsea as a "roughly circular" archipelago with a "diameter of some twenty thousand miles" and comprising hundreds of islands.[9] The largest island is Havnor, "the Great Island, heart and hearth of the Archipelago."[10] At over three-hundred miles across at its widest point and with a coastline which approximately mirrors the shape of the archipelago as a whole, Havnor is "commonly regarded by the people of Earthsea as the centre of the world itself."[11] This island, which lies north of the Inmost Sea, is both geographically central and the "core of the archipelago's political and commercial life."[12] Earthsea's "spiritual centre,"[13] however, lies approximately two-hundred miles due south of Havnor's South Port, on the small island of Roke, "the center of the Old Powers in all Earthsea,"[14] where the magic that pervades the whole archipelago is concentrated, especially at Roke Knoll and in the Immanent Grove. The wizardry school at Roke, a principal setting in the story of Earthsea, is protected by the island's "charmed waters," and by the "Roke-wind" that "keeps off evil powers from the Isle of the Wise."[15] Roke's magic is key to the "fictional fact" of Earthsea's geomorphology: "the roots of it were deep, deeper than the sea, reaching down even to the old, blind, secret fires at the world's core";

"the roots of Roke are the roots of all the islands."[16] Most of the islands of Earthsea belong to the Inner Lands surrounding Havnor, but the power and influence of Havnor and Roke extend into the South, West, East, and North Reaches. Together, the Inner Lands and the Reaches comprise the Hardic Lands, and their dark-skinned inhabitants share the Hardic language and culture, with some local differences especially on the island of Osskil northwest of Havnor and at the archipelago's outer reaches. The fair-skinned, blue- or grey-eyed peoples of the Kargad Lands, "four great islands to the northeast of the main Archipelago,"[17] are linguistically and culturally distinct from the Hardic peoples and "have held themselves apart from and often in enmity towards the Archipelagans for two or three millennia."[18] Throughout this world magical and sacred power is concentrated at sites on islands rather than in the waters that surround them, in "springs, caves, hills, stones, and woods,"[19] and while it is tempting to describe Earthsea as "nautical fantasy" for the amount of time characters spend on boats, land ("earth") has primacy in this world. The people of Earthsea know of no lands beyond the Open Sea that encircles the Reaches: some believe that "[t]here is nothing but water till world's edge," and others "imagine other Archipelagoes or vast undiscovered lands on the other face of the world."[20]

Kenneth J. Zahorski and Robert H. Boyer, in their important early study of world-building in fantasy fiction, point to Earthsea as an exemplar of a self-contained secondary world distant from our own: "Readers can get as far away as the remote islands of Earthsea, or they can go to as close a place as Wales."[21] However, Zahorski and Boyer's description of Earthsea as "a maritime secondary world of countless islands and vast oceans" with "no connection" to our own is contradicted by their overarching contention that individual secondary worlds contribute to a common atlas of fantasy: "Perilous realm, legendary land, mythic country, Faërie, home of the gods: these are a few of the generic names for the landscape or 'secondary world' [...] of high fantasy."[22] Similarly, Le Guin begins her 1973 essay, "From Elfland to Poughkeepsie," by suggesting that fantasy writers share a collective secondary world, or what Tolkien called "faërie": "Elfland is what Lord Dunsany called the place. It is also known as Middle Earth, and Prydain, and the Forest of Broceliande, and Once Upon a Time; and by many other names."[23] In these terms, Earthsea is one manifestation of fantasy fiction's project to imagine an alternate reality, a secondary world different to our own (or Poughkeepsie, New York in Le Guin's case). Later in the essay, however, she insists that "in fantasy there is nothing but the writer's vision of the world. [...] There is only a construct built in a void."[24] This same contradiction, between inclusivity and exclusivity, generality and particularity, runs through Le Guin's commentary on Earthsea, most notably in her repeated claims that she is not so much the archipelago's creator as its explorer: "I did not deliberately invent Earthsea. I did not think 'Hey wow—islands are archetypes and archipelagoes are superarchetypes and let's build us an archipelago!' I am not an engineer, but an explorer. I discovered Earthsea."[25]

In an Afterword written for the 2012 release of the six Earthsea books as a set—the first time they appeared as a "unified edition"—Le Guin explains that she thinks of these books not as a "cycle," as her publishers have packaged them, but "simply as Earthsea."[26] She does, however, permit "Earthsea Trilogies, in the plural" to acknowledge the difference between the first three novels (1968–1972), which were written and marketed for young adult readers, and the second three (1990–2001), which are not aimed specifically at adolescent readers.[27] By the time she came to write the second trilogy, nearly two decades after the publication of *The Farthest Shore*, Le Guin had, due to the sheer passage of time, herself become a reader or "explorer" of Earthsea: "I lose my way on islands I thought I knew by heart."[28] *Tales from Earthsea* includes five stories set at various points in the archipelago's history and also the encyclopaedic "A Description of Earthsea," which she compares to the "first big map" she drew of "all the Archipelago and Reaches" when she began work on *A Wizard of Earthsea*: "I needed to know where things are, and how to get from here to there—in time as well as in space."[29] In the 2012 editions, Le Guin positions herself as a devoted reader of, and virtual traveller in, Earthsea, albeit one who has privileged access to what she terms the "Archives of the Archipelago," by sketching a frame tale in which she is cast as geographer, historian, ethnographer, and storyteller. This artistic conceit—not uncommon in fantasy fiction—is, however, compromised by the hand-drawn and lettered map included in the recent editions. Le Guin's signature in the map's bottom-right corner emphatically identifies her as the creator, not the surveyor, of this "entirely *im*possible" world.[30]

Le Guin's own accounts of finding enjoyment in Earthsea are as much about world-building, or what we might call here imaginary archipelagraphy, as they are about crafting characters or telling stories. It is significant that she identifies drawing a map of the archipelago as a creative entry point, both when she commenced the first book and when she returned to the world over three decades later. For Christian Jacob, the fictional map is an "invitation to narrative and adventure" for both writers and readers: "It results from a double-edged drive: the simple freedom of the graphic gesture and the pleasure of fiction."[31] He points to Robert Louis Stevenson's famous map of *Treasure Island* (1883) as an exemplar of cartography as "the initial stage, the generative site of the fiction."[32] "*[I]solated* from the rest of the world," individual islands "occupy a privileged place" in fictional cartography because of their eminent suitability for "vertical, cartographic viewing."[33] Jacob turns to Jules Verne's map in *The Mysterious Island* (1874) to explore the treatment of islands as containers for fiction ("The island is well suited to all the dreams of

Putting Islands on the Fantasy Map 157

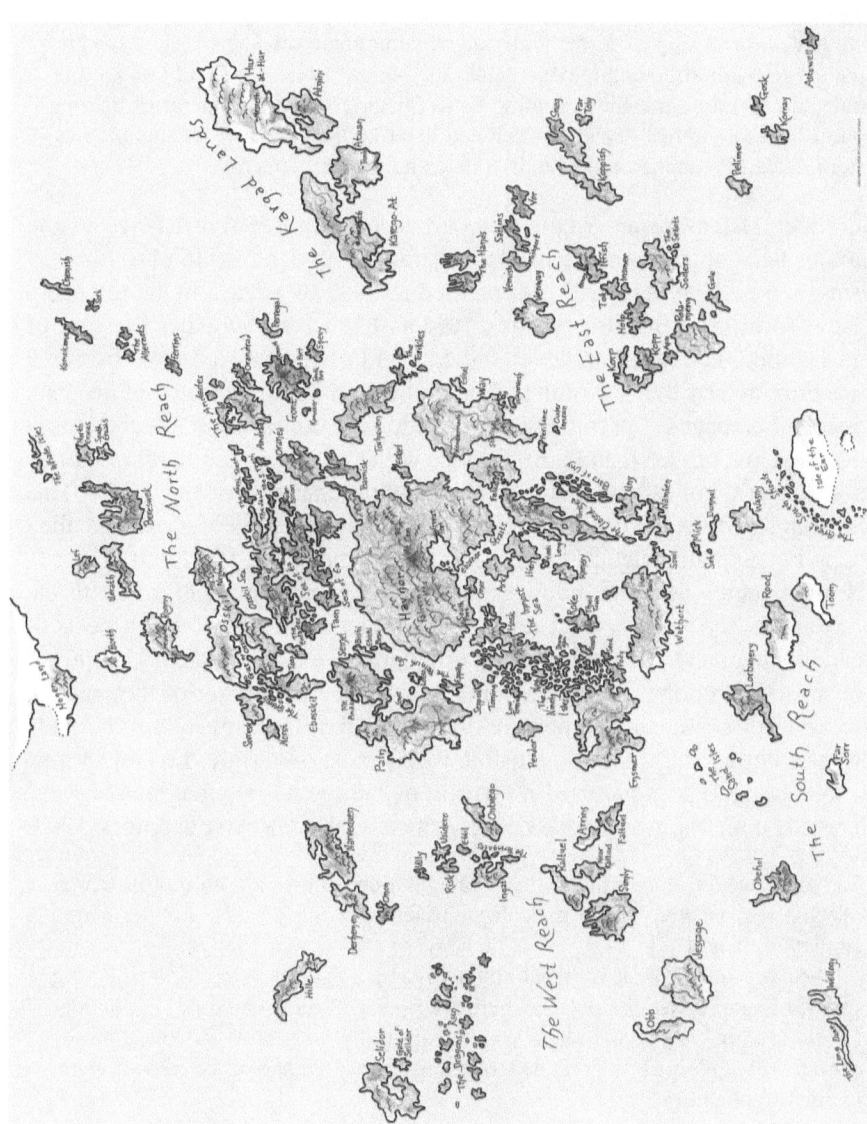

Figure 11.1. Map of Earthsea drawn by Ursula K. Le Guin, 2001 (ursulakleguin.com).

the microcosm"[34]) and uses Earthsea to show that the mapping of a fictional archipelago operates somewhat differently:

> Offering a dissemination of forms and names, the map of an imaginary archipelago tends to decenter the viewer's gaze and attention. [...] Here [with Earthsea] we have a profusion of forms with jagged contours, a dusting of islands, as in the subset within the archipelago called the Ninety Isles. A map of this kind is indeed a narrative machine, inviting us to imagine voyages, itineraries linking one island to another, each of which can itself be the center of an autonomous story. Here the map exceeds the discourse and the written story.[35]

The Ninety Isles are an excellent example of Earthsea's resistance to the finitude and containment of enisled characters and plots. In *A Wizard of Earthsea*, when the hero Ged is appointed as the new wizard in the township of Low Torning in the Ninety Isles, readers learn that "whether the sum of them is ninety is a question never settled."[36] Furthermore, the view from the house provided by the Isle-Men to Ged grants him an archipelagic rather than an insular perspective: "From the door one looked out on other thatched roofs and groves and gardens, and other islands with their roofs and fields and hills, and amongst them all the many bright winding channels of the sea."[37] This archipelagic perspective is implicit also in characters' awareness that they occupy but a small space in Earthsea's "vast scene of sea-girt lands."[38]

Brian Attebery sees the Indonesian archipelago as a "model" for Earthsea. Lenz demurs and suggests instead a correspondence between some aspects of the archipelago and Europe.[39] But the rough map Le Guin "redrew" in 2001 is unmistakably fictional in that it seems to carry the remainder of the creative process of inventing an archipelago for the telling of fantastic tales rather than as an analogue for Earth or a plausible world in its own right. Le Guin's map can thus be seen as a pictorial rendering of the mental or imaginative work she recalls undertaking when asked to write a book for young people in 1967:

> For some weeks or months I let my imagination go groping around in search of what was wanted, in the dark. It stumbled over the Islands, and the magic employed there. [...]
>
> The story of the book is essentially a voyage, a pattern in the form of a long spiral. I began to see the places where the young wizard would go. Eventually I drew a map. Now that I knew where everything was, now was the time for cartography. Of course a great deal of it only appeared above water, as it were, in drawing the map.

Here, Le Guin evokes the idea of "literary cartography" according to which "narratives are in some ways devices or methods used to map real-and-imagined spaces of human experience."[40] Further, her account of inventing Earthsea chimes with John Clute's well-known definition of fantasy as a "self-coherent story set in a world which is impossible." To adapt Clute's term, the world of Earthsea, is "story-shaped"⁴¹; it is both the site and the mechanism for Le Guin's brand of utopian fantasy-adventure.

The opening sentence of *A Wizard of Earthsea* employs time-honoured tropes for the representation of small islands as solitary and peculiar: "The island of Gont, a single mountain that lifts its peak a mile above the storm-wracked Northeast Sea, is a land famous for wizards."⁴² Singular and sea-girt, Gont calls to mind the thinking about islands encapsulated in Tolkien's naming of Tol Eressëa, or the Lonely Isle, a land famous for elves ("Tol" is Tolkien's term for an isle "rising with sheer sides from the sea or from a river"); in Stephen Donaldson's more prosaic toponym for the mystical and remote Isle of the One Tree; and in Margo Lanagan's redolent Rollrock Island.⁴³ The second sentence, however, shifts attention from insularity to connectivity: "From the towns in its high valleys and the ports on its dark narrow bays many a Gontishman has gone forth to serve the Lords of the Archipelago in their cities as wizard or mage, or, looking for adventure, to wander working magic from isle to isle of all Earthsea."⁴⁴ From the outset, readers are alerted to the suitability of an archipelagic setting to the highly episodic structure of the adventure tale and invited to follow the novel's Gontish hero "from isle to isle of all Earthsea." Together, these opening sentences begin the charting of the first novel's narrative map, positioning readers to anticipate journeys across and between islands and to look forward to the island stops on the protagonist's itinerary. More importantly, the tone of excitement and suspense of this opening passage is a product of both insular and archipelagic tropes: each island stands alone and so can promise a new adventure, but these micro-adventures take on a larger significance because each island is always part of a greater whole. So, while chapters in *A Wizard of Earthsea* typically begin or end with scenes of arrival on or departure for new islands, the goal of "working magic from isle to isle," a structural description which holds for all of the books, is to reunite the "sea-divided lands."⁴⁵

The narrative mapping of Earthsea evinces the tension between localism and globalism which is unavoidable in literary archipelagraphy. Each island (and each islander) is at once unique and a small part of the archipelago. The guiding spatial binary in the story of Earthsea opposes and integrates concepts of home and world as a series of young protagonists leave the protection and familiarity of their island homes and come to recognise themselves as citizens of their world of islands, with all of the rights and responsibilities that entails. We learn on the first page of *A Wizard of Earthsea* that the Gontish child, Duny, becomes the "greatest voyager" of Earthsea, the dragonlord and Archmage known as Sparrowhawk and immortalised in the *Deed of Ged* and other songs of the archipelago.⁴⁶ In *The Tombs of Atuan*, Ged leads the Kargish girl, Tenar, away from the sacred site of the title where she has been held captive to her role as Arha, the Priestess Ever Reborn, and she glimpses the sea for the first time, "a kind of joyous shimmering off on the edge of the world."[47] Ged reassures Tenar that she will see many islands: "It is marvellous to see them: the new lands rising from the sea as your boat comes towards them."[48] *The Farthest Shore* begins at the Great House of Roke, where Arren, the son of the Prince of Enlad and the Enlades, has recently arrived with a message from his father, for Ged, now the Archmage: "Only in these last few weeks had he seen lands that were not his own homeland, become aware of distance and diversity, and recognized that there was a great world beyond the pleasant hills of Enlad, and many people in it."[49] This preoccupation with characters who venture beyond the horizon of their known environment and community and a concomitant investment in geographical symbols and stories also runs through the later three books, and, in this regard, Earthsea is not exceptional. For, as Lucie Armitt, explains, "[i]rrespective of which fantasy text one is discussing, borders and parameters remain its key themes, and spatial and topographical concerns its key motifs."[50] In Earthsea, however, fantasy's world-building enterprise is all about the raising of islands.

The epigraph of *A Wizard of Earthsea* quotes a text from within the storyworld: *The Creation of Éa*, the "oldest of all songs"[51] in the archipelago and the foundation of education across the islands. Earthsea's creation myth is told and retold throughout the cycle. The archipelago's creator, Segoy, "raised the islands of the world from the Open Sea"[52] by naming them into being, a fantastic literalisation of theories of linguistic determinism: the islands only exist as a product of language. Le Guin provides a summary of the song in "A Description of Earthsea":

> Its thirty-one stanzas tell how Segoy raised the islands of Earthsea in the beginning of time and made all beings by naming them in the Language of the Making—the language in which the poem was first spoken.
>
> The ocean, however, is older than the islands; so say the songs.
>
> > *Before bright Éa was, before Segoy*
> > *Bade the islands be,*
> > *The wind of dawn blew on the sea ...*[53]

Segoy, variously described as a deity and the Earth itself, is worshipped throughout the archipelago on the night of the Long Dance, a ritual and celebration practiced even by the islandless Raft-People who live on floating platforms beyond the South Reach. The paired images of an island rising from the water and an island sinking into the water are the fulcrum of Le Guin's world-building in Earthsea. Time and again, her central characters look back to islands that sink into the sea and ahead to islands that rise from the sea, often from Ged's aptly named boat *Lookfar*. In this aspect, Earthsea is highly (and productively) repetitive as the archipelagic literary cartography enables and takes delight in the conduciveness of islandscapes to episodic or serial storytelling.

Earthsea eschews the closed system narrativisation of so many island genre fictions. This is perhaps clearest in the brief Robinsonade Le Guin inserts into chapter 8 of *A Wizard of Earthsea*, the tale of which quickly becomes part of the archipelago's oral storytelling tradition. Ged is shipwrecked, "flung [...] up like a stick of driftwood on the sand" on a "nameless isle" in the middle of the ocean where he finds an elderly couple, a brother and sister, who had been marooned there as children to live alone "in the utter desolation of the empty sea."[54] They refuse to leave and give the young wizard half of the legendary ring of Erreth-Ekbe (he later finds the other half in the Tombs of Atuan, but it is beyond the scope of this chapter to recount Earthsea's epic narrative). Before he leaves the island, Ged thanks the couple for their kindness by charming their salty spring to run clear and constant, and thus their home comes to be named Springwater Isle. From an island studies perspective, the interest of this episode is in the pointed misalignment of the classic castaway narrative and epic fantasy. The resolutely archipelagic sensibility underlying Earthsea is reinforced numerous times throughout the series, not least in the celebration of the awesome mobility of dragons for whom the world is uncompromisingly vast and open. At the heart of Earthsea, as the very name of Le Guin's fantasy world suggests, is the question of balance or equilibrium in the spiritual and political life of the archipelago, which is manifested throughout in the highly contingent hydrogeomorphology of land and water.

NOTES

1. Jonathan Pugh, "Island Movements: Thinking with the Archipelago," *Island Studies Journal* 8, no. 1 (2013): 9, accessed 12 May 2015, http://www.islandstudies.ca/sites/islandstudies.ca/files/ISJ-8-1-2013-Pugh_0.pdf.

2. Pugh, "Island Movements," 9.

3. Elizabeth DeLoughrey, "'The Litany of Islands, The Rosary of Archipelagoes: Caribbean and Pacific Archipelagraphy," *Ariel: A Review of International English Literature* 32, no. 1 (2001): 23.

4. Stefan Ekman, *Here Be Dragons: Exploring Fantasy Maps and Settings* (Middletown: Wesleyan UP, 2013), Kindle, location 123.

5. Millicent Lenz, "Ursula K. Le Guin," in *Alternative Worlds in Fantasy Fiction*, by Peter Hunt and Millicent Lenz (2001; repr., London: Continuum, 2003), 74.

6. Peter Hunt, "Introduction: Fantasy and Alternative Worlds," in *Alternative Worlds in Fantasy Fiction*, by Peter Hunt and Millicent Lenz (2001; repr., London: Continuum, 2003), 5.

7. Hunt, "Introduction: Fantasy and Alternative Worlds," 5.

8. Ursula K. Le Guin, foreword to the first edition of *Tales from Earthsea* (2001; repr., Boston: Graphia, 2012), xiv.

9. Alberto Manguel and Gianni Guadalupi, *Dictionary of Imaginary Places* (New York: Macmillan Publishing Co., 1980), 105.

10. Ursula K. Le Guin, *A Wizard of Earthsea* (1968; repr., Boston: Graphia, 2012), 38.

11. Manguel and Guadalupi, *Dictionary of Imaginary Places*, 162.

12. Manguel and Guadalupi, *Dictionary of Imaginary Places*, 105.

13. Manguel and Guadalupi, *Dictionary of Imaginary Places*, 105.

14. Ursula K. Le Guin, "A Description of Earthsea," in *Tales from Earthsea* (2001; repr., New York: Graphia-Houghton Mifflin Harcourt, 2012), 412.

15. Le Guin, *A Wizard of Earthsea*, 53, 134.

16. Le Guin, *A Wizard of Earthsea*, 81; Ursula K. Le Guin, "The Finder," in *Tales from Earthsea*, 100.

17. Le Guin, "A Description of Earthsea," 379.

18. Le Guin, "A Description of Earthsea," 380.

19. Le Guin, "A Description of Earthsea," 412.

20. Le Guin, *A Wizard of Earthsea*, 241, 243.

21. Kenneth J. Zahorski and Robert H. Boyer, "The Secondary Worlds of High Fantasy," in *The Aesthetics of Fantasy Literature and Art*, ed. Roger C. Schlobin (Notre Dame: University of Notre Dame Press, 1982), 80.

22. Zahorski and Boyer, "The Secondary Worlds of High Fantasy," 80, 56.

23. Ursula Le Guin, "From Elfland to Poughkeepsie," in *From Elfland to Poughkeepsie*, ed. David Sandner (1973; repr., Westport: Praeger, 2004), 144.

24. Le Guin, "From Elfland to Poughkeepsie," 154.

25. Ursula K. Le Guin, "Dreams Must Explain Themselves," *The Language of the Night: Essays on Fantasy and Science Fiction*, by Le Guin, ed. Susan Wood (New York: Ultramarine Publishing, 1980), 49–50.

26. Ursula K. Le Guin, afterword to the 2012 edition of *The Other Wind* (New York: Graphia-Houghton Mifflin Harcourt, 2012), 307.

27. Le Guin, afterword to the 2012 edition of *The Other Wind*, 307–308.

28. Le Guin, foreword to the first edition of *Tales from Earthsea*, xvii.

29. Le Guin, foreword to the first edition of *Tales from Earthsea*, xiv.

30. Katherine Buse, "Genre, Utopia, and Ecological Crisis: World-Multiplication in Le Guin's Fantasy," *Green Letters: Studies in Ecocriticism* 17, no. 3 (2013): 266, accessed 19 April 2016, http://dx.doi.org/10.1080/14688417.2013.860556.

31. Christian Jacob, *The Sovereign Map: Theoretical Approaches in Cartography Through History*, ed. Edward H. Dahl, trans. Tom Conley (Chicago: University of Chicago Press, 2006), 281.

32. Jacob, *The Sovereign Map*, 281.

33. Jacob, *The Sovereign Map*, 286.

34. Jacob, *The Sovereign Map*, 286.

35. Jacob, *The Sovereign Map*, 289.

36. Le Guin, *A Wizard of Earthsea*, 104.

37. Le Guin, *A Wizard of Earthsea*, 105.

38. Ursula K. Le Guin, *The Farthest Shore* (1973; repr., London: Saga Press, 2012), 8.

39. Lenz, "Ursula K. Le Guin," 45

40. Robert T. Tally Jr., "Introduction: Mapping Narratives," in *Literary Cartographies: Spatiality, Representation, and Narrative*, Geocriticism and Spatial Literary Studies. ed. Robert T. Tally Jr. (New York: Palgrave Macmillan, 2014), 3.

41. John Clute and John Grant interviewed by David Langford, 1999, in *Crosstalk: Interviews Conducted by David Langford* (Reading: Ansible Editions, 2015), 18.

42. Le Guin, *A Wizard of Earthsea*, 1.

43. J. R. R. Tolkien, *The Silmarillion*, ed. Christopher Tolkien (London: George Allen & Unwin, 1977), 365; Stephen Donaldson, *One Tree*, Second Chronicles of Thomas Covenant 2 (Melbourne: Fontana/Collins, 1982); Margo Lanagan, *The Brides of Rollrock Island* (2012; repr., London: David Fickling Books, 2013).

44. Le Guin, *A Wizard of Earthsea*, 1.

45. Le Guin, *A Wizard of Earthsea*, 75.

46. Le Guin, *A Wizard of Earthsea*, 1.

47. Ursula K. Le Guin, *The Tombs of Atuan* (1971; repr., London: Saga Press, 2012), 192–93.

48. Le Guin, *The Tombs of Atuan*, 196.

49. Le Guin, *The Farthest Shore*, 7.

50. Lucie Armitt. *Fantasy Fiction: An Introduction* (New York: Continuum, 2005), 58.

51. Le Guin, *A Wizard of Earthsea*, 57.

52. Le Guin, *A Wizard of Earthsea*, 160.

53. Le Guin, "A Description of Earthsea," 390

54. Le Guin, *A Wizard of Earthsea*, 192, 196.

Chapter Twelve

An Imaginary Water World
Robin Hobb's The Liveship Traders Trilogy

The map (figure 12.1) included at the beginning of each book of Robin Hobb's Liveship Traders trilogy—*Ship of Magic* (1998), *The Mad Ship* (1999), and *Ship of Destiny* (2000)—is the first indication that the treatment of the archipelagic setting of this series is not "terrecentric."[1] Explanatory text on the broken coastline of the Cursed Shores marks the region, but not the shores, interiors, or waterways of the Pirate Islands, or Pirate Isles, as they are often referred to in the trilogy. "Not reliably charted" due to "steam fogs, sand and silt," the "islands shift in storms."[2] As the crow, or, more aptly, as the dragon flies, the Pirate Islands lie roughly halfway between Jamaillia City in the map's south-western corner and Bingtown, its northernmost named settlement, behind a chain of barrier islands which run the length of the Cursed Shores. The continental landmass that comprises roughly a third of the map is largely empty. An arrow in the Wild Sea on the map's eastern border points the way to the "Barrens," a group of distant islands that feature in the first novel, but there is no indication of the scale or topography of the unnamed continent. Furthermore, while no rivers extend from the four estuarine areas on its coastline, the "marsh" north of Jamaillia City and nearby Candletown and the "bad water" south of Bingtown anticipate a narrative in which the boundary between land and sea is ever open.

Jon Anderson and Kimberley Peters frame their recent edited collection, *Water Worlds: Human Geographies of the Ocean*, with the statement, "Our world is a water world."[3] Following the ocean studies scholar Phillip E. Steinberg, Anderson and Peters describe geography as a largely "landlocked" discipline. Their objectives are to move beyond thinking of "the oceans as a flat, empty space, or one of only abstract representation, to a space that is living, and has its own agencies," and "to consider the various *lives* that 'fill' ocean space and the manifold *things* that surface 'on' or

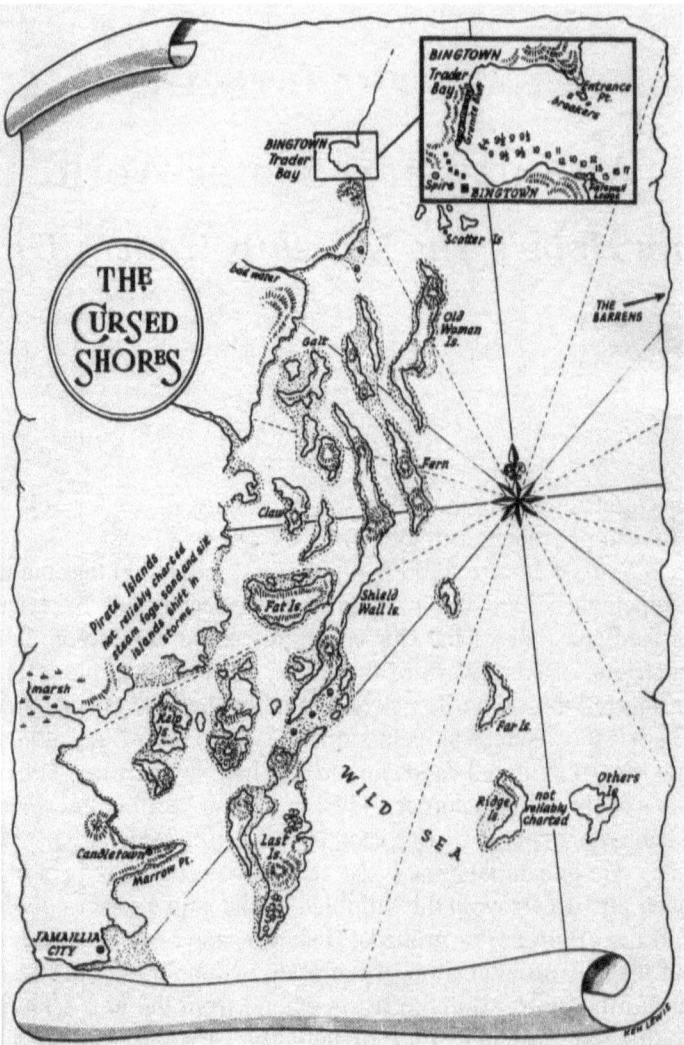

Figure 12.1. Map of The Cursed Shores in Robin Hobb's The Liveship Traders (1998–2000).

'within' the sea, as well as taking seriously the very *matter* of water itself."[4] In short, Hobb's trilogy imagines a water world in exactly such terms. The surfaces and depths of the Wild Sea and the channels and bodies of water to which it is connected are anything but "empty space." Instead, they are, to borrow a description from Steinberg and Peters, "indisputably voluminous, stubbornly material, and unmistakably undergoing continual reformation."[5] There are numerous descriptions of the trilogy's setting as one dominated by water, for its volume, its varying composition, and its constant movement. A dragon's-eye view presents the ocean as a "rippling fabric, the islands scattered toys,"[6] but for the most part Hobb eschews descriptions that make water a surface significant only for what breaks through or floats upon it. Instead, the descriptions of the islands and of the continent's coastline emphasise water's function as an actant in the landscape, for its turbulence, its changing phases, and its chemistry: "the many small streams of the islands were full and rushing. Some meandered out into the saltwater; others fell in sheets of silver as waterfalls from the steeper, rockier islands. All contributed freshwater that floated for a time atop the salt, changing the colours of the waters they moved through so serenely"; "The corrosive waters of the river ruled the world, and flowed where they wished"; and "The rains of winter had filled the rivers and streams of this region to overflowing. At high tide, saltwater and river water mingled in the brackish bogs."[7] More important, as these quotations show, the "waterscape"[8] over which the titular liveships sail is not depicted as a world apart but as one that exists in a conceptual and material interrelationship with the sky and land, the "Three Realms" that the human and non-human characters must learn to share if they and their world are to endure.

One way to examine the conceptualisation and representation of islands in The Liveship Traders might be through Philip Hayward's concept of "aquapelagos," which he proposes as a solution to the overemphasis on island-to-island relations in recent calls for the development of "Archipelago Studies."[9] Hayward defines aquapelagos as "entities created when humans occupy and interact with integrated land and aquatic spaces."[10] They are, he explains, "performatively constituted" social and geographical assemblages where humans are essential but only one type in a diversity of "actants"[11]: "The air above the waters and land, the weather that occurs in it, the windblown seeds and species that are born by it and the birds that inhabit the air, sea and land are just as much part of the integrated space of the aquapelago."[12] This holistic view highlights the centrality of water to defining and understanding archipelagos; understands islands within a complicated meshwork of land, sea, and air; and acknowledges that any island-marine environment is a "human construct."[13] Hayward's conceptualisation of the aquapelago resonates with Hobb's approach to world-building in The Liveship Traders and with the series' implicit environmental politics. His insights have thus informed the analyses to follow. However, like Godfrey Baldacchino we are not persuaded that island studies need the neologism "aquapelago" to appreciate the myriad ways in which islands and their surrounding waters fold into each other.[14] Instead, as our chapter title indicates, we draw on recent scholarship in ocean studies to analyse Hobb's imaginary "water world."

The series opens with a brief prologue in which Maulkin, the leader of a "tangle" of great serpents, rises from the sea-floor and announces that the "time has come" for them to migrate north.[15] The serpents' perspective on the world introduces each of the novels: for them, the oceans are the "Plenty" and the space above the water is the "Lack." This neat inversion of the land/ocean binary runs against the grain of dominant ways of thinking about the space beneath the water's surface as a void. By beginning the series in the "scratchy dirt" and "filtered blue sunlight" of the "sea-bottom,"[16] Hobb immerses readers in a secondary world distinct from but reflecting our own. John Mack, in his discussion of the history of representation of the Mediterranean, argues that the sea has been largely understood as "the space in between" the coastal areas of islands and continents. Seas are, for the most part, "portrayed either as the backdrop to the stage on which the real action is seen to take place—that is, the land—or they are portrayed simply as the means of connection between activities taking place at coasts and in their interiors."[17] Hobb's main human characters are initially oblivious to the life of the sea, except to the extent that it intrudes on the smooth passage of ships between land settlements for trade and migration. By the series' end, however, the humans and non-humans (serpents, dragons, liveships) have reached a mutual understanding that, while their perspectives on and experiences of the world differ in essential ways, in ecological terms they share a common (water) world.

The Liveship Traders begins in the "bottom muck"[18] of the Wild Sea and ends on the muddy banks of the Serpent River, where the survivors of Maulkin's tangle wait in cocoons for the summer sun to trigger their emergence as dragons. Over the course of the series, we learn that the great serpents are not the monsters of the deep humans imagined them to be but dragons in their larval phase "caught twixt times"[19] by the long aftermath of a massive volcanic eruption. Once imagined as mythical by sailors and pirates, the serpents become increasingly visible, first as scavengers trailing slave ships and then as canny predators attracted to the liveships which give the series its name.

The map of the Cursed Shores bears more than a passing resemblance to that of Robert Louis Stevenson's map of Treasure Island, not least because of the rhumb lines extending from its compass rose. The homage to Stevenson's famous maritime adventure tale is reinforced by the design of the ornament at the beginning of each chapter in the trilogy, a near-exact copy of the compass rose on the Treasure Island map, and is amplified in the portrayal of the first human character we meet in the series. Chapter 1 of *Ship of Magic*, "Of Priests and Pirates," begins on Others' Island, the furthest landmass from the Cursed Shores marked on the map. The pirate, Kennit, walks the tideline of Treasure Beach. His ship is anchored on the other side of the island, in "notorious" Deception Cove, and he is anxious to return before the "fanged rocks" devour his ship; coming ashore had felt to Kennit "like stepping into some creature's half-open mouth."[20] The isolated island and its topography are personified through a familiar metaphorics: the salt waves "lick the sandy beach clean of his tracks"; as the tide turns, the waves lose their "pleading grasp upon the land" and reveal the "worn molars of shale."[21] Kennit and Genkis, the older pirate who accompanies him, are aware that the "hazards of visiting this island [are] legendary."[22] They recall stories of the island, including the "ancient tale of Kaven Ravenlock," who visited the island for fifty years and returned as if no time had passed, but with golden hair, red eyes, and singing "true songs that told of the future in twisted rhymes."[23] Textually such moments assist with building a coherent and engaging secondary world (The Liveship Traders is one of five series set in Hobb's more expansive fictional world, known as the realm of the Elderlings[24]), but the description of Others' Island as "legendary" and "notorious" also gestures beyond Hobb's fiction as does the naming of the island and its locations. Not only does the topography and flora of Others' Island, with "evergreens so dark they were nearly black,"[25] recall Stevenson's island, but Kennit is a charismatic villain in the mould of Stevenson's Long John Silver and J. M. Barrie's Captain Hook. Like Silver, Kennit is linked to another legendary pirate, Igrot the Bold (Hobb's Captain Flint); like Hook, he is supported by a series of Smee-like figures, beginning with Genkis, and loses his leg to a sea-dwelling reptile; and like both Silver and Hook, he mentors a young boy whom he attracts and repels in equal measure. In *The Mad Ship*, Kennit returns to Others' Island with the boy, Wintrow, who nearly dies freeing a serpent imprisoned in a cave by the "cold and squamous"[26] amphibians, the Others who give the island their name. Finding an island's secret in a cave is a trusted storytelling device across genres. The serpent's imprisonment on Others' Island is a dark twist on the aquatic "tank" Ralph Rover and his companions create to hold sea creatures in R. M. Ballantyne's *The Coral Island* and of which he imagines himself "master."[27]

By beginning her epic tale on this isolated and "sorcerous place"[28] that is so clearly derivative of classic literary islands, Hobb offers an implicit critique of insular secondary worlds, both for the limits they place on storytelling and for their lack of verisimilitude. The latter is especially relevant in this series which invites consideration as an eco-fantasy. The "long stretch of islands" along the coastline was once a mountain range and the "wide swamp" on the continent's edge once "richly fertile inland plains."[29] From the perspective of the dragon, Tintaglia, who flies the skies of the Cursed Shores in *Ship of Destiny*, "Humans [have] multiplied like fleas on a dying rabbit. Their dirty, smoky settlements littered the world."[30] Her question,

"How dared humans assume they were masters of the world?,"[31] is an invitation to readers to trace the similarities between the realm of the Elderlings and our own world.

The naming of Others' Island evokes, of course, the long association in Western culture between remote islands and fear of racial difference. Beginning this epic fantasy on its shores positions readers to appreciate the history and geopolitics of its secondary world as a reflection of our primary one. The Others, who the entrapped serpent thinks of as the "Abominations," exist only in the unreality of their remote island, jealous guards of its peculiar magic. The place and its inhabitants are co-constitutive. This interest in what we would call performative geographies persists throughout the series; for example, slaves who have moved from master to master, and place to place, are known as "map-faces" for the number of tattoos on their faces; and people who live on the shores of the Rain Wild river grow distinctive "lumps and wattles of flesh."[32] Kennit first visits Others' Island to seek treasures on its aptly named beach, which he lays for "soothsaying" before the island's oracle.[33] He asks the venomous, fish-eyed creature one question as permitted by the Others' rituals: "Shall I succeed in what I aspire?"[34] Kennit's ambition is to be the "first King of the Pirate Isles,"[35] but, like the Others/Abominations, in the end his megalomania is his undoing.

Raised by his father on Key Island, a small island in the bay of Keyhole Island, "a wall of forest-topped cliffs, shaped like a near-closed horseshoe,"[36] Kennit has a skewed utopian sensibility. He is happiest when drawing plans to rebuild settlements in the Pirate Isles: "It was like creating his own world, a tidy and orderly world where things made sense and were arranged to their best advantage."[37] Like his father before him, however, Kennit is a perverse sub-creator, overinvested in the impossible fantasy of a "perfect little world on a hidden island,"[38] and unable to recognise that connecting with other people and places is a higher virtue than standing apart from the greater world.

Hobb drip-feeds readers Kennit's tragic backstory, which explains his aspiration to captain a liveship and become King of the Pirate Isles. His father, Lucto Ludluck—a Liveship Trader—was murdered by Captain Igrot who burned the settlement on Key Island, commandeered the family's liveship, and imprisoned Kennit to rape and torture him mercilessly. In the third book, it is revealed that the boy and the Ludluck's ship, Paragon, worked together to kill Igrot and vowed to keep their shared trauma a secret. Paragon is a main character in the series, the eponymous "mad ship" of the second book; when the series opens he lies on a Bingtown beach, abandoned by his human family, but still alive. Liveships are sentient tall ships; their keels, figureheads, and the planking of their hulls are made of "wizardwood" by the people of the Rain Wild River who harvest the mysterious material and guard its origins. Old Trader families of Bingtown and the Rain Wild Traders are kin, descendants of colonisers from Jamaillia who settled the Cursed Shores generations earlier. When the third member of a liveship's family dies on its decks and the wizardwood absorbs his or her "anma," the ship quickens, its figurehead transfigures into a living, speaking being, and the ship is able to share thoughts and feelings with people on board, especially members of the family that owns it. Liveships are, as it turns out, not built from timber, but from the cocoons of dragons, unearthed from the ruins of a magnificent Rain Wild city buried long ago by a volcano. Their "life" comes from the memories woven into the cocoons. The Liveship Traders trilogy is, in effect, a ghost ship narrative: the ships carry the spirits of the dragons who died when their cocoons were split open and sawn into planks. Liveships are thus simultaneously characters and settings; importantly, as beings made of memories they are also a kind of text, palimpsests that are added to by the people and events on their decks.

The Vestrit family liveship, Vivacia (her name becomes ironic), is quickened by the death of Ephron Vestrit early in *Ship of Magic*. His daughter, Althea, expects to inherit the ship and its captaincy but feels betrayed when her father's will leaves Vivacia in the charge of her sister, Keffria, and thus positions her brother-in-law, Kyle Haven, to become its captain. Kyle satisfies the ship's need to have a Vestrit on board by forcing his son, Wintrow, to sail with him. Althea's opposition to Kyle becomes more passionate when she learns of his plans to convert Vivacia into a slave ship, contravening Bingtown's historical opposition to slavery and risking her beloved and newly quickened ship's sanity through involvement in the brutality of the slave trade. The maritime toponymy of the series—ships sail the Inner Passage between Jamaillia City and Bingtown—clearly draws on the history of slavery (which in turn recalls the Middle Passage and the islands of the Caribbean) as do the descriptions of the ships as "floating cemeteries."[39] Althea spends much of the series plotting to reclaim her ship, first from Kyle, and then from Kennit, who captures Vivacia and maroons Kyle on Key Island, keeping Wintrow on board to placate the ship. After Wintrow abandons the ship in Jamaillia and is arrested for giving succour to imprisoned slaves, he is purchased by his father and tattooed with Vivacia's likeness, becoming a slave to the ship. The Liveship Traders is an epic fantasy with a large cast of characters, multiple narrative strands, and a multifaceted imagined world. It is worth reiterating here that our analysis is necessarily limited by our focus on genre fiction's approach to islands. This trilogy exhibits and questions fantasy fiction's abiding islophilia by positioning its characters (and readers) to consider islands from the water.

Baldacchino acknowledges that island studies will benefit from turning its attention to the water: "Land-based is land-biased. We really need to get wet."[40] Hobb's seafaring characters do go ashore on a number of islands, including beautiful Claw Island, inhospitable Stink Island, and the unnamed isle where the pirates have their stronghold at Divvytown, but they encounter many more named and unnamed islands from offshore, glimpsing them as low "hummocks" on the horizon, navigating to avoid their rocky shores, or anchoring in their bays. The offshore (or waterborne) perspectives on islands such as Pointless Island, Hawser Island, Last Island, and Shield Island add detail to Hobb's narrative map of a world of islands, which is expanded by references to islands in the realm's further reaches, including the Perfume Isles and the Spice Isles. The "shifting islands" and "unreliable shores"[41] of the Pirate Islands are mostly viewed from a distance, from water rather than land, by the crew and passengers of liveships, and by the ships themselves—especially Paragon and Vivacia, but also Ophelia and Kendry. For example, early in *The Mad Ship*, Wintrow leans on the "bow rail […] staring out over the choppy water."[42] Vivacia, now captained by Kennit, is "bound for some pirate stronghold," and the boy is both deeply aware of his ignorance of the channels and islands on their route and attentive to the phase changes of water (especially from liquid to vapour and vice versa) that impede any efforts to chart the islands:

> To the west, the horizon disappeared into the foggy coast of the Cursed Shores. The swift-running steaming rivers of that region dumped their warm and silty waters into this channel, which created near permanent mists and fogs that cloaked an ever-changing shoreline of shoals and shallows. Sudden, violent storms were common in the winter months, and not unknown even in the kinder days of summer. The pirate islands were uncharted. What sense was there in charting a coast that changed almost daily?[43]

Much later, his cousin Althea is similarly awed by the region's resistance to cartography: "The Pirate Isles were not only uncharted and infested with pirates, they were an uncertain place to visit, for storms and inland floods often changed the contour of the islands, river mouths and waterways."[44] The terrestrial and marine environment of the Cursed Shores is thus depicted as an unstable nexus of sea, land, and sky, in which water prevails.

Anderson and Peters ask us to reconceptualise "our (water)world as one which is in flux, changeable, processual and in a constant state of becoming."[45] From the perspective of island (literary) studies reading The Liveship Traders is one place to begin:

> The whole section of "coast" known as the Pirate Isles was constantly in flux. Some claimed that the multitude of rivers and streams that dumped into the Inside Passage around the Pirate Isles were actually one great river, eternally shifting in its many-channelled bed. Brashen didn't much care if the steaming waters that emptied out into the channel were from one river or many. The facts were that although the warm water mellowed the climate of the Pirate Isles, it also stank, fouled boat bottoms at a prodigious rate, weakened ropes and lines and created billowing fogs in every season of the year.[46]

To follow Elizabeth DeLoughrey, what we might call the imaginary "archipelagraphy"[47] of The Liveship Traders is mostly drawn from on or above the water. However, Hobb uses the point-of-view of the serpents to take us beneath the waves. Whereas the passage above presents the "dry" perspective of Bingtown-born Brashen Trell, the serpents are unmistakably "wet." For instance, after the serpent known as "She who Remembers," is freed from her prison on Others' Island she makes a mental map of the journey ahead of her: "Beyond the islands was the mainland, and in the mainland was the mouth of the river that led to the cocooning grounds. That was her destination."[48] Not only does the serpent's point of view foreground islands, it is also based on the knowledge that islands are defined as much by the water that surrounds them as by their landmass.

Steinberg and Peters argue that a concept of "wet ontology" "can reinvigorate, redirect, and reshape debates that are all too often restricted by terrestrial limits."[49] For most of us, thinking from the water—"*through*, and also *under*"[50] the sea—requires a leap of imagination. The richly nuanced wet ontology of The Liveship Traders demonstrates the capacity of fantasy fiction to show us other ways to think about islands. Whereas ships afford us a view of islands from on the water, such a perspective is—even when it is raining or waves are crashing on the decks—still a predominantly dry one. The liveships are, in this sense, like floating islands. In the final book of Hobb's trilogy, Vivacia breaks her bond with Wintrow and he is suddenly aware of his insignificance in the water world: "In a dizzying instant, he was aware of how immense the sea and the world around him were."[51] By marooning Wintrow's father—the cruelly named Kyle Haven—on Key Island, Hobb invokes the trope of the maroon, from Robinson Crusoe to Ben Gunn in Stevenson's *Treasure Island*, and from the finding of the skeleton of the unlucky castaway in Ballantyne's *The Coral Island* to the allusion to this scene in Clive Cussler's *Shock Wave* (1996). However, this fantasy series does not use the figure of the castaway to interrogate the relationship between its characters and their world as novels like Defoe's *Robinson Crusoe* do. Rather, when Kyle Haven is banished, he disappears from the tale and only reappears briefly before dying towards the end of the trilogy. The Liveship Traders thus shows an impatience with the overemphasis on insularity in literary history and asks us to appreciate islands in the context of a water world.

NOTES

1. Phillip E. Steinberg, "Of Other Seas: Metaphors and Materialities in Maritime Regions," *Atlantic Studies* 10, no. 2 (2013): 163, accessed 28 April 2016, http://dx.doi.org/10.1080/14788810.2013.785192.

2. Robin Hobb, *Ship of Magic*, The Liveship Traders 1 (1998; repr., London: HarperVoyager, 2012), n.p.

3. Jon Anderson and Kimberley Peters, "'A perfect and absolute blank': Human Geographies of Water Worlds," in *Water Worlds Human Geographies of the Ocean*, ed. Anderson and Peters (Farnham: Ashgate, 2014), 3.

4. Anderson and Peters, "'A perfect and absolute blank,'" 8.

5. Phillip Steinberg and Kimberley Peters, "Wet Ontologies, Fluid Spaces: Giving Depth to Volume Through Oceanic Thinking," *Environment and Planning D: Society and Space*, 33, no. 2 (2015): 248, accessed 5 May 2016, http://dx.doi.org/10.1068/d14148p.

6. Robin Hobb, *Ship of Destiny*, The Liveship Traders 3 (2000; repr. London: HarperVoyager, 2012), 743.

7. Hobb, *Ship of Magic*, 491; Robin Hobb, *The Mad Ship,* The Liveship Traders 2 (1999; repr., London: HarperVoyager, 2012), 801; Hobb, *Ship of Destiny*, 339.

8. Hobb, *Ship of Destiny*, 203.

9. Philip Hayward, "Aquapelagos and Aquapelagic Assemblages: Towards an Integrated Study of Island Societies and Marine Environments," *Shima: The International Journal of Research into Island Cultures* 6, No. 1 (2012): 1–11, accessed 12 May 2015, http://www.shimajournal.org/issues/v6n1/c.-Hayward-Shima-v6n1-1-11.pdf; see also Peter Hayward, "The Constitution of Assemblages and the Aquapelagality of Haida Gwaii," *Shima: The International Journal of Research into Island Cultures* 6, no. 2 (2012): 1–13, accessed 5 March 2015, http://www.shimajournal.org/issues/v6n2/c.-Hayward-Shima-v6n2-1-14.pdf.

10. Hayward, "The Constitution of Assemblages and the Aquapelagality of Haida Gwaii," 2.

11. Hayward, "The Constitution of Assemblages and the Aquapelagality of Haida Gwaii," 3.

12. Hayward, "The Constitution of Assemblages and the Aquapelagality of Haida Gwaii," 2.

13. Hayward, "Aquapelagos and Aquapelagic Assemblages," 2.

14. Godfrey Baldacchino, "Getting Wet: A Response to Hayward's Concept of Aquapelagos," *Shima: The International Journal of Research into Island Cultures* 6, No. 1 (2012): 23, accessed 12 May 2015, http://www.shimajournal.org/issues/v6n1/f.-Baldacchino-Shima-v6n1-22-26.pdf.

15. Hobb, *Ship of Magic*, xi–xii.

16. Hobb, *Ship of Magic*, xi.

17. John Mack, *The Sea: A Cultural History* (London: Reaktion Books, 2011), 19.

18. Hobb, *Ship of Magic*, xi.

19. Hobb, *Ship of Magic*, xi.

20. Hobb, *Ship of Magic*, 3.

21. Hobb, *Ship of Magic*, 3.

22. Hobb, *Ship of Magic*, 4.

23. Hobb, *Ship of Magic*, 5.

24. The Cursed Shores are part of Hobb's fictional realm of the Elderlings, the setting for this and four other series (The Farseer Trilogy, The Tawny Man, The Rain Wild Chronicles, and The Fitz and the Fool Trilogy), a stand-alone novel (*The Willful*

Princess and the Piebald Prince [2013]) and three short stories ("Homecoming," "The Inheritance," and "Cat's Meat," in *The Inheritance*, by Robin Hobb and Megan Lindholm [London: HarperVoyager, 2011]). Examining the islands of this much larger world would be a fascinating project, but it is beyond the scope of this chapter. For instance, Hobb, who moved to Kodiak Island, Alaska in 1970, based the geography of the Six Duchies in the realm's north on "the panhandle of Alaska." See Interview with Robin Hobb, *Lightspeed: Science Fiction and Fantasy* no. 23 (April 2012), accessed 9 May 2016, http://www.lightspeedmagazine.com/nonfiction/interview-robin-hobb/.

25. Hobb, *Ship of Magic*, 3.
26. Hobb, *Ship of Magic*, 27.
27. Robert Michael Ballantyne, *The Coral Island*, ed. Ralph Crane and Lisa Fletcher (1857; repr. Richmond: Valancourt Books, 2015), 221.
28. Hobb, *Ship of Magic*, 32.
29. Hobb, *Ship of Destiny*, 403.
30. Hobb, *Ship of Destiny*, 403.
31. Hobb, *Ship of Destiny*, 403.
32. Hobb, *Ship of Magic*, 370.
33. Hobb, *Ship of Magic*, 27.
34. Hobb, *Ship of Magic*, 29.
35. Hobb, *Ship of Magic*, 36.
36. Hobb, *The Mad Ship*, 372.
37. Hobb, *The Mad Ship*, 740.
38. Hobb, *The Mad Ship*, 741.
39. Hobb, *Ship of Destiny*, 357.
40. Baldacchino, "Getting Wet," 22.
41. Hobb, *The Mad Ship*, 249.
42. Hobb, *The Mad Ship*, 19.
43. Hobb, *The Mad Ship*, 22.
44. Hobb, *Ship of Destiny*, 95.
45. Anderson and Peters, "'A perfect and absolute blank,'" 5.
46. Hobb, *The Mad Ship*, 248.
47. Elizabeth DeLoughrey, "'The Litany of Islands, The Rosary of Archipelagoes: Caribbean and Pacific Archipelagraphy," *Ariel: A Review of International English Literature* 32, no. 1 (2001): 21–52.
48. Hobb, *The Mad Ship*, 906.
49. Steinberg and Peters, "Wet Ontologies, Fluid Spaces," 247.
50. Steinberg and Peters, "Wet Ontologies, Fluid Spaces," 253.
51. Hobb, *Ship of Destiny*, 161.

Epilogue

Island Genres, Genre Islands plots a path for the investigation of the operations of popular genres in contemporary thinking about islands. It argues the case for attending more closely to the significance of setting in literary and popular fiction studies, by analysing the conceptualisation and representation of small islands across a wide selection of novels from four popular genres. In doing so it adds "genre"—and a range of associated terms and concepts—to the critical lexicon of island studies. Further, from a geocritical perspective, this book acknowledges that geography and genre are mutually informing: islands influence popular genres; popular genres influence islands.

This book maps in detail the insular topography of the four "islands" of crime, thrillers, romance, and fantasy through a combination of comparative survey and detailed textual analysis. At the same time, it takes an archipelagic view of the contemporary world of genres through the pan-generic arguments developed across the four sections. In each genre we consider, islands both play distinctive roles determined by the requirements of that genre and conform to expectations that are shared across the field of popular fiction. These shared conventions of representation are not, however, owned by any or all of the four genres discussed here but are found, too, in other genres such as horror and science fiction as well as in broader literary and cultural fields.

Popular fiction clearly reinforces habits of thinking about islands in contemporary Western culture. This would be evident to any island studies scholar who, for example, looked at crime writer Peter May's Lewis trilogy, set in the Outer Hebrides, or Tracey Alvarez's Due South romance series, set in New Zealand's Stewart Island. As we have demonstrated, reading genre novels enables the identification of dominant notions of islandness and the typical roles of islands in conventional narrative structures. But islands are not one-dimensional settings in popular fiction. Rather, islands in popular fiction function in myriad, complex ways, on which the texts themselves often reflect. This self-reflexivity can be found in novels which may at first appear to be written to templates for island storytelling, most obviously in popular romance novels and thrillers, which frequently alert readers to the games the genres play with tropes of space and place. Reading novels and series in which archipelagoes, rather than individual islands, are foregrounded, facilitates interrogation of recent calls for archipelagic or aquapelagic approaches to island studies. This is most apparent when islands appear in thrillers and fantasy fiction, both of which are globally or world-oriented genres.

Island Genres, Genre Islands attends to the textual life of islands in contemporary popular novels and advocates for more scholarly attention to the kinds of texts it discusses. The next step towards a rich understanding of islands in the popular imagination might be to look beyond books, to the fictional islands of film, television, and video games, or to the "real" islands of reality television, documentaries, and social media. Each of these topics could be considered singularly or through comparative approaches. Such research might be based in textual or discourse analysis, but the burgeoning field of the GeoHumanities creates opportunities for adding digital mapping to the analytical toolbox for island studies. The use of Geographic Information Systems (GIS), for example, has far-reaching possibilities for building new knowledge about where real-and-imagined islands fit in our world. As we indicated in chapter 1, Outer Hebrides tourism has already developed a Peter May Trail (complete with GIS coordinates) for visitors. But island scholars have yet to tap into the potential such technologies offer for the modelling and analysis of literary islands. Island studies is an obvious umbrella for this type of interdisciplinary scholarship.

Bibliography

PRIMARY SOURCES—CRIME

Adler-Olson, Jussi. *The Hanging Girl*. Translated by William Frost. New York: Penguin, 2015.
Allingham, Marjery. *Mystery Mile*. 1930. Reprint, London: Vintage, 2005.
Bale, Tom. *Terror's Reach*. 2010. Reprint, London: Arrow, 2011.
Barr, Nevada. *A Superior Death*. 1994. Reprint, New York: Berkley, 2003.
———. *Endangered Species*. 1997. Reprint, New York: Berkley, 2008.
———. *Blind Descent*. 1998. Reprint, New York: Berkley, 2009.
———. *Deep South*. 2000. Reprint, New York: Berkley, 2001.
———. *Flashback*. 2003. Reprint, New York: Berkley, 2004.
———. *Winter Study*. 2008. Reprint, New York: Berkley, 2009.
Beaton, M. C. *Death of a Snob*. 1991. Reprint, London: C&R Crime, 2011.
———. *Agatha Raisin and the Terrible Tourist*. 1997. Reprint, London: Constable, 2010.
Billingham, Mark. *The Bones Beneath*. London: Sphere, 2014.
Christie, Agatha. *The Mysterious Affair at Styles*. 1920. Reprint, London: HarperCollins, 2007.
———. *The Murder of Roger Ackroyd*. 1926. Reprint, London: HarperCollins, 1995.
———. *The Murder at the Vicarage*. 1930. Reprint, London: HarperCollins, 2002.
———. *Murder on the Orient Express*. 1934. Reprint, London: HarperCollins, 2015.
———. *And Then There Were None*. 1939. Reprint, London: HarperCollins, 2013.
———. *Evil Under the Sun*. 1941. Reprint, London: HarperCollins, 2008.
———. *A Caribbean Mystery*. 1964. Reprint, London: HarperCollins, 2006.
Cleeves, Ann. *Raven Black*. 2006. Reprint, London: Pan, 2010.
———. *Blue Lightening*. 2010. Reprint, London: Pan, 2010.
———. *Thin Air*. 2014. Reprint, London: Pan, 2015.
Cornwell, Patricia. *Isle of Dogs*. London: Little, Brown, 2001.
Derr Biggers, Earl. *The House Without a Key*. 1925. Reprint, Chicago: Academy Chicago, 2008.
Disher, Garry. *Port Vila Blues*. 1996. Reprint, New York: Soho Press, 2012.

Downie, Jill. *Daggers and Men's Smiles*. Toronto: Dundurn, 2011.
Duncan, Sandy Frances, and George Szanto. *Never Sleep with a Suspect on Gabriola Island*. Islands Investigations International Mystery 1. Surrey, BC: Touch Wood Editions, 2009.
———. *Always Kiss the Corpse on Whidbey Island*. Islands Investigations International Mystery 2. Surrey, BC: Touch Wood Editions, 2010.
———. *Never Hug a Mugger on Quadra Island*. Islands Investigations International Mystery 3. Surrey, BC: Touch Wood Editions, 2011.
———. *Always Love a Villain on San Juan Island*. Islands Investigations International Mystery 4. Surrey, BC: Touch Wood Editions, 2013.
Enright, John. *Pago Pago Tango*. Las Vegas: Thomas & Mercer, 2012.
———. *Fire Knife Dancing*. Las Vegas: Thomas & Mercer, 2013.
———. *The Dead Don't Dance*. Seattle: Thomas & Mercer, 2014.
———. *Blood Jungle Ballet*. Seattle: Thomas & Mercer, 2014.
Ewan, Chris. *The Good Thief's Guide to Venice*. 2011. Reprint, New York: Minotaur, 2012.
———. *Safe House*. 2012. Reprint, London: Faber, 2013.
———. *Dark Tides*. London: Faber, 2014.
———. *Long Time Lost*. London: Faber, 2016.
Flint, Shamini. *A Bali Conspiracy Most Foul*. London: Piatkus, 2009.
———. *The Singapore School of Villainy*. London: Piatkus, 2010.
Fois, Marcello. *The Advocate*. 1998. Translated by Patrick Creagh. London: Harvill, 2003.
George, Elizabeth. *A Place of Hiding*. London: Hodder & Stoughton, 2003.
Hamer, Gillian E. *Crimson Shore*. N.p. G. E. Hamer, 2014.
Hughes, Chip. *Murder on Moloka'i*. 2004. Reprint, Kailua, HI: Slate Ridge, 2011.
James, P. D. *The Skull Beneath the Skin*. London: Faber, 1982.
———. *The Lighthouse*. London: Faber, 2005.
Jungstedt, Mari. *Unseen*. 2003. Translated by Tiina Nunnally. London: Corgi, 2008.
Kaye, M. M. *Death in Cyprus*. 1956/1984. Reprint, New York: St Martin's Minotaur, 2001.
———. *Death in Zanzibar*. 1959/1983. Reprint, New York: St Martin's Minotaur, 1999.
———. *Death in the Andamans*. 1960/1985. Reprint, New York: St Martin's Minotaur, 2000.
Kelly, Jim. *Death's Door*. London: Severn House, 2012.
Kent, G. W. *Devil-Devil*. London: Robinson, 2011.
———. *One Blood*. London: Robinson, 2012.
———. *Killman*. London: C&R Crime, 2013.
Lackberg, Camilla. *Buried Angels*. 2011. Translated by Tiina Nunnally. London: Harper, 2014.
Larsson, Stieg. *The Girl with the Dragon Tattoo*. 2005. Translated by Reg Keeland. London: MacLehose/Quercus, 2008.
Lehane, Dennis. *Shutter Island*. 2003. Reprint, London: Bantam Books, 2004.
Leon, Donna. *Death in La Fenice*, 1992. Reprint, London: Arrow, 2009.
McGuire, Matt. *Dark Dawn*. London: Constable & Robinson, 2012.

———. *When Sorrows Come*. London: C&R Crime, 2014.
May, Peter. *The Blackhouse*. Lewis Trilogy 1. London: Quercus, 2011.
———. *The Lewis Man*. Lewis Trilogy 2. London: Quercus, 2012.
———. *The Chessmen*. Lewis Trilogy 3. London: Quercus, 2013.
———. *Entry Island*. London: Quercus, 2014.
Mayle, Peter. *The Corsican Caper*. 2014. Reprint, New York: Vintage, 2015.
Mills, Mark. *The Information Officer.* London: Harper, 2009.
Owen, David. *Pig's Head*. 1994. Reprint, Sydney: Arrow, 2003.
Padura, Leonardo. *Havana Blue*. 2000. Translated by Peter Bush. London: Bitter Lemon Press, 2006.
Quigley, Sheila. *Thorn in My Side*. Holy Island Trilogy 1. Houghton-le-Spring, Co Dur: Burgess Books, 2011.
———. *Nowhere Man*. Holy Island Trilogy 2. Houghton-le-Spring, Co Dur: Burgess Books, 2012.
———. *The Final Countdown*. Holy Island Trilogy 3. Houghton-le-Spring, Co Dur: Burgess Books, 2013.
Robertson, Craig. *The Last Refuge*. London: Simon & Schuster, 2014.
Rowson, Pauline. *Blood on the Sand*. 2010. Reprint, Hayling Island, Hants: Fathom, 2011.
Silva, Daniel. *The English Girl*. 2013. 2000. Reprint, New York: Harper, 2014.
Titasey, Catherine. *My Island Homicide*. St Lucia: University of Queensland Press, 2013.
Vichi, Marco. *Death in Sardinia*. 2004. Translated by Stephen Sartarelli. London: Hodder & Stoughton, 2012.
Wheelaghan, Marianne. *Food of Ghosts*. Edinburgh: Pilrig Press, 2012.
———. *The Shoeshine Killer*. Edinburgh: Pilrig Press, 2015.
Zouroudi, Anne. *The Messenger of Athens*. 2007. Reprint, London: Bloomsbury, 2011.
———. *The Taint of Midas*. 2008. Reprint, London: Bloomsbury, 2011.
———. *The Doctor of Thessaly*. 2009. Reprint, London: Bloomsbury, 2010.
———. *The Lady of Sorrows*. 2010. Reprint, London: Bloomsbury, 2011.
———. *The Whispers of Nemesis*. 2011. Reprint, London: Bloomsbury, 2012.
———. *The Bull of Mithros*. 2012. Reprint, London: Bloomsbury, 2013.
———. *The Feast of Artemis*. 2013. Reprint, London: Bloomsbury, 2014.

PRIMARY SOURCES—THRILLERS

Allen, Chris. *Hunter: Intrepid 2*. Sydney: Momentum, 2012.
Amis, Kingsley [writing as Robert Markham]. *Colonel Sun*. 1968. Reprint, London: Vintage, 2015.
Bagley, Desmond. *Wyatt's Hurricane*. 1966. Reprint, London: Fontana, 1970.
———. *Running Blind*. 1970. Reprint, London: Fontana, 1971.
———. *Bahama Crisis*. 1980. Reprint, London: Fontana, 1982.
Besson, Bernard. *The Greenland Breach*. 2013. Reprint, New York: Le French Book, 2014.
Bolton, Sharon. *Sacrifice*. 2008. Reprint, London: Corgi, 2009.

———. *Little Black Lies*. 2015. Reprint, London: Corgi, 2015.
Buchan, John. *The Island of Sheep*. 1936. Edited by Ian Duncan. Oxford World's Classics. Reprint, Oxford: Oxford University Press, 1997.
Childers, Erskine. *The Riddle of the Sands*. 1903. Edited by David Trotter. Oxford World's Classics. Reprint: Oxford: Oxford University Press, 2008.
Coonts, Stephen, and William H. Keith, *Deep Black: Death Wave*. 2011. Reprint, New York: St Martin's Press, 2011.
Crichton, Michael. *State of Fear*. New York: HarperCollins, 2004.
———. *Pirate Latitudes*. 2009. Reprint, London: Harper, 2010.
Crichton, Michael [writing as John Lange]. *Grave Descend*. 1970. Reprint, New York: Hard Case Crime, 2006.
Cussler, Clive. *The Mediterranean Caper*. 1973. Reprint, New York: Berkley, 2008.
———. *Dragon*. 1990. Reprint, New York: Pocket Books, 2006.
———. *Treasure*. 1993. Reprint, London: HarperCollins, 2005.
———. *Shock Wave*. 1996. Reprint, New York: Pocket Star Books, 2008.
Duns, Jeremy. *The Moscow Option*. London: Simon & Schuster, 2012.
Fleming, Ian. *Casino Royale*. 1953. Reprint, London: Vintage, 2012.
———. *Live and Let Die*. 1954. Reprint, London: Vintage, 2012.
———. *Dr No*. 1958. Reprint, London: Vintage, 2012.
———. *Goldfinger*. 1959. Reprint, London: Vintage, 2015.
———. *For Your Eyes Only*. 1960. Reprint, London: Vintage, 2012.
———. *Thunderball*. 1961. Reprint, London: Vintage, 2012.
———. *On Her Majesty's Secret Service*. 1963. Reprint, London: Vintage, 2012.
———. *You Only Live Twice*. 1964. Reprint, London: Vintage, 2012.
———. *The Man with the Golden Gun*. 1965. Reprint, London: Vintage, 2012.
Follett, Ken. *Eye of the Needle*. 1978. Reprint, New York: Harper, 2010.
Hayder, Mo. *Pig Island*. London: Bantam, 2006.
Higgins, Jack. *The Dark Side of the Island*. 1963. Reprint, London: Harper, 2010.
———. *Night Judgement at Sinos*. 1970. Reprint, London: Coronet, 1971.
Hoeg, Peter. *Miss Smilla's Feeling for Snow*. 1992. Translated by F. David. 1993. Reprint, London: HarperCollins, 1994.
Isaksen, Jógvan. *Walpurgis Tide*. 2005. Translated by John Keithsson. London: Norvik Press, 2016.
Lackberg, Camilla. *The Lost Boy*. 2009. Translated by Tiina Nunnally. London: HarperCollins, 2013.
MacLean, Alistair. *Bear Island*. 1971. Reprint, New York: Sterling, 2012.
———. *Santorini*. London: Collins, 1986.
Poyer, David. *Hatteras Blue*. 1989. Reprint, n.p.: Northampton House Press, 2013.
———. *Bahamas Blue*. 1991. Reprint, n.p.: Northampton House Press, 2014.
———. *Louisiana Blue*. 1994. Reprint, n.p.: Northampton House Press, 2014.
Preston, Douglas, and Lincoln Childs. *The Lost Island*. New York: Grand Central Publishing, 2014.
Stone, Nick. *Mr Clarinet*. 2006. Reprint, London: Penguin, 2011.
———. *Voodoo Eyes*. London: Sphere, 2011.
Theorin, Johan. *Echoes from the Dead*. 2008. Translated by Marlaine Delargy. Öland Quartet 1. 2008. Reprint, London: Black Swan, 2009.

———. *The Darkest Room*. 2008. Translated by Marlaine Delargy. Öland Quartet 2. 2009. Reprint, London: Black Swan, 2010.

———. *The Quarry*. 2011. Translated by Marlaine Delargy. Öland Quartet 3. 2011. Reprint, London: Black Swan, 2012.

———. *The Voices Beyond*. 2013. Translated by Marlaine Delargy. Öland Quartet 4. 2015. Reprint, London: Black Swan, 2016.

Wheatley, Dennis. *Strange Conflict*. 1941. Reprint, London: Arrow, 1959.

———. *The Island Where Time Stands Still*. London: Hutchinson, 1954.

———. *Dangerous Inheritance*. 1965. Reprint, London: Hutchinson, 1970

PRIMARY SOURCES—ROMANCE

Andresen, Julie Tetel. *Swept Away*. 1989. Reprint, Durham: Helix-Windows on History, 1997.

Archer, Zöe. *Skies of Gold*. Ether Chronicles. Sydney: Avon Impulse, 2013. Kindle edition.

Cole, Kresley. *The Price of Pleasure*. New York: Pocket Books, 2004. Kindle edition.

Deveraux, Jude. *True Love*. Nantucket Brides 1. London: Headline Eternal, 2013. Kindle edition.

Donald, Robyn. *Island of Secrets*. Sexy eBooks. Chatswood, NSW: Harlequin Mills & Boon, 2013. Kindle edition.

Freeman, Kimberley. *Ember Island*. 2013. Reprint, New York: Touchstone, 2014.

Graves, Tracey Garvis. *On the Island*. 2011. Reprint, London: Penguin, 2012. Kindle edition.

———. *Uncharted: An On the Island Novella*. London: Penguin, 2013. Kindle edition.

Gray, Ginna. *Always*. New York: Silhouette, 1994.

Hilton, Margery. *Girl Crusoe*. London: Mills & Boon, 1969.

Holt, Victoria. *Lord of the Far Island*. 1975. Reprint, New York: St Martin's Griffin, n.d.

Kantra, Virginia. *Carolina Home*. New York: Berkley Sensation, 2012. Kindle edition.

Kinsale, Laura. *Seize the Fire*. 1989. Reprint. New York: Open Road Integrated Media, 2014. Kindle edition.

Krentz, Jayne Ann. *A Coral Kiss*. New York: Warner, 1987.

Krentz, Jayne Ann, writing as Jayne Castle. *Canyons of the Night*. Arcane Society. Harmony Series 8. London: Hachette Digital, 2011. Kindle edition.

Laurens, Stephanie. *The Brazen Bride*. Black Cobra Quartet 1. New York: HarperCollins e-books, 2010. Kindle edition.

Mallery, Susan. *Three Sisters*. Blackberry Island 2. Chatswood, NSW: Harlequin MIRA, 2013. Kindle edition.

Marsh, Anne. *Pleasing Her SEAL*. 2016. 2 Great Reads edition with Lisa Childs, *Red Hot*. Blaze 0116. Sydney: Harlequin Mills & Boon, 2016.

Marsh, Nicola. *Deserted Island, Dreamy Ex*. 2011. Sexy. Reprint, North Sydney: Harlequin Mills & Boon, 2015. Kindle edition.

Marshall, Darlene. *Castaway Dreams*. Indian Hills: Amber Quill, 2012.
Mather, Anne. *Leopard in the Snow*. 1974. Reprint, London: Mills & Boon, 2014.
———. *Stay Through the Night*. 2005. In *Dark Seductions*. By Request. Reprint. North Sydney: Harlequin Mills & Boon, 2014. Kindle edition.
Michaels, Barbara [Elizabeth Peters]. *The Sea King's Daughter*. 1975. Reprint, New York: HarperTorch, 2005.
Miller, Linda Lael. *Pirates*. 1995. Reprint, New York: Pocket Books, n. d. Kindle edition.
Neri, Penelope. *No Sweeter Paradise*. New York: Zebra, 1993.
O'Neill, Ellie. *The Enchanted Island*. London: Simon & Schuster, 2015.
Osburn, Terri. *Meant to Be*. Anchor Island. Las Vegas: Montlake Romance, 2013. Kindle edition.
Parv, Valerie. *The Monarch's Son*. Carramer Crown 1. Sweet Romance 4791. Chatswood, NSW: Harlequin Mills & Boon, 2000.
Phillips, Susan Elizabeth. *Heroes Are My Weakness*. Sydney: William Morrow-HarperCollins, 2014. Kindle edition.
Porter, Margaret Evans. *Kissing a Stranger*. New York: Avon Books, 1998.
———. *Kissing a Stranger*. Revised eBook edition. Islanders. N.p.: Margaret Evans Porter, 2012. Kindle edition.
———. *The Seducer*. New York: Avon Books, 1999.
———. *The Seducer*. Revised eBook edition. Islanders. N.p.: Margaret Evans Porter, 2012. Kindle edition.
———. *Improper Advances*. New York: Avon Books, 2000.
———. *Improper Advances*. Revised eBook edition. Islanders. N.p.: Margaret Evans Porter, 2012. Kindle edition.
Proctor, Candice. *Beyond Sunrise*. New York: Ivy Books, 2003.
Robards, Karen. *Island Flame*. 1981. Reprint, New York: Pocket Star Books, 2012.
Roberts, Nora. *Island of Flowers*. 1982. Reprint, London: Hachette Digital, 2012. Kindle edition.
———. *Risky Business*. 1986. Reprint, New York: Silhouette Books, 2010.
———. *Treasures Lost, Treasures Found*. 1986. PST Special Releases. Reprint, Chatswood: Mills & Boon, n. d. Kindle edition.
———. *The Welcoming*. 1989. Reprint, London: Harlequin Mills & Boon, 2012.
———. *Sanctuary*. 1997. Reprint, London: Hachette Digital, 2008. Kindle edition.
———. *A Dance Upon the Air*. Three Sisters Island 1. New York: Jove Books, 2001.
———. *Heaven and Earth*. Three Sisters Island 2. New York: Jove Books, 2001.
———. *Face the Fire*. Three Sisters Island 3. New York: Jove Books, 2002.
———. *The Search*. 2010. Reprint, New York: Piatkus, 2012.
———. *Stars of Fortune*. Guardians Trilogy 1. London: Piatkus, 2015.
———. *Bay of Sighs*. Guardians Trilogy 2. London: Piatkus, 2016.
Shepherd, Kandy. *The Castaway Bride*. N.p.: Kandy Shepherd, 2011. Kindle edition.
Sinclair, Kira. *Bring It On*. Island Nights 1. Chatswood, NSW: Harlequin Mills & Boon, 2012. Kindle edition.
———. *Take it Down*. Island Nights 2. Chatswood, NSW: Harlequin Mills & Boon, 2012. Kindle edition

———. *Rub it In*. Island Nights 3. Chatswood, NSW: Harlequin Mills & Boon, 2012. Kindle edition.
Sorenson, Jill. *Stranded with Her Ex*. 2011. Romantic Suspense. Reprint, Chatswood, NSW: Harlequin Mills & Boon, 2012. Kindle edition.
Stephens, Susan. *Bought: One Island, One Bride*. Greek Tycoons. 2008. Reprint, Chatswood, NSW: Harlequin Mills & Boon, 2011. Kindle edition.
Whitney, Phyllis A. *Lost Island*. 1971. Reprint, London: Pan, 1980.
Winspear, Violet. *Beloved Castaway*. 1968. Toronto: Harlequin, 1971.

PRIMARY SOURCES—FANTASY

Brooks, Terry. *Magic Kingdom for Sale Sold!* 1986. Reprint, London: Orbit, 1991.
———. *The Elf Queen of Shannara*. 1992. Heritage of Shannara 3. Reprint, London: Orbit, 2006.
Butcher, Jim. *Turn Coat*. Dresden Files 11. London: Hachette Digital, 2009. Kindle edition.
———. *Cold Days*. Dresden Files 14. London: Hachette Digital, 2012. Kindle edition.
———. *Skin Game*. Dresden Files 15. London: Orbit, 2014. Kindle edition.
Carey, Jacqueline. *Kushiel's Dart*. 2001. Reprint, New York: Tor, 2002.
———. *Kushiel's Chosen*. New York: Tor, 2002.
———. *Kushiel's Avatar*. New York: Tor, 2003.
Donaldson, Stephen. *One Tree*. Second Chronicles of Thomas Covenant 2. London: Fontana/Collins, 1982.
Eddings, David. *Castle of Wizardry*. 1984. Belgariad 4. Reprint, London: Corgi, 1987.
Eddings, David, and Leigh Eddings. *The Rivan Codex: Ancient Texts of the Belgariad and the Mallorean*. Illustrated by Geoff Taylor. 1998. Reprint, London: Voyager, 1999.
Hobb, Robin. *The Ship of Magic*. Liveship Traders 1. 1998. Reprint, London: HarperVoyager, 2012.
———. *The Mad Ship*. Liveship Traders 2. 1999. Reprint, London: HarperVoyager, 2012.
———. *Ship of Destiny*. Liveship Traders 3. 2000. Reprint, London: HarperVoyager, 2012.
———. *The Willful Princess and the Piebald Prince*. London: HarperVoyager, 2013.
Hobb, Robin, and Megan Lindholm. *The Inheritance*. London: HarperVoyager, 2011.
Jemisin, N. K. *The Hundred Thousand Kingdoms*. Inheritance 1. New York: Orbit, 2010.
———. *The Broken Kingdoms*. Inheritance 2. New York: Orbit, 2010.
———. *The Kingdom of Gods*. Inheritance 3. New York: Orbit, 2011.
Kerr, Katharine. *Daggerspell*. Deverry Series 1. 1986. Reprint, London: Grafton, 1988.
———. *Darkspell*. Deverry Series 2. 1988. Reprint, London: Grafton, 1989.
———. *Dawnspell: The Bristling Wood*. Deverry Series 3. 1989. Reprint, London: Grafton, 1996.
———. *Dragonspell: The Southern Sea*. Deverry Series 4. 1990. Reprint, London: Grafton, 1998.
———. *A Time of Omens*. 1992. Westlands Cycle 2. Reprint, London: Voyager, 1996.

Lanagan, Margo. *The Brides of Rollrock Island*. 2012. Reprint. Oxford: David Fickling Books, 2013.
Larke, Glenda. *The Aware*. Isles of Glory 1. Sydney: Voyager, 2003.
———. *Gilfeather*. Isles of Glory 2. 2003. Reprint, n.p.: Fablecroft Publishing, 2013. Kindle edition.
———. *The Tainted*. Isles of Glory 3. 2004. Reprint, n.p.: Fablecroft Publishing, 2014. Kindle edition.
Lebbon, Tim. *The Island*. 2009. Reprint, London: Allison & Busby, 2010.
Le Guin, Ursula K. *A Wizard of Earthsea*. 1968. Reprint. Earthsea Cycle 1. Boston: Graphia, 2012.
———. *The Tombs of Atuan*. 1972. Reprint. Earthsea Cycle 2. London: Saga Press, 2012.
———. *The Farthest Shore*. 1973. Reprint. Earthsea Cycle 3. London: Saga Press, 2012.
———. *Tehanu*. 1990. Reprint. Earthsea Cycle 4. New York: Simon Pulse, 2012.
———. *Tales from Earthsea*. 2001. Reprint. Earthsea Cycle 5. Boston: Graphia, 2012.
———. *The Other Wind*. 2001. Reprint. Earthsea Cycle 6. Boston: Graphia, 2012.
Lynch, Scott. *The Lies of Locke Lamora*. Gentleman Bastard Sequence 1. 2006. Reprint. London: Gollancz, 2007.
———. *Red Seas Under Red Skies*. Gentleman Bastard Sequence 2. 2007. Reprint. London: Gollancz, 2007.
———. *The Republic of Thieves*. Gentleman Bastard Sequence 3. 2013. Reprint. London: Gollancz, 2014.
Staveley, Brian. *The Last Mortal Bond*. Chronicle of the Unhewn Throne 3. London: Tor, 2016.
Tolkien, J. R. R. *The Hobbit, or, There and Back Again*. 1937. Reprint, London: Longmans, 1966.
———. *The Fellowship of the Ring*. Lord of the Rings 1. 1954. Reprint, London: Allen & Unwin, 1978.
———. *The Two Towers*. Lord of the Rings 2. 1954. Reprint, London: Allen & Unwin, 1974.
———. *The Return of the King*. Lord of the Rings 3. 1955. Reprint, London: Allen & Unwin, 1974.
———. *The Silmarillion*, edited by Christopher Tolkien. London: George Allen & Unwin, 1977.

PRIMARY SOURCES—OTHER

Ballantyne, Robert Michael. *The Coral Island*. 1857. Edited by Ralph Crane and Lisa Fletcher. Richmond, VA: Valancourt Books, 2015.
———. *Gascoyne, The Sandal-Wood Trader: A Tale of the Pacific*. 1864, Reprint, London: Blackie, 1915.
Barrie, J. M. *Peter Pan in Kensington Gardens and Peter and Wendy*. 1904/1911. Edited by Peter Hollindale. Oxford World's Classics. Reprint, Oxford: Oxford University Press, 2008.

Buchan, John. *The Thirty-Nine Steps*. 1915. Edited by Christopher Harvie. Oxford World's Classics. Reprint, Oxford: Oxford University Press, 2008.

Cowper, William. "Verses, Supposed to be written by Alexander Selkirk, during his solitary abode in the island of Juan Fernandez." In *Selected Poems*, edited by Nick Rhodes, 38–40. New York: Routledge, 2003.

Defoe, Daniel. *Robinson Crusoe*. 1719. Edited by Thomas Keymer. Oxford World's Classics. Reprint, Oxford: Oxford University Press, 2007.

Donne, John. *Devotions Upon Emergent Occasions and Death's Duel*. London: Vintage, 1999.

Homer, *The Odyssey*. Translated by Robert Fagles. 1996. Reprint, New York, Penguin, 1997.

Kipling, Rudyard. *Kim*. 1901. Edited by Alan Sandison. Oxford World's Classics. Reprint, Oxford: Oxford University Press, 2008.

Laymon, Richard. *Island*. 1991. Reprint, New York: Leisure, 2002.

O'Donnell, Peter. *Modesty Blaise*. 1965. Reprint, London: Pan, 1966.

Poe, Edgar Allan. "MS. Found in a Bottle." In *Complete Stories and Poems of Edgar Allan Poe*, 148–55. New York: Doubleday, 1984.

Sabatini, Rafael. *Captain Blood: His Odyssey*. London: Hutchinson, 1922.

Shakespeare, William. *The Tempest*. 1611. Edited by Stephen Orgel. Oxford World's Classics. Reprint, Oxford: Oxford University Press, 2008.

Stacpoole, H. de Vere. *The Blue Lagoon: A Romance*. 1908. Edited by Adrienne E. Gavin. Kansas City: Valancourt Books, 2010.

Stevenson, Robert Louis. *Treasure Island*. 1883. Edited by Peter Hunt. Oxford World's Classics. Reprint, Oxford: Oxford University Press. 2011.

Verne, Jules. *A Voyage Round the World. In Search of the Castaways: A Romantic Narrative of the Loss of Captain Grant of the Brig Britannia and of the Adventures of His Children and Friends in His Discovery and Rescue*. 1873. Reprint, Philadelphia: Lippincott, 1874.

———. *The Mysterious Island*. 1874. Translated by Jordan Stump. New York: Modern Library, 2004.

Wells, H. G. *The Island of Doctor Moreau*. 1896. Reprint, London: Penguin, 2005.

SECONDARY SOURCES

Amis, Kingsley. Introduction to *Colonel Sun*, by Kingsley Amis, writing as Robert Markham, xi-xv. 1991. Reprint, London: Vintage, 2015.

Anderson, Jon, and Kimberley Peters. "'A perfect and absolute blank': Human Geographies of Water Worlds." In *Water Worlds: Human Geographies of the Ocean,* edited by Anderson and Peters, 3–19. Farnham: Ashgate, 2014.

Armitt, Lucie. *Fantasy Fiction: An Introduction*. New York: Continuum, 2005.

Bakhtin, M. M. "Forms of Time and of the Chronotope in the Novel." In *The Dialogic Imagination: Four Essays by M. M. Bakhtin,* edited by Michael Holquist. Translated by Caryl Emerson and Michael Holquist, 84–258. Austin: University of Texas Press, 1981.

Baldacchino, Godfrey. "Getting Wet: A Response to Hayward's Concept of Aquapelagos." *Shima: The International Journal of Research into Island Cultures 6*, no. 1 (2012): 22–26. Accessed 12 May 2015, http://www.shimajournal.org/issues/v6n1/f.-Baldacchino-Shima-v6n1-22-26.pdf.

———. "The Lure of the Island: A Spatial Analysis of Power Relations." *Journal of Marine and Island Cultures* 1, no. 2 (2012): 55–62.

Barlow, Linda, and Jayne Ann Krentz. "Beneath the Surface: The Hidden Codes of Romance." In *Dangerous Men and Adventurous Women: Romance Writers on the Appeal of the Romance*, edited by Jayne Ann Krentz, 15–29. Philadelphia: University of Pennsylvania Press, 1992.

Barnhill, Blythe. Review of *Improper Advances*, by Margaret Evans Porter. *All About Romance*. Accessed 3 March 2016, http://www.likesbooks.com/cgi-bin/bookReview.pl?BookReviewId=4246.

Beer, Gillian. "Island Bounds." In *Islands in History and Representations*, edited by Rod Edmond and Vanessa Smith, 32–42. London: Routledge, 2003.

Bennett, Tony, and Janet Woollacott, *Bond and Beyond: The Popular Career of a Popular Hero*. London: Macmillan, 1987.

Berlant, Lauren. *Desire/Love*. Brooklyn: Punctum Books, 2012. Adobe PDF eBook.

Black, Jeremy. *The Politics of James Bond: From Fleming's Novels to the Big Screen*. 2000. Reprint, Lincoln: University of Nebraska Press, 2005.

Bourne, Sam, aka Jonathan Freedland. Introduction to *Dr No*, by Ian Fleming, ix-xviii. London: Vintage, 2012.

Brace, Catherine, and Adeline Johns-Putra. "The Importance of Process." In *Process: Landscape and Text*. Spatial Practices: An Interdisciplinary Series in Cultural History, edited by Catherine Brace and Adeline Johns-Putra, 29–44. Geography and Literature, edited by Robert Burden and Stephan Kohl. Amsterdam: Rodopi, 2010.

Brager, Jill. Review of *The Seducer*, by Margaret Evans Porter. Accessed 3 March 2016, http://www.rtbookreviews.com/book-review/seducer.

Buse, Katherine. "Genre, Utopia, and Ecological Crisis: World-Multiplication in Le Guin's Fantasy." *Green Letters: Studies in Ecocriticism* 17, no. 3 (2013): 264–280. Accessed 19 April 2016, http://dx.doi.org/10.1080/14688417.2013.860556.

Bushell, Sally. "The Slipperiness of Literary Maps: Critical Geography and Literary Cartography." *Cartographica* 47, no. 3 (2012): 149–60.

Christian, Ed. "Ethnic Postcolonial Crime and Detection (Anglophone)." In *The Cambridge Companion to Crime Fiction*, edited by Martin Priestman, 283–95. Cambridge: Cambridge University Press, 2003.

Clute, John, ed. *Encyclopedia of Fantasy*. June 1997. Accessed 26 April 2016, http://sf-encyclopedia.uk.

Crane, Ralph. "Reading the Club as Colonial Island in E. M. Forster's *A Passage to India* and George Orwell's *Burmese Days*." *Island Studies Journal* 6, no. 1 (2011): 17–28. Accessed 12 May 2015, http://www.islandstudies.ca/sites/islandstudies.ca/files/ISJ-6-1-2011-Crane_0.pdf.

Cresswell, Tim. "Towards a Politics of Mobility," *Environment and Planning D: Society and Space* 28, no. 1 (2010): 17–31.

Cuddon, J. A. *Dictionary of Literary Terms and Literary Theory*. 5th ed. Rev. by M. A. R. Habib. Chichester: Wiley-Blackwell, 2013.

DeLoughrey, Elizabeth. "The Litany of Islands, The Rosary of Archipelagoes: Caribbean and Pacific Archipelagraphy." *Ariel: A Review of International English Literature* 32, no. 1 (2001): 21–52.

Denning, Michael. *Cover Stories: Narrative and Ideology in the British Spy Thriller*. London: Routledge and Kegan Paul, 1987.

———. "Licensed to Look: James Bond and the Heroism of Consumption." In *The James Bond Phenomenon: A Critical Reader*, edited by Christoph Lindner, 2nd ed., 2006, 56–75. Reprint, Manchester: Manchester University Press, 2014.

Derrida, Jacques. "The Law of Genre." *Glyph* 7 (1980): 202–32.

Ekman, Stefan. *Here Be Dragons: Exploring Fantasy Maps and Settings*. Middletown, CT: Wesleyan University Press, 2013. Kindle edition.

Feltham, John. *A Tour through the Island of Man, in 1797 and 1798; Comprising Sketches of Its Ancient and Modern History, Constitution, Laws, Commerce, Agriculture, Fishery, &c. Including Whatever Is Remarkable in Each Parish, Its Population, Inscriptions, Registers, &c.* Bath: R. Cruttwell, 1798. Google eBook. Accessed 20 March 2016, https://books.google.com.au/books?id=MJY9AAAAYAAJ&source=gbs_navlinks_s.

Fletcher, Lisa. *Historical Romance Fiction: Heterosexuality and Performativity*. Aldershot, UK: Ashgate, 2008.

———. "'... some distance to go': A Critical Survey of Island Studies." *New Literatures Review* nos. 47–48 (2011): 17–34.

———, ed. *Genre Settings: Spatiality and Popular Fiction*. London: Palgrave Macmillan, 2016.

Fonstad, Karen Wynn. *The Atlas of Middle-Earth*. Rev. ed. New York: Houghton Mifflin, 1991.

Frantz, Sarah S. G., and Eric Murphy Selinger, eds. *New Approaches to Popular Romance Fiction: Critical Essays*. Jefferson, NC: McFarland, 2012. Kindle.

Freitag, Barbara. "The Gaelicization of Brasil Island: From Cartographic Error to Celtic Elysium." In *Shipwreck and Island Motifs in Literature and the Arts*, edited by Brigitte le Juez and Olga Springer, 123–34. Leiden: Brill Rodopi, 2015.

Frow, John. *Genre*. The New Critical Idiom, edited by John Drakakis. 2005. Reprint, London: Routledge, 2009.

———. "'Reproducibles, Rubrics, and Everything You Need': Genre Theory Today." *PMLA* 122, no. 5 (2007): 1626–34.

Gelder, Ken. *Popular Fiction: The Logics and Practices of a Literary Field*. London: Routledge, 2004.

Gleason, William. "The Inside Story: Jennifer Crusie and the Architecture of Love." In Fletcher, Genre Settings, 79–93.

Glover, David, and Scott McCracken, eds. *The Cambridge Companion to Popular Fiction*. Cambridge: Cambridge University Press, 2012.

———. Introduction to *The Cambridge Companion to Popular Fiction*. In Glover and McCracken, 1–14.

Goris, An. "Body, Mind, Love: Nora Roberts and the Evolution of Popular Romance Studies." *Journal of Popular Romance Studies* 3, no. 1 (2012): n.p. Accessed 7

October 2014, http://jprstudies.org/2012/10/mind-body-love-nora-roberts-and-the-evolution-of-popular-romance-studies-by-an-goris/.

———. "From Romance to Roberts and Back Again: Genre, Authorship and the Construction of Textual Identity in Contemporary Popular Romance Novels." PhD diss., University of Leuven, 2011.

———. "Happily Ever After … and After: Serialization and the Popular Romance Novel." *Americana: The Journal of American Popular Culture 1900 to Present* 12, no. 1 (2013). Accessed 5 May 2015, http://www.americanpopularculture.com/journal/articles/spring_2013/goris.htm

Gornall, John. "John Buchan's *The Island of Sheep* and *Faereyinga Saga.*" *Saga-Book* 24, no. 5 (1997): 351–54.

Griswold, John. *Ian Fleming's James Bond: Annotations and Chronologies for Ian Fleming's Bond Stories.* Bloomington, IN: AuthorHouse, 2006.

Grossvogel, David. "Agatha Christie: Containment of the Unknown." In *The Poetics of Murder*, edited by Glenn W. Most and William W. Stowe, 252–65. New York: Harcourt Brace Jovanovich, 1983.

Hall, Edward T. *The Hidden Dimension.* 1966. Reprint, New York: Anchor Books, 1990.

Halloran, Vivian. "Tropical Bond." In *Ian Fleming and James Bond: The Cultural Politics of 007*, edited by Edward P. Comentale, Stephen Watt, and Skip Willman, 158–77. Bloomington: Indiana University Press, 2005.

Harrington, Pat and Noah Wardrip-Fruin, eds. *Third Person: Authoring and Exploring Vast Narratives.* Cambridge, MA: MIT Press, 2009.

Hartmann, Britta. "Island Fictions: Castaways and Imperialism." PhD dissertation, University of Tasmania, 2014.

Hau'ofa, Epeli. "Our Sea of Islands." In *A New Oceania: Rediscovering Our Sea of Islands,* edited by Eric Waddell, Vijay Naidu, and Epeli Hau'ofa, 2–16. Suva: University of the South Pacific, 1993.

Hay, Pete. "A Phenomenology of Islands." *Island Studies Journal* 1, no. 1 (2006): 19–42. Accessed 7 October 7 2014, http://www.islandstudies.ca/sites/vre2.upei.ca.islandstudies.ca/files/u2/ISJ-1-1-2006-Hay-pp19-42.pdf.

———. "The Poetics of Island Place: Articulating Particularity." *Local Environment* 8, no. 3 (2003): 553–58.

———. "What the Sea Portends: A Reconsideration of Contested Island Tropes." *Island Studies Journal* 8, no. 2 (2013): 209–32. Accessed 3 March 2015, http://www.islandstudies.ca/sites/islandstudies.ca/files/ISJ-8-2-2013-Hay.pdf.

Hayward, Philip. "Aquapelagos and Aquapelagic Assemblages: Towards an Integrated Study of Island Societies and Marine Environments." *Shima: The International Journal of Research into Island Cultures* 6, no. 1 (2012): 1–11. Accessed 12 May 2015, http://www.shimajournal.org/issues/v6n1/c.-Hayward-Shima-v6n1-1-11.pdf.

———. "The Constitution of Assemblages and the Aquapelagality of Haida Gwaii." *Shima: The International Journal of Research into Island Cultures* 6, no. 2 (2012): 1–13. Accessed 5 March 2015, http://www.shimajournal.org/issues/v6n2/c.-Hayward-Shima-v6n2-1-14.pdf.

Heath, Stephen. "The Politics of Genre." In *Debating World Literature*, edited by Christopher Prendergast, 163–74. London: Verso, 2004.

Hones, Sheila. "Text as It Happens: Literary Geography." *Geography Compass* 2, no. 5 (2009): 1301–17.

Humble, Nicola. "The Reader of Popular Fiction." In Glover and McCracken, 86–102.

Hunt, Peter. "Introduction: Fantasy and Alternative Worlds." In *Alternative Worlds in Fantasy Fiction*, by Peter Hunt and Millicent Lenz, 1–41. 2001. Reprint, London: Continuum, 2003.

Jacob, Christian. *The Sovereign Map: Theoretical Approaches in Cartography Throughout History*, edited by Edward H. Dahl, translated by Tom Conley. Chicago: Chicago University Press, 2006.

Jones, Diana Wynne. *The Tough Guide to Fantasyland*. Revised edition. New York: Firebird, 2006.

Knight, Stephen. *Crime Fiction Since 1800: Detection, Death, Diversity*. 2nd edition. London: Palgrave Macmillan, 2010.

———. *Form and Ideology in Crime Fiction*. London: Macmillan, 1980.

———. "The Golden Age." In *The Cambridge Companion to Crime Fiction*, edited by Martin Priestman, 77–94. Cambridge: Cambridge University Press, 2003.

Leane, Elizabeth. "Unstable Places and Generic Spaces: Thrillers in Antarctica." In Fletcher, *Genre Settings*, 25-43.

Leggett, Bianca. "Departures: The Novel, the Non-Place and the Airport." *Alluvium* 1, no. 4 (2012): n.p. Accessed 6 May 2015, http://dx.doi.org/10.7766/alluvium.v1.4.03.

Le Guin, Ursula. "From Elfland to Poughkeepsie." In *From Elfland to Poughkeepsie*, edited by David Sandner, 144–155. 1973. Reprint, Westport, CT: Praeger, 2004.

Le Guin, Ursula K. "Dreams Must Explain Themselves." *The Language of the Night: Essays on Fantasy and Science Fiction*, by Le Guin, edited by Susan Wood, 47–56. New York: Ultramarine Publishing, 1980.

Lenz, Millicent. "Ursula K. Le Guin." In *Alternative Worlds in Fantasy Fiction*, by Peter Hunt and Millicent Lenz, 42–85. 2001. Reprint, London: Continuum, 2003.

Light, Alison. *Forever England: Femininity, Literature and Conservatism Between the Wars*. London and New York: Routledge, 1991.

Litte, Jane. "Once Upon a Desert Isle Keeper." *Dear Author*. 26 September 2008. Accessed 3 March 2016, http://dearauthor.com/features/letters-of-opinion/once-upon-a-desert-isle-keeper/.

Lowenthal, David. "Islands, Lovers, and Others." *Geographical Review* 97, no. 2 (2007): 202–29.

Luria, Sarah. "Spatial Literacies: Geotexts." In *Geohumanities: Art, History, Text at the Edge of Place*, edited by Michael Dear, Jim Ketchum, Sarah Luria, and Doug Richardson, 67–70. London: Routledge, 2011. ePub eBook.

Lycett, Andrew. *Ian Fleming*. New York: St Martin's Press, 1995.

MacDonald, George. Preface to *The Light Princess, and Other Fairy Tales*. iii-vii. New York: G. P. Putnam's Sons, 1893. Accessed 26 April 2016, https://archive.org/details/lightprincessoth00macd.

Mack, John. *The Sea: A Cultural History*. London: Reaktion Books, 2011.

Manguel, Alberto and Gianni Guadalupi. *Dictionary of Imaginary Places*. Illustrated by Graham Greenfield. Maps and Charts by James Cook. New York: Macmillan Publishing Co., 1980.

McCracken, Scott. *Pulp: Reading Popular Fiction.* Manchester: Manchester University Press, 1999.

———. "Reading Time: Popular Fiction and the Everyday." In Glover and McCracken, 103–21.

Mendlesohn, Farah and Edward James. *A Short History of Fantasy.* 2009. Revised edition. Faringdon, UK: Libri Publishing, 2012. Kindle edition.

Merrill, Robert. "Christie's Narrative Games." In *Theory and Practice of Classic Detective Fiction*, edited by Jerome H. Delamater and Ruth Prigozy. Contributions to the Study of Popular Culture 62. 87–101. Westport, CT: Greenwood, 1997.

Messent, Peter. *The Crime Fiction Handbook.* Chichester: Wiley-Blackwell, 2013.

Moore, Peter. "GW Kent: The Secrets Behind His Solomon Island Murder Mysteries." *Wanderlust*, 19 July 2012. Accessed 1 June 2015, http://www.wanderlust.co.uk/magazine/articles/interviews/g-w-kent-the-secrets-behind-his-solomon-island-murder-mysteries?page=all.

Moretti, Franco. "Clues." In *Signs Taken for Wonders: On the Sociology of Literary Forms,* 130–56. 1983. Reprint, London: Verso, 2005.

Morris, Meaghan. "Transnational Imagination in Action Cinema: Hong Kong and the Making of a Global Popular Culture." *Inter-Asia Cultural Studies* 5, no. 2 (2004): 181–99.

Parker, Matthew. *Goldeneye: Where James Bond Was Born: Ian Fleming's Jamaica.* London: Hutchinson, 2014.

Parrinder, Patrick. "John Buchan and the Spy Thriller." In *The Bloomsbury Introduction to Popular Fiction*, edited by Christine Berberich, 200–212. London: Bloomsbury, 2015.

Parv, Valerie. *The Art of Romance Writing: Practical Advice from an International Bestselling Romance Writer.* Revised edition. Crows Nest, NSW: Allen & Unwin, 2004. Kindle edition.

Pearce, Lynne. "Another Time, Another Place: The Chronotope of Romantic Love in Contemporary Feminist Fiction." In *Fatal Attractions: Re-Scripting Romance in Contemporary Literature and Film*, edited by Lynne Pearce and Gina Wisker, 98–111. London: Pluto Press, 1998.

———. "Popular Romance and Its Readers." In *A Companion to Romance: From Classical to Contemporary*, edited by Corinne Saunders, 521–38. Malden, MA: Blackwell, 2004.

———. *Romance Writing.* Cambridge: Polity, 2007.

Pezzotti, Barbara. *The Importance of Place in Contemporary Italian Crime Fiction: A Bloody Journey.* 2012. Reprint, Madison, NJ: Fairleigh Dickinson University Press, 2014.

Phifer, Michell. Review of *Improper Advances*, by Margaret Evans Porter. *RT Book Reviews.* Accessed 3 March 2016, http://www.rtbookreviews.com/book-review/improper-advances.

———. Review of *Kissing a Stranger*, by Margaret Evans Porter. *RT Book Reviews.* Accessed 3 March 2016, http://www.rtbookreviews.com/book-review/kissing-stranger.

Porter, Margaret Evans. "Isle of Man." Margaret Evans Porter. Accessed 20 March 2016, http://margaretevansporter.com/iom.html.
Pratchett, Terry [with the Discworld Emporium]. *The Compleat Discworld Atlas, of General and Descriptive Geography Which Together With New Maps and Gazetteer Forms a Compleat Guide to Our World and All It Encompasses.* London: Transworld, 2015.
Pratt, Mary Louise. *Imperial Eyes: Travel Writing and Transculturation.* London: Routledge, 1992.
Prieto, Eric. *Literature, Geography, and the Postmodern Poetics of Place.* London: Palgrave Macmillan, 2013.
Pugh, Jonathan. "Island Movements: Thinking with the Archipelago." *Island Studies Journal* 8, no. 1 (2013): 9–24. Accessed 12 May 2015, http://www.islandstudies.ca/sites/islandstudies.ca/files/ISJ-8-1-2013-Pugh_0.pdf.
Ramsdell, Kristin. *Romance Fiction: A Guide to the Genre.* 2nd edition. Santa Barbara: Libraries Unlimited, 2012. Kindle edition.
Regis, Pamela. *A Natural History of the Romance Novel.* 2003. Reprint, Philadelphia: University of Pennsylvania Press, 2007.
Relph, Edward. *Place and Placelessness.* London: Pion, 1976.
Roach, Catherine M. *Happily Ever After: The Romance Story in Popular Culture.* Bloomington: Indiana University Press, 2016. Kindle edition.
Scaggs, John. *Crime Fiction.* The New Critical Idiom, edited by John Drakakis. London and New York: Routledge, 2005.
Schaberg, Christopher. *The Textual Life of Airports: Reading the Culture of Flight.* New York: Continuum, 2012. Adobe PDF eBook.
Seed, David. "Crime and the Spy Genre." In *A Companion to Crime Fiction*, edited by Charles J. Rzepka and Lee Horsley, 233–44. Chichester: Wiley-Blackwell, 2010.
———. "Spy Fiction." In *The Cambridge Companion to Crime Fiction*, edited by Martin Priestman, 115–34. Cambridge: Cambridge University Press, 2003.
Seidel, Kathleen Gilles. "Judge Me by the Joy I Bring." In *Dangerous Men and Adventurous Women: Romance Writers on the Appeal of the Romance*, edited by Jayne Ann Krentz, 159–179. Philadelphia: University of Pennsylvania Press, 1992.
Selinger, Eric Murphy. "How to Read a Romance Novel (and Fall in Love with Popular Romance)." In Frantz and Selinger.
Sepeda, Toni. *Brunetti's Venice: Walks Through the Novels.* 2008. Reprint, London: Heinemann, 2009.
Staveley, Brian. "Cartography and Its Discontents." *Tor.com* (blog), 11 April 2016. Accessed 22 April 2016, http://www.tor.com/2016/04/11/cartography-and-its-discontents/.
Steinberg, Phillip E. "Of Other Seas: Metaphors and Materialities in Maritime Regions." *Atlantic Studies* 10, no. 2 (2013): 156–69. Accessed 28 April 2016, http://dx.doi.org/10.1080/14788810.2013.785192.
Steinberg, Phillip and Kimberley Peters. "Wet Ontologies, Fluid Spaces: Giving Depth to Volume Through Oceanic Thinking." *Environment and Planning D: Society and Space* 33, no. 2 (2015): 247–64. Accessed 5 May 2016, http://dx.doi.org/10.1068/d14148p.

Symons, Julian. *Bloody Murder: From the Detective Story to the Crime Novel: A History*. London: Faber, 1972.

Tally Jr., Robert T. "Introduction: On Geocriticism." In *Geocritical Explorations: Space, Place, and Mapping in Literary and Cultural Studies*, edited by Tally, 1–9. New York: Palgrave Macmillan, 2011. Adobe PDF eBook.

———. "Introduction: Mapping Narratives." In *Literary Cartographies: Spatiality, Representation, and Narrative*, edited by Robert T. Tally Jr. Geocriticism and Spatial Literary Studies, 1–12. New York: Palgrave Macmillan, 2014.

Taylor, Andrew. Introduction to *Live and Let Die*, by Ian Fleming, ix-xvii. London: Vintage, 2012.

Todorov, Tzvetan. "The Typology of Detective Fiction." In *The Poetics of Prose*, translated by Richard Howard, 42–52. Oxford: Blackwell, 1977.

———. *Introduction to Poetics*. Translated by Richard Howard. Minneapolis: University of Minnesota Press, 1981.

Tolkien, J. R. R. "To Colonel Worskett [A Letter to a Reader of *The Lord of the Rings*]." In *The Letters of J.R.R. Tolkien*, edited by Humphrey Carpenter with the assistance of Christopher Tolkien, 333–35. 1995. Reprint, Boston: Houghton Mifflin Company, 2000.

———. "On Fairy-Stories." In *Tree and Leaf*. Location 84–1040. 1964. Reprint, London: HarperCollins, 2012. Kindle edition.

Tuan, Yi-Fu. *Space and Place: The Perspective of Experience*. Minneapolis: University of Minnesota Press, 1977.

Turner, Louis, and John Ash. *The Golden Hordes: International Tourism and the Pleasure Periphery*. London: Constable, 1975.

Valeo, Christina A. "The Power of Three: Nora Roberts and Serial Magic." In Frantz and Selinger.

Vannini, Phillip. "Constellations of Ferry (Im)mobility: Islandness as the Performance and Politics of Insulation and Isolation." *Cultural Geographies* 18, no. 2 (2011): 249–71.

Vivanco, Laura. *For Love and Money: The Literary Art of the Harlequin Mills & Boon Romance*. Penrith: Humanities-Ebooks, 2011. Kindle edition.

Weaver-Hightower, Rebecca. *Empire Islands: Castaways, Cannibals, and Fantasies of Conquest*. Minneapolis: University of Minnesota Press, 2007.

Wendell, Sarah, and Candy Tan. *Beyond Heaving Bosoms: The Smart Bitches' Guide to Romance Novels*. New York: Fireside, 2009.

Wilkins, Kim. "From Middle Earth to Westeros: Medievalism, Proliferation, and Paratextuality." In *New Directions in Popular Fiction: Genre, Reproduction, Distribution*, edited by Ken Gelder, 201–221. London: Palgrave Macmillan, 2016.

———. "Popular Genres and the Australian Literary Community: The Case of Fantasy Fiction." *Journal of Australian Studies* 32, no. 2 (2008): 276, Accessed 13 January 2015, http://dx.doi.org/10.1080/14443050802056771.

———. "The Process of Genre: Authors, Readers, Institutions." *Text* 9, no. 2 (2005): 265–278. Accessed 27 July 2015, http://www.textjournal.com.au/oct05/wilkins.htm.

Wilson, Dominique Beth. "Myth and Re-Imagined Religion in *Kushiel's Legacy*." *Literature and Aesthetics* 19, no. 9 (2009): 247–61. Accessed 19 May 2016, http://openjournals.library.usyd.edu.au/index.php/LA/article/view/5013.

Wolf, Mark J. P. *Building Imaginary Worlds: The Theory and History of Subcreation*. New York: Routledge, 2013. Adobe PDF eBook.

Young, Helen. *Race and Popular Fantasy Literature: Habits of Whiteness*. New York: Routledge, 2016.

Zahorski, Kenneth J. and Robert H. Boyer. "The Secondary Worlds of High Fantasy." In *The Aesthetics of Fantasy Literature and Art*, edited by Roger C. Schlobin, 56–81. Notre Dame, IN: University of Notre Dame Press, 1982.

Index

Adler-Olson, Jussi, *The Hanging Girl* 4
Allen, Chris, *Hunter* 47, 52
Allingham, Margery, *Mystery Mile* 5, 9–10
Alvarez, Tracey, Due South romance series 177
Amis, Kingsley, *Colonel Sun* 46
Anderson, Jon 165–6, 172
Andresen, Julie Tetel, *Swept Away* 94
Andress, Ursula 65–6, 70n52
Archer, Zoë, *Skies of Gold* 88
Armitt, Lucie 160
Ash, John 47, 65
Attebery, Brian 158

Bagley, Desmond
  Bahama Crisis 47, 50
  Running Blind 48
  Wyatt's Hurricane 47
Bakhtin, M. M. 108
Baldacchino, Godfrey 122, 167, 171
Bale, Tom, *Terror's Reach* 5
Ballantyne, Robert Michael, *The Coral Island* 24–5, 77, 79, 169, 173
Barlow, Linda 92
Barnhill, Blythe 105
Barr, Nevada 3, 16n34
  Endangered Species 10
  Flashback 10
  Winter Study 10
Barthes, Roland 111–12
Beaton, M. C. 4
  Death of a Snob 5
Beer, Gillian 22–3
Bennett, Tony 65
Berlant, Lauren 129
Besson, Bernard, *The Greenland Breach* 48
Billingham, Mark, *The Bones Beneath* 5, 7, 12, 23
Black, Benjamin (John Banville) 5
Black, Jeremy 60
Bloch, Ernest, *The Principle of Hope* 89
Bolton, Sharon
  Little Black Lies 48, 49, 50–51, 53, 63
  Sacrifice 48
Boyer, Robert H. 155
Boyer, Susan M. 4
Brager, Jill 105
Brooks, Terry 142–3
Buchan, John
  The Island of Sheep 48, 74
  The Thirty-Nine Steps 74
Bushell, Sally 10, 25, 26–7, 139
Butcher, Jim, *Turn Coat* 147–8

Camilleri, Andrea 3, 15
Carey, Jacqueline, Kushiel Legacy series 143–4
Child, Lincoln, *The Lost Island* 49–50
Childers, Erskine 49
   The Riddle of the Sands 46
Christian, Ed 33, 34
Christie, Agatha 3
   A Caribbean Mystery 7, 20–21, 25
   And Then There Were None 9, 20, 22, 23–4, 25, 28n6
   Evil Under the Sun 7, 10, 12–14, 20, 21, 25–6, 36, 40
   island locations 7, 19–28, 60
   Murder on the Orient Express 25
   The Murder of Roger Ackroyd 21–2, 26–8
   The Mysterious Affair at Styles 19, 21–2, 25
Cleeves, Ann 5, 9, 15, 21, 36
   Blue Lightening 24
   Raven Black 7–8
   Thin Air 9, 27
Clute, John 138, 143, 158–9
   Encyclopedia of Fantasy 140, 143–4
Cole, Kresley, *The Price of Pleasure* 91
Coonts, Stephen, *Deep Black: Death Wave* 48
Cornwell, Patricia, *Isle of Dogs* 4
Cresswell, Tim 53
Crichton, Michael
   Grave Descend 47
   Pirate Latitudes 60
   State of Fear 47
crime fiction
   clue-puzzle mysteries 19–20
   golden age 19–25
   island locations 3–17, 19–28
   postcolonial settings 31–42
   Scandinavian crime novels 4–5
   use of maps 10–12, 25–6
   whodunit mysteries 19–20
Cussler, Clive 45, 48–9, 50, 53

Dirk Pitt Adventure series 71–83
   Dragon 48–9, 53, 61–2, 71, 73, 76–9
   Shock Wave 48–9, 71, 73–4, 79–82, 173
   The Mediterranean Caper 48–9, 71–3, 75–6

Defoe, Daniel, *Robinson Crusoe* 24–5, 66, 67, 173
DeLoughrey, Elizabeth 153, 173
Denning, Michael 57, 65
Derr Biggers, Earl, *The House Without a Key* 3
detective fiction *see* crime fiction
Deveraux, Jude, Nantucket Brides trilogy 129
Disher, Garry, *Port Vila Blues* 3
Donald, Robyn, *Island of Secrets* 87
Donaldson, Stephen 159
Donne, John 14–15
Douglas, Michelle 90
Downie, Jill 5
Duncan, Sandy Frances 3–4, 10
Duns, Jeremy, *The Moscow Option* 48

Eddings, David 143
Ekman, Stefan 139, 140
   Here Be Dragons 137
Enright, John 3, 9, 35, 36
   Fire Knife Dancing 62
Ewan, Chris
   Dark Tides 9, 21, 48
   Long Time Lost 48
   Safe House 5, 21, 48
   The Good Thief's Guide to Venice 3

Falk, Kathryn 103
fantasy fiction 137–51, 153–63, 165–75, 178
   use of maps 139–40, 145, 156–8, 165–6, 168–9
   world building 137–51, 156
Feist, Raymond E. 140

Fermor, Patrick Leigh, *The Traveller's Tree* 61
Fleming, Ian 45, 47, 52, 53
  Casino Royale 59
  Dr No 49, 50, 57, 58–9, 62–7, 68
  For Your Eyes Only 57
  Goldfinger 57
  island locations 57–70
  Live and Let Die 46, 47, 50, 53, 57–8, 59–60, 62, 64, 68
  On Her Majesty's Secret Service 67–8, 70n52
  The Man With the Golden Gun 57, 62
  Thunderball 57, 58, 59, 64, 67, 68
  You Only Live Twice 59
Fletcher, Lisa 106–7
Flint, Shamini
  A Bali Conspiracy Most Foul 3–4
  The Singapore School of Villainy 3–4
Fois, Marcello, *The Advocate* 4
Follett, Ken, *Eye of the Needle* 48, 51–2, 54n13
Force, Marie 98

Gelder, Ken 49
George, Elizabeth, *A Place of Hiding* 5
Gleason, William 93
Gold, Laurie 107
Goodreads website 107, 119
Goris, An 125, 129
Gornall, John 48
Gracie, Anne 90, 106
Graves, Tracey Garvis
  On the Island 88, 95–6
  Uncharted 96
Gray, Ginna, *Always* 94
Guadalupi, Gianni, *Dictionary of Imaginary Places* 141, 154

Hall, Edward T. 121
Halloran, Vivian 57
Hamer, Gillian E., *Crimson Shore* 5
Hanson, Donna Maree 145

Harrington, Pat 141
Hartmann, Britta 94, 96
Hau'ofa, Epeli 80–81, 82
Hay, Pete 106–7
Hayder, Mo, *Pig Island* 48
Hayward, Philip 167
Heath, Stephen 45
Higgins, Jack
  Night Judgement at Sinos 47
  The Dark Side of the Island 47
Hilton, Margery, *Girl Crusoe* 94
Hobb, Robin 141, 146, 174–5n24
  Liveship Traders trilogy 165–75
  Ship of Destiny 165, 169–70
  Ship of Magic 165, 168–70, 171
  The Mad Ship 165, 170, 172
Hoeg, Peter, *Miss Smilla's Feeling for Snow* 48, 51
Holt, Victoria 97–8
  Lord of the Far Island 98
Hughes, Chip, *Murder on Moloka'i* 3
Humble, Nicola 140
Hunt, Peter 154

Indridason, Arnaldur 4
island locations
  Bond novels 57–70
  crime fiction 3–17, 19–28
  fantasy fiction 137–51, 153–63, 165–75, 178
  romance fiction 87–101, 103–118, 119–33
  thrillers 45–53, 71–83

Jacob, Christian 25–6, 31, 156–8
James, P. D., *The Lighthouse* 5
Jemisin, N. K. 144
Jungstedt, Mari 48
  Unseen 4

Kantra, Virginia, *Carolina Home* 93
Kaye, M. M. 4
  Death in the Andamans 24

Keith, William H., *Deep Black: Death Wave* 48
Kelly, Jim, *Death's Door* 5
Kent, G. W. 3, 14
  Solomon Island Series 31–42
  Devil-Devil 31, 32, 35–6, 37–8, 40–41
  Killman 31, 32, 37, 39–40, 41, 42n41
  One Blood 31, 32, 33–5, 36, 37, 38–9, 41, 42n16
Kerr, Katharine 140
  A Time of Omens 143
  Dragonspell 143
Kinsale, Laura, *Seize the Fire* 88
Kipling, Rudyard, *Kim* 74
Kleypas, Lisa 98
Knight, Stephen 19, 26, 34
  Form and Ideology in Crime Fiction 8
Krentz, Jayne Ann 92
  A Coral Kiss 93
  Canyons of Night 88

Lackberg, Camilla 4, 49
  The Lost Boy 48
Lanagan, Margo 159
Larke, Glenda, Isles of Glory trilogy 144–6
Larsson, Stieg, *The Girl with the Dragon Tattoo* 9–10, 26
Laurens, Stephanie 90
  The Brazen Bride 94
Laymon, Raymond, *Island* 22
Le Guin, Ursula K. 140, 141, 146, 153–63
  Earthsea series 153–63
  A Wizard of Earthsea 153, 159, 160–61
  Tales from Earthsea 153
  Tehanu 153
  The Farthest Shore 153, 160
  The Other Wind 153
  The Tombs of Atuan 153, 159–60

Leane, Elizabeth 45–6
Lebbon, Tim, *The Island* 147
Lehane, Dennis, *Shutter Island* 6
Lenz, Millicent 154, 158
Leon, Donna 3, 12, 16n32
Light, Alison 19, 25
Lowenthal, David 109
Lycett, Andrew 59
Lynch, Scott 138, 146–7

McCall Smith, Alexander 31–3
MacDonald, George 138
McGuire, Matt 5
Mack, John 168
MacLean, Alistair
  Bear Island 48, 50, 63
  Santorini 52
Mallery, Susan 98
  Three Sisters 90–91, 93
Manguel, Alberto, *Dictionary of Imaginary Places* 141, 154
Marsh, Anne, *Pleasing her SEAL* 91
Marsh, Ngaio 3
Marsh, Nicola, *Deserted Island, Dreamy Ex* 94–5
Marshall, Darlene, *Castaway Dreams* 88
Martin, George R. R. 138, 144
Mather, Anne
  Leopard in the Snow 88
  Stay Through the Night 92–3
May, Peter 5, 12, 13, 15, 177
  Entry Island 4, 6–7, 24
  The Blackhouse 7, 8
  The Chessmen 10
Mayle, Peter, *The Corsican Caper* 3
Mayo, Kat 103
Messent, Peter 14, 25, 35
Michaels, Barbara 97–8
  The Sea King's Daughter 98
Miéville, China 138
Miller, Linda Lael, *Pirates* 93
Mills, Mark, *The Information Officer* 4, 11–12

Moretti, Franco 33
Morris, Meaghan 57

Neri, Penelope, *No Sweeter Paradise* 94

O'Donnell, John, *Modesty Blaise* 61
O'Neill, Ellie, *The Enchanted Island* 96–7
Osburn, Terri 98
  Meant to Be 90
Owen, David 3, 5–6
  Pig's Head 8

Padura, Leonardo, *Havana Blue* 4
Parker, Matthew 58
Parrinder, Patrick 48
Parv, Valerie 87
  The Monarch's Son 94
Pearce, Lynne 88–9, 91–2, 108–9, 110, 111, 113
Peters, Kimberley 141, 165–6, 172, 173
Pezzotti, Barbara 8–9, 15
  The Importance of Place in Contemporary Italian Crime Fiction 6
Phifer, Michell 105
Phillips, Suzanne Elizabeth, *Heroes Are My Weakness* 91
Poe, Edgar Allan 24–5
popular fiction *see* crime fiction; fantasy fiction; romance fiction; thrillers
Porter, Margaret Evans
  The Islanders series 103–118
  Improper Advances 103, 104–6, 113–14
  Kissing a Stranger 103, 104, 105, 109–110, 114
  The Seducer 103, 104, 105, 110–113, 114
Poyer, David
  Bahamas Blue 47
  Hatteras Blue 47

Louisiana Blue 46
Pratchett, Terry 138, 139
Pratt, Mary Louise 35
  Imperial Eyes 60–61, 64
Preston, Douglas, *The Lost Island* 49–50
Prieto, Eric 14
Proctor, Candice, *Beyond Sunrise* 88
Pugh, Jonathan 153

Quigley, Sheila 5

Rankin, Ian 14
Regis, Pamela, *A Natural History of the Romance Novel* 124–5
Relph, Edward 53
Roach, Catherine M. 90
Roberts, Nora 25
  Sanctuary 98, 120
  Three Sisters trilogy 119–33
  Dance Upon the Air 119, 120–21, 123–6, 127–8
  Face the Fire 119, 121, 126, 128–9
  Heaven and Earth 119, 121, 126–7, 128
Robertson, Craig, *The Last Refuge* 4
romance fiction 87–101
  common tropes 103–4, 110–112
  definition 89–90
  island locations 87–101, 103–118, 119–33
Romantic Times book review website 103
Rowson, Pauline 5

Sabatini, Rafael, *Captain Blood* 60
Scaggs, John 10, 12
Seed, David 52
Seidel, Kathleen Gilles 93
Selinger, Eric Murphy 119
Sepeda, Toni, *Brunetti's Venice* 12
Shepherd, Kandy, *The Castaway Bride* 94
Sigurdardottir, Yrsa 4

Silva, Daniel, *The English Girl* 4
Sinclair, Kira 93
Singh, Nalini 90
Sorenson, Jill, *Stranded with Her Ex* 95
Staveley, Brian 139–40
Steinberg, Phillip E. 141, 165, 166, 173
Stephens, Susan, *Bought: One Island, One Bride* 87–8
Stevenson, Robert Louis, *Treasure Island* 24–5, 60, 156, 168, 173
Stewart, Mary 97–8
Stone, Nick, *Mr Clarinet* 47, 50
Symons, Julian 19
Szanto, George 3–4, 10

Tally, Robert T. 126, 140
Tan, Candy 103
Taylor, Andrew 46
Theorin, Johan
   Echoes from the Dead 4, 48
   The Darkest Room 48
   The Quarry 48
   The Voices Beyond 48
Thomas, Paul 3
thrillers 45–53, 178
   island locations 45–53, 71–83
   use of maps 50–51, 71–2
Titasey, Catherine, *My Island Homicide* 5–6, 35
Todorov, Tzvetan 7, 41, 45, 52–3
Tolkien, J. R. R. 137–9
   The Fellowship of the Ring 139
   The Hobbit 138–9
   The Lord of the Rings 137–8, 140, 144
   The Silmarillion 138
Tuan, Yi-Fu 14
Turner, Louis 47, 65

Valeo, Christina A. 119, 129
Vannini, Phillip 53
Verne, Jules
   In Search of the Castaways 24–5
   The Mysterious Island 24–5, 156–7
Vichi, Marco, *Death in Sardinia* 4
Vivanco, Laura 92

Wardrip-Fruin, Noah 141
Weaver-Hightower, Rebecca 57–8, 64
Wendell, Sarah 103
Wheatley, Dennis
   Dangerous Inheritance 47
   Strange Conflict 47, 61
   The Island Where Time Stands Still 47
Wheelaghan, Marianne 3, 21
   Food of Ghosts 21, 35
   The Shoeshine Killer 35
Whitney, Phyllis A. 97–8
   Lost Island 98
Wilkins, Kim 21, 91, 139, 140, 142, 144–5
Wilson, Dominique Beth 144
Winspear, Violet, *Beloved Castaway* 93, 94
Winterson, Jeanette, *The Powerbook* 113
Wolf, Mark J. P. 141
   Building Imaginary Worlds 137
Woollacott, Janet 65
Wynne Jones, Diana 142

Young, Helen 144

Zahorski, Kenneth J. 155
Zouroudi, Anne 14, 16n37
   The Messenger of Athens 4, 10–11

www.ingramcontent.com/pod-product-compliance
Lightning Source LLC
Chambersburg PA
CBHW020912020526
44114CB00039B/348